DEFENDING

THE CITY

OF GOD

A MEDIEVAL QUEEN, THE FIRST CRUSADES,
AND THE QUEST FOR PEACE IN JERUSALEM

SHARAN NEWMAN

palgrave
macmillan

First published in 2014 by PALGRAVE MACMILLAN® in the U.S.—
a division of St. Martin's Press LLC, 175 Fifth Avenue, New York, NY 10010.

Where this book is distributed in the UK, Europe and the rest of the world,
this is by Palgrave Macmillan, a division of Macmillan Publishers Limited,
registered in England, company number 785998, of Houndmills, Basingstoke,
Hampshire RG21 6XS.

Palgrave Macmillan is the global academic imprint of the above companies and
has companies and representatives throughout the world.

Palgrave® and Macmillan® are registered trademarks in the United States, the
United Kingdom, Europe and other countries.

ISBN: 978-1-137-27865-4

The Library of Congress has catalogued the hardcover edition as follows:
Newman, Sharan.
    Defending the City of God : a medieval queen, the first Crusades, and the
quest for peace in Jerusalem / Sharan Newman.
        pages   cm
    Includes index.
    ISBN 978-1-137-27865-4 (hardback : alkaline paper)
    1. Jerusalem—History—Latin Kingdom, 1099–1244. 2. Melisende, Queen
of Jerusalem, -1161. 3. Queens—Jerusalem—Biography. 4. Jerusalem—Politics
and government. 5. Jerusalem—History, Military. 6. Crusades. 7. Cultural
pluralism—Jerusalem—History—To 1500. 8. Social change—Jerusalem—
History—To 1500. 9. Jerusalem—Social conditions. I. Title.
D182.N49 2014
956.94'42032—dc23
                                                                2013049594

A catalogue record of the book is available from the British Library.

Design by Letra Libre

First edition: April 2014

10 9 8 7 6 5 4 3 2 1

Printed in the United States of America.

This book is for

Dr. Georgia Sommers Wright,

friend, refuge, scholar, and gentle woman,

to whom I owe more than I can ever repay.

CONTENTS

INTRODUCTION

THE WORD "CRUSADE" HAS ENTERED OUR MYTHOL-
ogy as a single-minded fight for a cause. "Crusader" often conjures up an
image of pennants fluttering in the wind and stalwart knights on horseback
galloping across the desert to meet the foe. Over the centuries the migration
from Western Europe to the Near East at the end of the eleventh century has
been viewed through multiple lenses, some highly distorting.

The Crusades have been seen as a selfless religious battle to free Christians from Muslim tyrants. This is what Pope Urban, Peter the Hermit,
Bernard of Clairvaux, and others preached at that time to persuade the first
Crusaders to go. Later historians saw the Crusades as a series of colonial
invasions, a useful activity for troublesome younger sons, who could either
make their fortune or die. While this is still a popular notion, it isn't borne
out by the facts. Many families sent all their sons and some daughters on
the first crusade. This included the great noblemen who left their estates in
the care of others or even sold them in order to finance the armies headed
to Jerusalem.

Other historians have seen the crusades in terms of economics, viewing
the Crusaders as looters and cynical merchants who wanted a monopoly on
rare items from the east. There was an element of truth to this, especially
considering the deals that Italian city-states made with the Crusaders for a
share of the profits. Then there is the romantic image of chivalry, honor, and
justice that was reflected almost immediately in popular literature and has
lasted until the present day in stories of Richard the Lionheart, Saladin, and
the Templar and Hospitaller knights.

It's been more than nine hundred years since the armies of the West, drawn mainly from what is now France, Belgium, and Northern Italy, captured the Holy City of Jerusalem and set about creating a Latin Christian state. Almost without exception, they believed that they were liberating the land where Jesus had lived, died, and risen, and from which the Apostles had set out to convert the world. The Crusader States were formed to ensure that these holy sites would remain in Christian hands.

But once the land had been freed from its Muslim overlords, then what? There were people there and ruins from civilizations going back to the dawn of humanity. The inhabitants were of many faiths. Some welcomed the western armies, while others, including local Christians, were horrified. Only recently have scholars started to consider the many facets of the society that the Crusaders entered.

The seeds for this book grew from an article I read some time ago on Melisende, the first hereditary queen of Jerusalem and the first person to inherit the crown by succession. The first three rulers of Jerusalem, including Melisende's father, Baldwin II, had been elected by the nobles of the expedition. There had been women who inherited in their own right before, but never in a new state, far from Europe, in a precarious military situation.[1]

Melisende rose to the challenge. She was extremely active in governing her kingdom, first with her husband, then on her own after his death. She was the acknowledged queen and in her own lifetime no one questioned her status, and yet this article, written in 1973, treated her as a female usurper, emphasizing the actions of her husband, Fulk of Anjou, and her son, Baldwin III, pushing Melisende into the background. Although all the evidence we have indicates that Melisende was a strong ruler, many historians have either ignored her or criticized her for trying to control the kingdom rather than defer to her husband and son. Reading this article, the only one to focus on Melisende alone, I began to wonder how many other women had been vilified in the same way by overwhelmingly male writers reacting to the status of women in their own day.

The answer is, a large number of them. As I began to look for the women of the Crusader States, I noticed that there were many besides Melisende who had been respected in their own time but had later been left out or relegated to the edges of history. I realize that this is not always intentional. The women of the crusades have most often been the subject of either short academic monographs or historical romance. Most history written for general readers is still heavy on politics and battles. The majority of materials written during the crusading period deal with these topics as well, which were vital to the chroniclers. But, if one looks closely at the sources, one can find the women, the peasant farmers, the merchants, and the bewildering assortment of distinct religious sects: Melkites, Jacobites, Ishmaelites, Druze, Samaritans, Maronites, Karites, and many more. There were also distinct ethnic groups for the Europeans to learn about and interact with. There were Greeks, Turks, Arabs, Armenians, Syrian Christians, Syrian Jews, Bedouin, Persians, and others. It was clear to me that their stories had to be included in the narrative to make a complete picture of life in the Latin States.

While the new arrivals needed to learn the differences among these native groups, they were referred to by the locals as Franks no matter where they came from. I shall adopt this custom when I speak of the settlers as a group.

Since Melisende was the impetus for my writing, her life span, from about 1105 to 1161, comprises the boundaries of this book. But almost all the written records from this period have vanished, lost to time, war, and neglect. Nothing specific is known about her early life. We have a few letters written to her, but nothing written by her. As she entered the political sphere, there are more records about her, but not enough to write a traditional biography as one would about Queen Victoria or Catherine de Medici. In telling Melisende's story, understanding the world she lived in—that of her mother, sisters, and other women, and nameless pilgrims, settlers, natives, monks, brigands, and lunatics—becomes very important.

Therefore, the first section of *Defending the City of God* sets the scene and introduces the people who were important to Melisende, most of all her mother, Morfia, who is barely mentioned in the contemporary sources but who was obviously brave and loving and deserves to be remembered. Melisende's grandfather, the Armenian Gabriel of Meletine, seems to have been a nasty example of a man who saw a political vacuum and decided to fill it ruthlessly. He is typical of the independent warlords who took advantage of the chaos of the times. These freebooters were a breed of their own, not typical of any particular group, but endemic to all. He has been ignored by history but was a key player in the politics of Edessa, where Melisende was born.

It would be nice to write a history of the Near East and not mention any fighting. That is as impossible for the twelfth century as it is for the twenty-first. But I do try to see the many battles and skirmishes from the point of view of the people whose crops were being destroyed, whose families were slaughtered or sold into slavery, whose homes were put to the torch. I also present the amazing ways that people recovered and rebuilt after not only war, but earthquakes, floods, droughts, and plagues of locusts.

The Latin States covered parts of what are now the countries of Syria, Turkey, Israel, Jordan, Lebanon, and Egypt. Even before westerners entered the picture, towns that were largely Muslim or Christian changed overlords often, sometimes by the week. Occasionally, oppressed townspeople rose up and made their own decision to change rulers. Borders were always in flux.

I have been writing this to the accompaniment of a civil war in Syria that is now spilling into other countries. It would be nice to think that by the time you read this, it will all be over and everyone will be living together in peace. Sadly, history suggests that this won't be the case. This mountainous, partially arid land with no oil has been the scene of almost constant conquest since before history was recorded. Many of the causes of the current struggles have their roots in this time period. Religious fanatics, unscrupulous dictators, profiteering outsiders, all of these were major participants during Melisende's life, along with pious monks, hardworking farmers, vintners, leatherworkers, silk weavers, goldsmiths, and guides to sites held holy by three religions.

History is not written by winners or losers, but by historians. All the same, there is no way to escape having a bias or being influenced by current events. Most of my information is drawn from twelfth- and thirteenth-century observers, charters that are mainly records of land translations, a few law codes, and the work of archeologists. Many times I found that two or three chroniclers could have completely different impressions of the same event. I have passed these on to the reader to make their own judgment before I give mine. It's important to see history (and current events) through as many lenses as possible.

My goal is to give an alternate perspective that includes the actions of the voiceless. That does not mean I distort or ignore facts. While I have used mainly the chronicles and records of the time, there is still much we can only make an educated guess about. And I have certainly studied the work of scholars whose knowledge of the time and place I respect. Without their work, especially that of translators from Armenian and Arabic, I couldn't have even begun mine.

I don't know what the precise motivations of the people living then were. But I do know that humanity has changed little in the past nine hundred years. If we were different, we wouldn't still be fighting the same wars, only with deadlier weapons.

The life of Melisende and the world she lived in is a window into the past, but it is my hope that there will also be a reflection in the glass that might help us understand and heal the world we live in today.

THE KINGDOM OF JERUSALEM

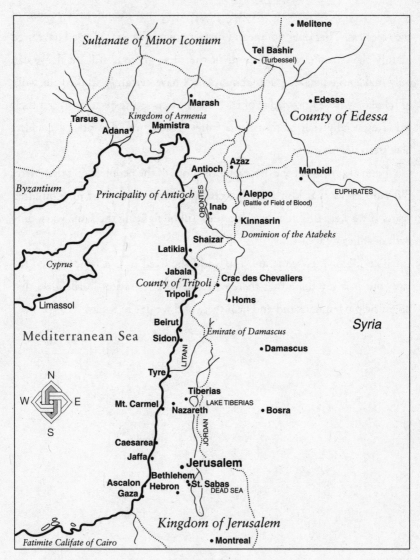

THE CITY OF JERUSALEM

Postern of
the Magdalene

Gate of St. Stephen

Church of
St. Mary Magdalen

Church of St. Anne

Gate of Jehoshaphat

Postern of St. Ladre

6

DOME OF THE ROCK

Church of
Holy Sepulchre

Golden Gate   *Mount
of Olives*

1 2 3 4

5

Templare

David's Gate
David's Tower

Templar Gate

Church of
St. James

CITY OF JERUSALEM

Gate of Zion

•Al- Aqsa Mosque

Mount Zion

1. *Hospital of the Knights of St.John*
2. *Covered Street*
3. *Street of Vegetables*
4. *Street of Bad Cookery*
5. *Syrian Exchange*
6. *Bathing Pool*

Melisende's Family Tree

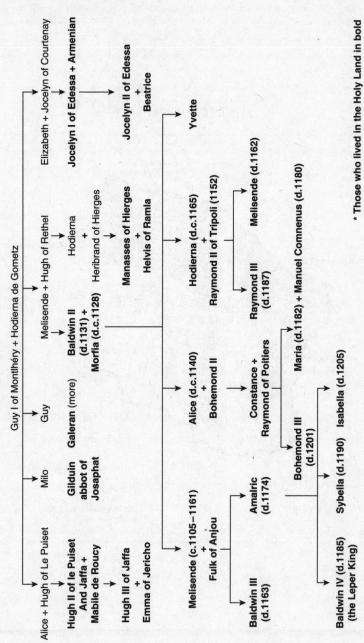

Guy I of Montlhéry + Hodierna de Gometz

Alice + Hugh of Le Puiset

Milo

Guy

Galeran (more)

Gilduin
abbot of
Josaphat

Melisende + Hugh of Rethel

Elizabeth + Jocelyn of Courtenay

Jocelyn I of Edessa + Armenian

Jocelyn II of Edessa
+
Beatrice

Hugh II of le Puiset
And Jaffa +
Mabile de Roucy

Hugh III of Jaffa
+
Emma of Jericho

Baldwin II
(d.1131) +
Morfia (d.c.1128)

Hodierna
+
Heribrand of Hierges

Manasses of Hierges
+
Helvis of Ramla

Melisende (c.1105–1161)
+
Fulk of Anjou

Alice (d.c.1140)
+
Bohemond II

Hodierna (d.c.1165)
+
Raymond II of Tripoli (1152)

Yvette

Baldwin III
(d.1163)

Amalric
(d.1174)

Constance +
Raymond of Poitiers

Melisende (d.1162)

Raymond III
(d.1187)

Bohemond III
(d.1201)

Maria (d.1182) + Manuel Comnenus (d.1180)

Baldwin IV (d.1185)
(the Leper King)

Sybella (d.1190)

Isabella (d.1205)

* Those who lived in the Holy Land in bold

PROLOGUE

BETHANY, KINGDOM
OF JERUSALEM, 1160

THE NUNS HAD PLACED HER IN A CHAIR BY A WIN-
dow facing west so she could be warmed by the afternoon sun. Her useless
arm was folded on her lap. Melisende, Queen of Jerusalem, was not yet sixty,
her dark hair threaded lightly with silver. This stroke was the only thing in
her life that she had not been able to fight.

Now she was trapped in the town of Bethany, in the convent she had ordered built for her baby sister, Yvette. Now little Yvette was the abbess of the
convent. It didn't seem possible that the invincible queen was now dependent
on her sisters and the nuns for even the most private of activities.

Melisende had always been the strong one. As the eldest child she had
been responsible for the others. A childhood full of uncertainty had taught
her to stand up for herself. In her life she had faced enemy armies, wily ambassadors, and ambitious bishops. Her husband had tried to usurp her power
and she had taught him his place. Her older son had finally won his right to
rule only after he had proved he had the strength to control the unruly kingdom. Sometimes Melisende wondered if her advice and example had even
convinced the young Queen Eleanor of France to leave her husband, Louis,
and marry Melisende's step-grandson, Henry II of England.

In her lifetime, Melisende was honored and obeyed. She wasn't alone
among noble women of the twelfth century in demanding and receiving

power, but the Latin Kingdom of Jerusalem was a challenge to govern, even for a man, and her right to rule was not questioned. In her own time, she was respected for her wisdom. Even after her son became king, he still asked for her counsel. It was not her contemporaries, but the historians, from the fourteenth through the late twentieth century, who denigrate her. They call her "Queen Mother" or "regent" for her son. They ignore her, preferring to dwell on the battles of her husband, Fulk. Melisende never thought of herself as regent or as just the king's mother or wife. Jerusalem was hers by inheritance. The Latin East was hers by birth. No one would have dared call her "regent" in her lifetime. To the day of her death Melisende remained queen of Jerusalem.

ONE

ARRANGING THE CHESSBOARD

THE HOLY LAND,
LATIN COUNTY OF EDESSA, 1105

DURING THE MIDDLE OF THE TWELFTH CENTURY, AT a time when the Crusader Kingdom of Jerusalem was barely established, it was ruled by a woman, Melisende, the daughter of a Crusader king and an Armenian noblewoman. Queen Melisende's path to the throne of Latin Jerusalem was not direct; it was marked by a series of fateful accidents. But the fact that the crusading armies of Europe had managed to create a Latin kingdom was in itself amazing—the work, many believed, of a divine hand.

It would have been a brave prophet who would have dared to predict that Melisende would become queen of anything. She was born around 1105, six years after the conquest of Jerusalem, in the city of Edessa, the Crusader foothold farthest inland.[1] Now the town of Urfa in Turkey, it lies between the Tigris and Euphrates rivers, away from the major cities and for travelers at that time, days north of Jerusalem. Her father was a minor lord from northern France, Baldwin of Le Bourq. He had been swept to the Holy Land along with thousands of other Europeans, following the call of Pope Urban II to take up arms and free Jerusalem from the Turkish invaders. He and his comrades were in the land to do God's work and, through his grace, they had succeeded.

At least that's the explanation for the success of the First Crusade that was believed in the West for many generations. How else could this cradle of civilization have been conquered and occupied so easily by Western Europeans?

No one really knows what the spark was that spurred thousands of people—men, women, and children from all walks of life—to sell all they owned and set off to free Jerusalem, which had been under Islamic rule for nearly four hundred years. In the nine hundred years since that First Crusade vats of ink have been emptied by historians and chroniclers trying to understand the cause. We know that the pope preached the expedition at the French town of Clermont and many other places, but what made people listen and then tell their friends and families? What made them heed this call?

The Byzantine princess Anna Komnene and the western monk Albert of Aachen observed the event from opposite ends of the Mediterranean. Both give the same explanation, which varies from that of later historians. They say that the expedition was ignited by a small incident that happened to one monk who became a pilgrim to Jerusalem in the early 1090s. As this man was attempting to visit all the sites of the life, death, and resurrection of Christ, he found himself continually harassed by the Turks who ruled the city and surrounding area. The pilgrim's name was Peter.

When Peter returned to the West, he supposedly began telling everyone that Christians must liberate the Holy City from the infidel. He told his story to Pope Urban, who was moved by the monk's tales of injustice and sent out a call for armed pilgrims to liberate the land that was sacred to Christianity. His preaching produced a fervent response among the nobility of the west.

Peter continued speaking out about the indignities he had suffered. He spoke in towns to local craftsmen and farmers, who were also galvanized by the fate of the Holy Land and joined his army by the thousands. Months before the troops sanctioned by the pope left, Peter led an undisciplined army drawn from many walks of life as far as Anatolia, where it was decimated.

Western historians know him as Peter the Hermit. From her palace in Constantinople, Princess Anna called him "Peter Coucou."[2] Peter's army was a group of ill-prepared pilgrims and soldiers, motivated more by enthusiasm than common sense.

Peter's preaching effectively whipped up the passions of Christians to free Jerusalem, but it was Pope Urban who gave an added incentive to those undertaking the journey. The pope promised the remission of sins to those who had fought, pillaged, cheated, thieved, and raped other Christians in their own countries. He reminded people that the Seljuk Turks were even then almost at the gates of Constantinople and that the emperor needed their help to keep the enemy from sweeping across Europe. To most, the call to liberate Jerusalem was more compelling than the desire to keep the Byzantine Empire afloat, but there were also political and monetary reasons to do so.

What Urban's private motives were is impossible to say. There had been an embassy from the Byzantine court to the papacy in 1095 and it may have contained a request for more mercenaries to replenish the imperial army, but all records of the actual event have been lost. At the time Urban was in a political quagmire. Although he was theoretically the leader of Christendom, Pope Urban wasn't speaking to William Rufus, the king of England. Philip, king of France, had been excommunicated and was living in contented adultery with Bertrada, the wife of the count of Anjou. And the Holy Roman emperor, Henry IV, had not only been excommunicated but had thumbed his nose at Urban and set up his own anti-pope.

Something was needed to bring faithful Christians together under the papal banner. Urban may have hoped that this expedition to restore Jerusalem for Christ would be the unifying force.

But the pilgrims who went on the crusade did not show any particular interest in helping the power of the papacy. They had generally not been inconvenienced by the problems their kings were having, and royal excommunication, though annoying to the clergy, did not have a big impact on their lives. The majority of them went in white-hot religious passion, ready to suffer for the Faith. What could have been missing in the lives of the thousands who answered the pope's call? They could have mended their sinful ways and entered convents and monasteries at home or devoted themselves to caring for the poor and sick rather than undertake such a dangerous and difficult journey.

I think that their response may have had less to do with faith and more with doubt. Perhaps what many needed was physical evidence of Christianity. They had to see the places sanctified by their lord, his mother, the apostles, and the saints. The dissension between the popes and lords must have been unsettling to their convictions, as well as the evidence all around that they were not living in a kingdom of God, although it was called Christendom. Adding to these uncertainties may have been wanderlust or a desire for wealth, but at the core of the original crusading movement was a desire to reaffirm wavering faith and to earn personal salvation.

When the Crusaders first arrived in the Holy Land in 1098, few people living there realized that these Europeans were an invading force. The Syrian gardener in Damascus, the Jacobite Hermit in the mountains, the Turkish sultan in Baghdad, the Armenian and Jewish merchants in Jerusalem may have heard of the Franks who were raiding along the northern coast but they were not unduly worried. They were used to western mercenaries. The Byzantine emperors had been hiring them for years. Saxons fleeing the Norman conquest of England had brought their swords to the Greek army. The Swedish Varangian Guard were trusted protectors of the Emperors of Byzantium. And, only a few years before, the Norman Robert Guiscard had invaded Byzantine territory in Greece, in the hope of conquering the empire. He was stopped in the Balkans.

It was some time before the inhabitants of the Holy Land realized that these warriors had come to stay, adding a new dimension that would rearrange the dynamics of an already complicated society. Within a generation these newcomers would become the "new Syrians," integrated into the social, religious, and political life of the Near East, changing it as it changed them.[3]

To most, the invaders from the West were little different from the others who had overrun this crescent of land from the Mediterranean Sea to the Tigris and Euphrates rivers over the millennia. In just the hundred years leading up to the First Crusade, the territory had been the center of wars among Greeks, Persians, Turks, and Egyptians. Some of the armies made lightning raids, looted their way across the landscape, and then staggered home with their booty. Others settled in the towns and exacted tribute from the surrounding villages. To the shepherds, farmers, and their families life didn't change much. There was a time of tumult, punctuated by terror, then a new master who wanted the same taxes.

This is their story as much as that of the Crusaders.

Most Crusade histories tell of the battles between Muslims and Christians, the conquest of Jerusalem and its eventual loss. The wives of these men are mentioned primarily as chess pieces. The children born to them tend to be regarded as identical to their fathers, with the same outlook and desires. Yet many of the women and most of the children were not Westerners. They had been born in the East. The Crusader states of Jerusalem, Edessa, Tripoli, and Antioch were the only homes they knew.

This is their story, too.

All the stories come together in Melisende's. Her life encompasses the conflicts that wounded a beautiful land, along with the deep faith and opportunism that created those conflicts. Melisende was descended from millennia of natives of the Near East but also forced by an accident of birth to be the representative of the most recent invaders. For her entire life she balanced on a knife's edge between two worlds.

So what was this place that Melisende was born into? In what sort of land would she spend her first years? To understand that, it's necessary to go back another generation, to the years just before the Crusades.

The old Arab dynasties had fallen apart by the middle of the eleventh century. In Egypt, Ismai'ili Shi'ite Muslims had overthrown the Sunni rulers of Jerusalem. Followers of the descendants of Muhammad's daughter Fatima and her husband, Ali, they considered the Sunni illegitimate leaders of Islam and fervently believed that they must be overthrown.[4] For a time, these Egyptian Fatimids held Jerusalem, but the city was taken from them in 1071 by the Seljuk Turks, newly arrived from their land in the east and only recently converted to Sunni Islam.

The Seljuk Turks were a tribe descended from or connected to a leader traditionally named Seljuk, who had lived in the tenth century in what is now roughly Turkmenistan. They were originally a nomadic people, moving from one area to another with their flocks. Their chieftains governed only with approval of the elders of the group. Leadership passed not from father to son but to the next oldest male relative.[5] When they were converted, it was to a militaristic form of Sunni Islam, which they had learned from the Ghazi, Turkic soldiers who lived on and guarded the frontiers of the Caliphate of Baghdad.[6] The Seljuks kept much of their social structure after conversion even as they began to take over towns in Syria and Iraq, settling among the Shi'ites, Syrian Christians, Samaritans, and others. It was a branch of this tribe, the Ortuqids, who were in charge of Jerusalem when Peter the Hermit had his life-changing experience there. To the native people, including Muslims, the Turks were newcomers with a language they didn't understand and strange customs. Like the western Europeans who followed them, the Turks may have been at first perceived as mercenaries in the pay of the Greek emperor.

Despite several centuries of Muslim rule, a large part of the Near East was still Christian, especially in the north: modern Lebanon, Syria, and Turkey. There were also substantial Jewish communities that had never been part of the diaspora. These groups included Christian and Jewish sects that were considered heretical by the mainstream of each religion, such as the Jewish Samaritans and Karites, the Armenian and Melkite Christians, and the Druze, who considered themselves Muslim but were rejected by both Sunni and Shi'ite. And then there were the Nizari, who are known in the west as Assassins. This group was autonomous in their Islamic beliefs, following a Shi'ite imam of their own sect, although their first leaders had come from the same Ismai'li beliefs as the Fatimids. The Assassins hatred of the Sunni led to the practice for which they were known and feared, political murder. They will appear throughout this story, sometimes in ways that go against the popular myths.

These Muslim groups, especially the Turks, still insecure in their control over the Levant, will be the main opponents of the Crusaders. The Egyptian

Fatimids, once they had lost Jerusalem, were mainly concerned with controlling the coastal cities, such as Tyre and Ascalon, then run by self-governing local lords. Especially in Melisende's life, they were not a continual presence but an occasional threat. Throughout the first half century after the conquest, Latin armies worked their way down the Mediterranean coast, taking control of the important trading cities: Tripoli, Beirut, Tyre, and, eventually, Ascalon. Melisende would have a part in the building of great fortresses that guarded the passes between Egypt and Jerusalem, many of which still stand today, if in ruins.

Once Peter the Hermit's mass of pilgrims had passed through, most lost either to death or slavery, the larger, more disciplined Crusader armies began to arrive. These came in groups, generally organized by region. Melisende's father, Baldwin of Le Bourq, arrived in the party of the three brothers, Eustace, Count of Boulogne; Godfrey, Duke of Lower Lorraine; and Baldwin of Boulogne. They came from the area that is now Belgium, the Netherlands, and northeastern France. The brothers, who soon became famous in legend, were cousins in some degree of Baldwin of Le Bourq although the exact connection isn't certain.

The youngest of the brothers, Baldwin of Boulogne, may have been planning to settle for he brought his wife, Godehilde de Toeni, with him. But we can't be sure of this. There were many in the armies who brought their wives and children on the journey and still returned to Europe, if they survived. Baldwin of Le Bourq seems to have traveled without any other immediate relatives, but, once he gained property in the Holy Land, he soon began to send for assorted sisters and cousins. Melisende would depend on the tight connections among her father's family for friendship and support throughout her life.

There were two other armies that supplied permanent settlers to the Latin States. One of these was led by a man who was a force of nature on his own. He came from the family that had stormed from Normandy into Italy and farther east in the previous generation. Bohemond of Taranto was not one of the original leaders of the expedition but through force of will and military skill he dominated others of higher rank. Bohemond came by this authority naturally. He was the eldest son of Robert Guiscard, a Norman adventurer, who had arrived in Italy in the early eleventh century, following some of his eleven brothers who had hired themselves out as mercenaries to Italian lords. After a time working for others, Robert went into business for himself, robbing travelers and monasteries for a while before slashing his way through a conquest of Greek-held southern Italy and Sicily.[7] Princess Anna Komnene loathed both Robert and his son for their ruthless and uncouth natures. But she had to admit they were striking. She described Robert as "a man of immense stature, . . . He had a ruddy complexion, fair hair, broad shoulders, eyes that all but shot out sparks of fire. In a well-built man, one looks for breadth here and slimness there; in him all was well-proportioned and elegant."[8] She also noted his loud and commanding voice. Anna added later that Bohemond resembled his father in all respects.[9] Bohemond may have been even larger. His given name was actually Marc, but his father called him Bohemond for a character in a now lost story who was known for his size and strength.[10] One might recall that the family was only a generation removed from their Viking ancestors, who had conquered Normandy. Anna viewed them with much the same wonder and fear that villagers must have felt when the Viking ships sailed up the rivers to their homes.

While Bohemond must have had some religious belief, it's probable that he took the pilgrim cross mainly to continue in the family tradition of conquest. Robert Guiscard had left his county of Apulia in southern Italy to Bohemond's younger half-brother, Roger. There may have been many reasons for this but Guiscard's single-minded series of assaults on Greek territory gives the impression that the Norman intended Bohemond to one day become the Byzantine emperor. Guiscard died of a fever while on campaign in 1085 at the age of seventy. Both his sons followed in his footsteps. With the huge number of relations from his father's family, Bohemond was able to recruit many cousins and nephews along on the Crusade. Three of them—a nephew, Tancred, a cousin, Richard, and Richard's son, Roger—would play important roles in Melisende's early life.

In the first wave of Crusaders there was also a force led by Raymond of St. Gilles, count of Toulouse and duke of Narbonne. When Raymond came to Constantinople, Anna found the nobleman from Provence much more civilized than the other Crusaders. She praised his intellect, piety, and honesty, noting that Raymond and her father, Emperor Alexis, became close friends.[11] She didn't mention his appearance or dwell on him the way she did with Robert Guiscard and Bohemond.[12] Of course, Robert was nearly sixty when he went on crusade and was accompanied by his pregnant third wife, Elvira.[13]

In contrast to the Normans, Raymond seems to have left his extensive lands from a sincere desire to free Jerusalem from the Muslims and to save his soul. He was lord of a much larger territory than that of the king of France. Provence had been settled by the Greeks and then the Romans and traces of Roman civilization remained. The land was not only wealthy but heir to over a thousand years of culture: art, literature, and philosophy, as well as fine wine. Raymond conquered the city of Tripoli and established an outpost county on the coast. But he died there of wounds received in a skirmish soon after his son, Alphonse Jordan, was born.[14] The county of Tripoli, settled by people from the south of France with frequent contact with the other Mediterranean lands, developed a society and culture unlike the others, becoming an important mercantile center.

Soon the new settlers would learn about the diverse peoples that they had conquered and the internecine wars that had made the conquest of Jerusalem, Antioch, Edessa, and Tripoli possible. But for the first few years they were busy adapting to their new lives.

SO NOW THE KNIGHTS, KINGS, AND BISHOPS ARE IN place. The pawns, as always, are scattered all over the chessboard, many already captured or slain.

The only piece missing is the queen.

TWO

CHILD OF THE FIRST CHRISTIAN CITY

EDESSA, 1105–1118

MELISENDE WAS BORN AND SPENT HER EARLY LIFE IN the city of Edessa. The state of Edessa under the Crusaders included much of what is now south-central Turkey and northern Syria. The city first fell into the hands of the Crusaders almost as a side trip, when Baldwin of Boulogne left the siege of Antioch looking for more adventure, but eventually it came into the hands of Melisende's father. The reason that the Crusaders were able to take a city so far inland is due to the machinations of Melisende's grandfather, the Armenian lord Gabriel of Melitine, who was as much an opportunist as the Norman Bohemond.

A literate knight who recorded his journey, writes of Edessa, "A very rich land lies between twin rivers, the Tigris and Euphrates. . . . Among the many cities which this land holds in its bosom, is one ancient, powerful, beautiful, wealthy with ore. . . . This city, whose name has been corrupted to Rohas, but in ancient times possessed the name Edessa . . . [is] where the patriarch Abraham lived."[1]

The borders around what became the county of Edessa were indistinct and constantly changing as small bands of independent freebooters fought for control of villages. This area of Anatolia was theoretically part of the Byzantine Empire. However, at the end of the eleventh century, the Byzantine emperor Alexis was trying to hold on to power in the region while simultaneously fighting against the Turks invading Anatolia from the east and a Norman army (under the same Norman Bohemond, continuing his father's plan), invading the Balkans from the west. Alexis hadn't the time or manpower to protect the scattered settlements on the southern edge of the empire. For an unprotected prize as rich as Edessa, there were many who were willing to risk their lives and fortunes and even make a detour to conquer it on their way to fulfill their promise to free Jerusalem.

The population of Edessa was largely Syrian Christian, with some Muslims and Armenian Christians. The citizens prided themselves on having been Christian from the time of Christ, before the crucifixion, as well as the home of the founder of Judaism, Abraham. According to the legend, the king in the time of Jesus, Abgar, heard of his miracles and sent a messenger asking him to preach to the Edessenes. Jesus instead sent a cloth miraculously imprinted with his likeness.[2] The city converted at once, even before the crucifixion and resurrection. While the tale is an invention, it is known that Edessa became Christian in the second century and the cloth, which appeared in the fourth century and was known as the Image of Edessa, was one of its most revered relics.[3]

Edessa had been conquered by Arab Muslims in the ninth century but stayed Christian and retained its pride in being one of the principal apostolic cities. Even the thirteenth-century Muslim chronicler Ibn al-Athir knew the history of Edessa and honored the site.[4]

The form of Christianity among the Syriac Edessenes was also particular to the place. The people revered native saints and relics and some of their practices were considered heretical by both the Latin and Greek churches. Throughout the centuries, the people of Edessa had held fast to their own convictions and customs. They had a fierce pride in their heritage and a strong sense of justice that they expected their ever-changing rulers to honor. More than one conqueror learned this to his destruction.

The Byzantines reconquered Edessa from the Arabs around 1030 and held it until the Seljuk Turks arrived in 1086. The Turks were in charge for only a few years until more Byzantines, along with the recent Armenian immigrants, took it again, just before the Crusaders arrived. Melisende's mother's family came from these Armenians who had been driven from their homeland in the east by the Turks a generation before and were now trying to carve out independent territories for themselves under distant Greek rule.

The religious significance of the city wasn't the only reason why Edessa was so often attacked. Some believed it was the site of the Garden of Eden, and it still seemed so to those who lived there. Citrus and olive trees grew in abundance as well as wheat and barley. The cooing of doves could be heard all over as every town kept dovecotes for both food and fertilizer. Ibis flew from Egypt to summer there. Most importantly, Edessa was a major stop on the trade route from the Persian Empire to the West.

On this same trade route was the town of Melitine, north of Edessa in Cappadocia, where Gabriel, the father of Melisende's mother, Morfia, was titular ruler. Gabriel was an Armenian but had many Greek contacts and had apparently converted to Greek Orthodoxy. Whether this was a spiritual or political conversion is open to debate. He had received the lordship of Melitine through his connection to another Greek/Armenian named Philaretos who was the deputy of Emperor Alexis in the city of Antioch. According to the account written by Anna Komnene, Philaretos was an opportunist who, when he saw that the Turks were nearing Antioch, "decided to join them and offered himself for circumcision, as was their custom. . . . [H]e arrived in Nicaea in a state of extreme distress."[5] The Armenian chronicler Matthew verifies this, saying that Philaretos renounced "the faith of Christ which he had not held in very pure manner to begin with."[6] This sort of battleground conversion was not unusual.[7]

Gabriel did not go as far as his mentor in currying the favor of the Muslim leaders, but he does seem to have been a man out for himself and not concerned with whom he used in the pursuit of his goals, even if they were his kin, as his cavalier treatment of his daughters will show. The maternal side of Melisende's family had a freewheeling, ruthless audacity that resembles that of the cattle barons of the early American West.

The European chroniclers make little mention of him, only noting that he was Baldwin of Le Bourq's father-in-law, but two Eastern writers have quite a bit to say. The first is Matthew, an Armenian monk of Edessa who was living in the city at the time. The second is Michael, the Syrian Patriarch of Antioch. Michael wasn't born until about 1122 but he grew up near Melitine and had heard stories about Gabriel from his elders.

Michael saw Gabriel as a villainous outsider who began his career in Melitine by murdering the Syrian bishop John because of a disagreement over surrendering the town to the Turks. John saw no harm in it as the Christians would not be harmed. Gabriel was not ready to hand over his city, which provided him with rich tithes and taxes. When Gabriel's guard refused to kill the bishop, Gabriel took the lance from his servant and did the job himself.[8]

Melitine was a wealthy town, also on the caravan routes, surrounded by apricot orchards. Michael says that Gabriel was infamous for shaking down merchants who were passing through.[9] Also, "he mistreated the poor worse than the Turks had."[10] In Michael's mind, Gabriel was nothing more than a warlord who had taken advantage of the chaos in the land in the wake of the Turkish invasions to grab all he could. Free of Greek supervision, local governors became independent dictators. This power vacuum full of petty lords and emirs at war with each other is one reason the Crusaders were able to conquer the land. It would be many years before this changed.

Gabriel seemed to have had his eye on Edessa, if not for himself, then for his descendants. He first married one of his daughters to another Greek/Armenian named Toros. Perhaps with Gabriel's help, Toros soon managed to take the citadel of Edessa from the Turks who then controlled it. The citadel, which still looms over the city, was a fortress to which the populace came for protection in times of attack.

Toros was not very popular, either with the Armenian or Syrian Christians, both of whom saw him as an outsider and traitor to his people. His title was *curopalates,* a Greek term meaning "keeper of the palace." However, like his father-in-law in Melitine, Toros seems to have seen Edessa as his private domain, and felt that he was not answerable to the Byzantine emperor. This was the situation in 1098, when the Crusaders, under Baldwin of Boulogne, arrived. They were fresh from the siege of Antioch, which had finally fallen to Bohemond of Taranto. While Emperor Alexis had expected Antioch to be returned to Byzantine control, Bohemond had laid claim to the city and, although they should have continued on to lay siege to Jerusalem, Baldwin and his followers, including Melisende's father, Baldwin of Le Bourq, decided to answer the call of the lord of Edessa for help against the Turks.

At the time of the taking of Antioch, Edessa was also under siege by local Turkish emirs. Toros was reluctant to ask the Byzantine emperor for help, especially since Alexis might not have sent any. Instead, he decided to invite Baldwin of Boulogne to come to Edessa and help him out. Baldwin was still looking for a city of his own, but the ruler of Edessa doesn't seem to have understood this. Toros probably did not expect the Flemish lord to become his successor but rather assumed he could pay the foreigner for his help and send him on his way.

It is agreed by both local commentators, Matthew and Michael, that Baldwin of Boulogne was welcomed in Edessa as a savior. He went through a local tradition with Toros in which the two men rubbed chests under the same shirt and so became family.[11] This is reported by western commentators as a bizarre eastern custom. But, apparently, the local citizens saw it as a binding agreement of mutual support.

Soon after Baldwin's arrival, Toros, his wife, and their children were killed by rebellious citizens. The stories about how this came about vary. Matthew says that men of the town conspired with Baldwin to overthrow Toros. When the *curopalates* saw that he was outnumbered, he surrendered, only asking that he and his family could leave in peace and go to his father-in-law, Gabriel, in Melitine. "Baldwin swore by all the saints" that Toros would be safe. But the next day Toros was beaten by the townspeople and thrown to his death from the top of the ramparts. "They put his head on a pole and vomited abuse upon him."[12] Others say that Baldwin knew nothing of the matter and that Toros was locked in the citadel by the townspeople and shot with a dozen arrows as he tried to escape down a rope, leaving his family behind. His wife and children aren't mentioned in that version but an anonymous chronicle states that they were also murdered.[13] Gabriel's daughter, whose name has not survived, was another nameless victim of an eternal power struggle. The reason the citizens of Edessa turned on their ruler is not clear. It was neither the first time nor the last that they would oust an unpopular lord. The Latin counts of Edessa would be wary of their subjects for the duration of the years they held it.

Undaunted by this setback to his plans, Gabriel offered his second daughter, Morfia, to the new Crusader prince of Antioch, Bohemond, in return for military aid. Why Baldwin of Boulogne wasn't considered as a husband for Morfia isn't clear. He was free, his wife having died in Marash in Anatolia on the journey. At this time Baldwin may already have been negotiating for his second wife, Arda, another Armenian heiress, the sister of Prince Leon.[14]

Bohemond seems to have considered the marriage offer and set out for Melitine to meet with Gabriel, but on the way he ran into a party of Turks under the Seljuk leader, Qilij Arslan, and was captured and held for ransom.[15] By the time Bohemond was released, he had lost his taste for Armenians. He returned to Antioch, which he ruled until he left for Europe in 1105 in search of fighting men and the funds to equip them. His goal was to return and conquer the Balkans and, ultimately, the Byzantine capitol of Constantinople.

While in Europe looking for recruits, Bohemond went to France, where he married Constance, the daughter of Philip I, king of France, an incredible coup. Their son, also named Bohemond, would later come to the Levant to take over his father's principality of Antioch and would play an important, if brief, role in the balance of power within the Crusader States. In Paris, Bohemond's wedding feast was arranged by Adela of Blois, the daughter of that other Norman conqueror, William. The groom used the opportunity to exhort the other guests to take the crusader's vow, called "taking the cross," and come with him.[16]

Bohemond of Taranto was the first of the heroes of the crusade to return to Europe. His fame had preceded him so that when he reached France, he

The Citadel of Edessa. The last bastion of defense for the city. Photograph courtesy of Penelope Adair.

was celebrated as one who had suffered for the Faith as much as any martyr. His conquest of Antioch was impressive, but it was his capture and release that touched a chord in those who had remained behind. Bohemond had endured imprisonment at the hands of the infidel. His first public act upon arriving in France was to fulfill a vow to visit the shrine of St. Leonard, the patron saint of prisoners. He left a pair of silver manacles as a thank you offering to the saint. What his admirers did not know was that Bohemond had been freed by Qilij Arlan's enemy, Danishmend, who wanted the Norman to continue his battle against their mutual enemy, the emperor of Byzantium.

He made a grand speaking tour of northern Europe visiting castles, monasteries, and cities. His popularity was such that he was asked to be godfather to a number of the infant sons of the nobility. "Hence, this celebrated name, which formally was unusual throughout the whole west, was now made common in Gaul."[17]

Bohemond was in his fifties by this time but had the stamina of his father, Robert. He mounted another "crusade" that was actually a continuation of his war of conquest against the Balkan territories of Emperor Alexis.

It was a disaster. After this failure, Bohemond never returned to Antioch, but went back to his land in Italy. He died on March 7, 1111.[18] Antioch was held in trust for his two-year-old son, Bohemond II. However, Bohemond's nephew, Tancred, left in charge, would soon style himself "Prince of Antioch" and mint coins in his own name.

Baldwin of Boulogne remained in Edessa for two years before being chosen king of Jerusalem on the death of his brother, Godfrey, in 1101. At that time he gave the county to his cousin, Baldwin of Le Bourq as a reward for his loyalty.

When Baldwin of Le Bourq became count, Morfia of Melitine was still on the marriage market and so her father, Gabriel, offered his remaining daughter to the new count.[19] Apparently the lord of Melitine wasn't worried about sending his child to live in the place where her sister had been murdered. He was also willing to give Baldwin 50,000 gold bezants as dowry.[20] The sum was more than the income of Edessa in a year. The count agreed. The marriage took place sometime around 1103. It seemed an ideal solution. Baldwin got money, Gabriel a militant son-in-law, and Edessa a strong leader. Morfia's opinion was not recorded.

It wasn't long after the marriage that Gabriel's brutal machinations caught up with him. Shortly after Morfia left for Edessa, Melitine was overrun by the Turkish army of Qilij Arslan. Michael the Syrian says that Gabriel was betrayed by the people of the town in revenge for his murder of their bishop and because, "without pity, he pillaged, despoiled and massacred."[21] Michael relates that the Turks who had captured Gabriel took him to the fortress of Qatya, which his wife was defending against the invaders.[22] They ordered him to make her surrender and he refused. With some satisfaction, Michael adds, "When the Turks learned [that he would not do as they demanded], they killed him and threw him to the dogs. They devoured him."[23]

There is no mention elsewhere of the fortress of Qatya or of Gabriel's wife, although one assumes that Morfia and her sister did have a mother. What happened to her after Gabriel's death is unknown. We don't know if Melisende ever met her grandmother or if she grew up with stories about her. Morfia herself is a shadowy figure, rarely mentioned in chronicles or even charters, the classic example of a woman who seems no more than a pawn. But there must have been a deep strength and intelligence in her, as the few hints about her life with—and often without—her husband will show.

Baldwin seems to have made himself respected in Edessa, partially by raiding Muslim territory and bringing back slaves, hostages, and "innumerable flocks of sheep and thousands of horses, cattle and camels," some of which the citizens shared in.[24] Baldwin also showed respect for the religion of the Armenians, another form of Christianity considered heretical by the Greeks and Latins. When the Armenian Patriarch Barsegh came from Ani to visit Edessa, "Baldwin received him with great honor, as is befitting a patriarch."[25] This earned him points with his Armenian subjects.

If Melisende was born in 1105, as records indicate, her Crusader father wasn't there to see his first child. Baldwin was languishing in prison in Mosul, having been captured during May 1104 in a raid on the nearby Muslim town of Harran. He was being held for a ransom that was slow in coming. His cousin, Jocelyn of Courteney, was captured as well, making him one of the first of many cousins to share in the bounty and danger of the Holy Land. Jocelyn had managed to raise his own ransom but was having a hard time getting the 60,000 bezants Baldwin's captors demanded.[26]

This situation could not have made life secure for Morfia and her newborn child.

So now we need to focus on Morfia. Her father had been slain and her home was in the hands of his enemies. She apparently was left with few relatives to turn to and her husband was in prison in Mosul, waiting for someone to appear with ransom money. Gabriel had died before Morfia's dowry was paid in full, so she must not have had funds of her own to secure her husband's freedom.

What was happening to her and their baby daughter? How did they survive?

Morfia may have stayed in Edessa and tried to keep a low profile while doing what she could toward getting Baldwin released. This may not have been much. There were few French in Edessa to seek help from. The Syrian and Armenian Christians may not have accepted her as their countess as she had been raised Greek Orthodox, which they considered traitorous as the religion of the tyrants who had ruled them. Her relationship with the native churches isn't clear at this time, although she donated to them later in her life. She may have gone to stay with her mother in Qatya, if it hadn't fallen to the Turks. The surviving records don't mention anything more about her family. All we know is that she and her firstborn child managed to stay alive.

Morfia's predicament is one that occurred many times in the Crusader States. Women were left to cope when towns and estates were attacked, their fathers or husbands gone to battle, captured, or slain. There are even reports of men of fighting age fleeing towns under attack, leaving their families to be slaughtered or enslaved. Morfia must have been resourceful to retain her position as countess of Edessa despite the likelihood that Armenian, Frank, and Muslim lords all had designs on the county. Because of her lack of family support and because she had so recently come to Edessa, it's doubtful that she had much say in the governing of the city.

Baldwin's cousin, Jocelyn, was released sometime in 1106 through the efforts of the people of his city of Tel Bashir, also called Turbessel. He did his best to raise the ransom for his cousin and may have tried to see that Baldwin's wife and child were taken care of, but no one knows.

The reason for the delay in Baldwin's ransom was not just that it was so high but that Bohemond of Antioch, who was at that time still in the east, and his nephew, Tancred, weren't eager to see the lord of Edessa freed. They had put Richard of Salerno, another of their many relatives, in charge of the city while Baldwin was out of commission, and Richard was milking everything he could out of it in the way of taxes and tithes.[27] The chronicler Albert of Aachen says that the county was worth 40,000 bezants a year.[28] Baldwin's compatriots were not interested in returning this lucrative property to him. It is likely that Morfia did not remain in Edessa during Richard's stay there, but even if she had, she could not have been welcomed by this rapacious steward.

Richard was not earning the trust of the people of Edessa. His military exploits in the area brought no wealth to the city and he apparently made no effort to learn the language or customs. Matthew, living in Edessa at the time, was scornful of his arrogance. Jokermish, the emir of Mosul, who had captured Baldwin, was still prowling the area when, Matthew sneers, "[Richard] unwisely made a sortie against the brave and militant Persian forces."[29] Richard's men were pushed into the moat by their opponents; Jokermish entered the city, looted it, slaughtered the local defenders, and left. "Thus on that day great sorrow fell upon Edessa, for cries and weeping issued forth from every household and blood flowed in all areas of the city."[30]

Matthew of Edessa's accounts are particularly interesting because they provide an eyewitness report of events. However, he is very much on the side of the Armenian natives, which forces the reader to critically examine this bias. Matthew was also positive that the end of the world was approaching soon and he saw apocalyptic signs everywhere, which led him to dwell on disasters in his accounts.

He was certain that the signs from heaven were against Richard. In 1105 the Cathedral of Saint Sophia in Edessa suddenly collapsed. Even more unnerving, on February 13 of that year, "a very awesome, yet marvelous comet appeared, one which instilled fear in those observing it."[31] Richard does not seem to have been one who heeded divine warnings, much to Matthew's disgust.

Richard doesn't seem to have been fazed even when Aplast'an, another Armenian town under Frankish rule, became so fed up with the avariciousness of their governance that they threw out the Frankish commander and went over to the Turks.[32] While there was no separation of Church and State, or even the concept of a totally secular government, the inhabitants of the Near East were happy to choose their overlords based on non-religious matters such as tax rates and military protection. Especially in this remote area, out of range of the emperor in Constantinople or the caliph in Baghdad, towns assumed as much autonomy as they could, and the authority of the native merchants and tradesmen in their own communities should not be underestimated.

The determination on the part of Bohemond and Tancred to keep Count Baldwin imprisoned was made even clearer when his captor in Mosul sent a legation to Antioch and Edessa with the offer to exchange the count in return for the release of a noblewoman of their house who had been captured when Antioch fell. From Jerusalem, King Baldwin I encouraged them to do this but the men wrote back that, "at this time it is necessary . . . to see if we can find a way to extract some money as well as our brother Baldwin himself in return for the restoration of the woman, for we are sadly in need of funds to repay the soldiers."[33] Melisende's father remained in chains for four years.

The intrigues, betrayals, and invasions being suffered in Edessa were endemic to the region, and the arrival of the Franks had only added another piece to the elaborate competition for power. The Damascene chronicler Ibn al-Qalanisi wrote, "In this year [1104] reports were brought to the effect that the peoples of Kurasan, Iraq and Syria were in a state of constant bickering and hatred, wars and disorder, and fear of one another, because their rulers neglected them and were distracted from the task of governing them by their dissension and mutual warfare."[34] Much of al-Qalanisi's account tells of the battles among the various Muslims, something that he laments since it allowed the Crusaders to become established.

Ibn al-Qalanisi wrote from the city of Damascus throughout most of this period. An Arab Muslim scholar and the director of the chancellery of Damascus, he is often just as annoyed with the squabbles of the Muslim rulers, both Arab and Turk, as he is by the raids of the Franks. He also reflects the attitude prevalent in the early years of the Latin States. To him, the new conquerors are just another in a line of infidels or heretics who have invaded his land. He doesn't like them as a group but finds some decent enough. Al-Qalanisi doesn't speak of *jihad,* holy war, against the Franks any more than he would against the Greeks or Fatimids. The Muslim religious war against the Crusaders comes later and reaches its pinnacle long after Melisende's death, with the rise of the Kurdish emir Saladin.

So Melisende's early years were likely spent not in a Frankish court but in a typical Near Eastern town, playing in the dusty streets or lush gardens kept green with wells. The city of Edessa also had water from a Byzantine canal centuries old when Melisende was born and an even more ancient irrigation system, ensuring the grain and fruit would thrive in the nearby fields.

There was always the danger of attack, if not from raiders, then from the lions, hyenas, and other wild beasts that still roamed the hills, but for a well-off child, Edessa would have been a comfortable place to live, except, of course, when the streets ran with blood.

Melisende's first language was certainly not the French of her father, but her mother's Armenian and perhaps the Arabic of the Syrian Christians. In her looks, dress, speech, and diet, Melisende was a native of the Near East. The only thing European about her was her name.

Her namesake grandmother, Melisende of Montlhéry, came from a prolific family that would provide Crusaders for several generations.

The Montlhéry family was a multi-branched dynasty that descended from Guy and Hodierna of Montlhéry. The couple had two sons, but it was the four redoubtable daughters—Alice, Melisende, Elizabeth, and Hodierna—who sent their sons and daughters to the Holy Land. Baldwin's cousin Jocelyn, to whom he gave the neighboring territory of Tel Bashir, was the son of Elizabeth.[35] Many other members of the family appear throughout this study. It is possible that Morfia was able to find shelter with some of her husband's cousins, although it's not clear from available records which of them other than Jocelyn had arrived by 1104. All through Melisende's adulthood this family connection would remain strong. Her Montlhéry cousins were among her staunchest supporters in all her struggles. And the Montlhéry women would be her role models, although not as much, I believe, as her mother.

Melisende became a bridge, first between her parents, neither of whom spoke the language of the other, then between the Frankish settlers and the eastern Christians she lived among. She was the first ruler of Jerusalem who could communicate directly with the Muslims in her land. But, at the beginning of her life, she was as subject to the machinations of men with swords and armies as any of her neighbors.

THREE

WORLDS COLLIDING

EDESSA AND
THE NORTH, 1108–1111

IN MANY WAYS, BALDWIN'S PREDICAMENT DURING captivity was much worse than Morfia's. Beyond having been defeated in battle and held for ransom, which couldn't have been pleasant, Baldwin was adrift in an alien culture. In the first six years that he had been in the east, most of his time had been spent with other northern, French-speaking Europeans. His main contact with the natives, apart from his wife, had been while trying to kill them and take their land. Now he was forced to live under their control. He ate what he was given and was subject to their customs. He must have managed to learn something of the language, if only for survival.

For most of his imprisonment, Baldwin was held in the town of Mosul, about 250 miles northwest of Baghdad, the center of Sunni power. Mosul lies on the west bank of the Tigris River not far from the ruins of Nineveh. At that time it was a flourishing city, ancient and wealthy. Like Edessa, it lay on the trade routes from India and China. Along with a mosque built by the Umayyad dynasty in the seventh century, there were Christian monasteries that had been continuously occupied since the fourth century.

He didn't start his imprisonment in Mosul. Baldwin had first been cap-tured by Ma'in ad-Daula Suqman ibn Ortek. Suqman was a Ortuqid Turk, a branch of the Seljuks descended from a man named Ortuq, the leader of those who had held Jerusalem when Peter the Hermit visited. He had lost Jerusalem to the Shi'ite Fatimids of Egypt just before the Crusaders arrived. Suqman's family was influential, with many brothers, sons, and cousins who would oppose the Franks over the next few generations.

After losing Jerusalem, Suqman moved north to the area around Edessa in the hope of carving out a new territory for himself in any place where the armies were weak, no matter what the religion. It was the threat of attack from Suqman that had driven Toros to call on Baldwin I for help.[1] In 1101, the Franks, including Baldwin of Le Bourq, had invaded a town Suqman had just captured and taken it from him.[2] So it must have pleased the Turk immensely to have captured the count of Edessa at Harran. However, Suq-man didn't hold Baldwin for long.

The leader of another section of the Turkish army was Jokermish, emir of Mosul. The two men had had a falling out because Jokermish had mur-dered Suqman's nephew.[3] Now, one of the many things the Crusaders and the Turks had in common was intense family loyalty and, although they had grudgingly agreed to fight the common foe, neither Suqman nor Jokermish felt any comradeship.

At the battle of Harran, Suqman had not only captured Baldwin and other noble Franks for ransom but a lot of booty as well. Jokermish's soldiers had collected little. "What shall we say to our people," they asked him, "If Suqman's men take all the spoils and we have nothing?"[4] What could Joker-mish say? He couldn't have his army humiliated. Baldwin and Jocelyn were seized from Suqman's tent by night and spirited off to Mosul.

While Melisende's father was cooling his heels in Mosul and Richard of Salerno was getting what he could out of Edessa, the conquest of the Holy Land proceeded. The Crusaders were no more united than the Muslims, as was shown by their lack of interest in freeing Baldwin. Money, property, and personal enmities were more important to the ruling class than religious principles. Especially in the early years of the conquest, politics often ignored boundaries of ethnicity and faith. This complexity was not acceptable to later historians writing from nationalistic or religious points of view, and was generally downplayed, especially in the seventeen and eighteenth centuries.

As part of this network, Baldwin was able to benefit from the ambition of his next captor, the newest ruler of Mosul, Jawali, who was rather like the Muslim counterpart of Richard in Edessa in his desire for power despite being only a lieutenant for a greater lord. Jawali had received the city to govern for the Turkish caliph, Qilij Arslan, who was based in Gabriel's old city of Melitine and stretched his influence as far as he could. Qilij Arslan had ordered Baldwin's captor, Jokermish, removed from office because "[Jokermish] did not carry out what he had said and found service and tribute burdensome."[5]

Mosul was therefore assigned to Jawali, but only if he could defeat Jokermish and remove him from the city. This grant gave Jawali free reign to attack Jokermish without worrying that Jokermish would receive help from allies. Baldwin's captor was soon defeated and slain, his head sent to Mosul as confirmation of his death. Baldwin now found himself part of the booty captured by Jawali, who became the emir of Mosul.

But if Qilij Arslan thought that Jawali would be a more tractable steward than Jokermish, the sultan was doomed to be disappointed. His new emir was no more inclined to obey than the last. Jawali fortified Mosul and prepared to defend it as his own. Along with the son of Jokermish, who was looking for revenge, Qilij Arslan set out to teach Jawali his place. But the lesson went awry for the sultan. In the blistering heat of June, so fierce that many of the horses died, Jawali fought and defeated Qilij Arslan, who was killed in the battle.[6] That accomplished, Jawali then went out to raid, forage, and plunder, according to tradition, leaving his wife in charge of the city. He took Baldwin with him, however, perhaps thinking the count was too valuable a prize to let out of sight.[7]

Ibn al-Athir tells us that, in Mosul, "Jawali's wife extorted money from those left in the city and oppressed the womenfolk of those who had left."[8] So, when Qilij Arslan's successor, Mawdud, attacked Mosul, the tradesmen of the city rose up, killed Jawali's troops and opened the gates.[9] They were no more tolerant of tyrants than the Christian Edessenes. Jawali's wife was allowed to leave safely and quickly retreated to her brother's estates. Mawdud took over Mosul. At this point Baldwin of Edessa had been the prisoner of three different Muslim emirs, each of whom had been defeated in a power struggle that had nothing to do with the Crusaders.

With Mosul in the hands of his enemy Mawdud, one can see why Jawali would be willing to finally make a deal for his most valuable prize of war. Jocelyn was able to raise part of Baldwin's ransom and offered himself as hostage for the rest, out of loyalty as both cousin and vassal. Along with the partial payment and Jocelyn's offer, Baldwin finally promised to free Muslim captives that he had taken earlier. He also swore to come to Jawali's aid, "with troops and money" if needed. In August 1108, Jawali gave him his freedom and "a robe of honor."[10]

Both men would respect the alliance.

Chroniclers who were more interested in battles and conquest didn't really care where Baldwin found his wife and child or what had been happening to them in the four plus years he'd been away. It's not even clear where Baldwin went upon his release. He may have tried to enter Edessa first and been turned back by Richard. The chronicler Fulcher of Chartres states that when Baldwin tried to gain entrance to Edessa, he was refused admittance. It is agreed that Tancred of Antioch refused to order his steward to give the county back to the count.[11]

Baldwin eventually went to Antioch to have it out with Tancred, but first he had to gather up his forces and find out who was loyal to him. So, my guess is that by this time Morfia and Melisende had taken refuge with "the most faithful"[12] Jocelyn at his fortress of Tel Bashir, west of Edessa. Since Jocelyn had only regained Tel Bashir the year before, they could not have been there longer than that. But it might have been long enough for both Melisende and her mother to learn the basics of her father's French. They might well have stayed at Tel Bashir for the short time that Jocelyn took Baldwin's place in captivity.

If the chronology is correct, this is when Melisende first met her father. She would have been around four years old. Throughout her life, Baldwin would rarely be with his family, even after he became king of Jerusalem. In effect, Melisende was raised by her Armenian mother. This would have made her keenly aware of the conditions of the native people around her.

Even without adding the destruction of war, people were rarely more than a harvest away from famine. Matthew of Edessa states that in 1099 there was a drought that led to such famine in the city that, "A Christian woman of the Roman faith cooked and ate her son. In the same way an infidel Muslim, pressured by the rigors of the famine, ate his wife."[13] Matthew sees this starvation as punishment for the Edessenes' treatment of Toros. But the drought stretched across the land. Near Antioch, a Norman knight wrote that a load of grain cost one hundred and twenty shillings. "Many of our people died there, not having the means to buy at so dear a price."[14]

Additionally, villagers were constantly threatened by warfare. This could range from exploitation by raiding and foraging parties to being stuck in the middle of a major battle. The soldiers who destroyed the land might be Christian or Muslim or both. The differences were slight to villagers, traders, and peasants. The worst part must have been that one never knew when or from what direction the next blow would come.

A prime example of this uncertainty is the bizarre series of battles that resulted from the failure of Tancred of Antioch and Richard of Salerno to return the county of Edessa to Baldwin.

Baldwin had spent his years in prison unable to do anything to safeguard or expand his own territory. Now he was determined to regain his lands. With Jocelyn, who had also been liberated, although the ransom had not yet been paid, he set out to force Tancred to return Edessa to him. Needing the help of allies to regain his territory, Baldwin turned to the Armenian prince, Kogh Vasil, lord of Ra'ban, north of Aleppo, who agreed to help. Baldwin may well have asked his Armenian wife to facilitate translations in making these arrangements. Most Frankish lords had bilingual *dragomen* or secretaries to translate for them, but Morfia could make sure they were accurate and not engaged in treachery.

The struggle between the prince of Antioch and the count of Edessa threatened to overwhelm the new, precarious settlements of the Europeans.

Finally, Bernard, the Latin Patriarch of Antioch, intervened. He convened the citizens and priests of Antioch at a council, where they swore that Bohemond, who had long since gone to Italy, had told Tancred that, if Baldwin were ever released, Edessa should be returned to him. With that testimony against him, Tancred was forced to turn over the city. Richard was given a smaller town near Antioch.

With the income from his holdings restored, Baldwin was able to pay the rest of his ransom to Jawali. On September 18, 1108, Baldwin took the money along with the promised Muslim captives to Mosul.[15]

For a few months after this there was peace in the region. Then, for some reason not given, the conflict between Baldwin and Tancred of Antioch was reignited. Baldwin had few men in Edessa to fill his army. So, in the face of this new threat from Antioch, he did something that horrified Matthew of Edessa: "Baldwin, in collusion with Jocelyn, did a wicked thing, something which was not pleasing in the eyes of God."[16] The count of Edessa called upon Jawali of Mosul, his former captor, for help against Tancred.

There is another version of this Muslim-Christian alliance. Ibn al-Athir, writing about a hundred years after the events, says that Jawali, still locked out of Mosul, wanted to attack Ridwan, emir of Aleppo. He promised to forget the final installment of Baldwin's ransom if the count would help him defeat Ridwan.[17] So the Muslim chronicler states that it was the Muslim emir who suggested that he and the Latin count join forces.

Both these accounts make it clear that Baldwin and Tancred had become embroiled in a long-established feud among the Muslim emirs. Jawali and Ridwan were both Sunni and Turks. Tancred and Baldwin were from different countries but supposedly still Roman Christian.

The animosity between Baldwin and Tancred had much the same root: Baldwin intended to hold Edessa; Tancred was determined to get it. The emirs of Mosul and Aleppo acted for the same reasons. There were no ethnic or religious ideals at stake, only power.

Much has been made of the differences between the European Christians and their Muslim enemies. But there were also many similarities. They seemed to follow the same rules of battle. Foot soldiers were killed, horsemen were taken for ransom, and noncombatants were either slain or enslaved. The reasons for fighting were clear to both sides. They were either territorial or personal. Both groups tended to see clan loyalty as more important than religious affiliation. This was the first time that the Latins and Turks would unite to fight against their co-religionists, but it was far from the last.

Ridwan of Aleppo learned of the coalition forming against him. By this time, Ridwan had established trade relations with Tancred at Antioch, as well as a tentative truce between the states that allowed farmers and merchants in the area of the two cities to continue working. Tancred, still furious at the loss of Edessa, agreed to join Ridwan to fight against Jawali and Baldwin, according to al-Athir. Whatever the instigation, the chronicles all agree that this ecumenical force clashed and that Tancred won.[18]

This was more to Ridwan's benefit than anyone elses', for Tancred was not able to take Edessa, which Baldwin retained. The effort of the campaign also left Tancred less able to invade Aleppo.

Sadly for Baldwin's cousin Jocelyn, the Edessan and Aleppan coalition armies met in his territory, near Tel Bashir, which was ravaged and this was not the last disaster the region suffered this year. Perhaps the comet that had hung in the sky for two weeks that June, with a "tail like a lance, pointing east," had been a warning to the citizens.[19] Just as they were recovering from the destruction caused by the conflict, harvesting what remained of their crops in September, the region was shaken by one of the frequent earthquakes that still strike the region.[20]

After the battle, Tancred returned to Antioch, Ridwan to Aleppo, and Baldwin and Jocelyn to Edessa. Jawali, whose men had broken ranks and fled, was forced to sneak away in disguise. "Jawali realized that he was able to preserve himself neither in the Jazeera nor in Syria."[21] His career as an independent conqueror was over. Eventually, he wound up as a vassal of the sultan in Isfahar and appears no more in the tales of the Crusader States.

In these early years, when alliances were formed based on need and common cause, not religion, it must have been confusing for the foot soldiers. The man fighting at a soldier's side today might be trying to kill him tomorrow. Local villagers, who provided the fields of battle, must have been equally traumatized by the sight of the combined armies.

Baldwin may have thought his troubles were finally over, but his return to Edessa was less triumphal than he expected. A rumor had reached the city that Tancred had prevailed in the battle. Therefore, they were in some doubt about which lord would come through the gates next and how to receive him. Many thought that Baldwin was dead. According to Matthew, the uncertain townspeople got together and consulted with the Latin bishop, who advised them to barricade themselves in the citadel until they knew what was going on. The Edessenes had no intention of letting Richard of Salerno rule them again.[22]

Now, one would think that when Baldwin and Jocelyn showed up the next day, everyone would have breathed a sigh of relief, cheered the victory, and that would be that. Instead, Baldwin seemed very upset to find the citadel had been barricaded. "They [Baldwin's knights?] proceeded to wantonly pillage everything in sight and to put out the eyes of many innocent people."[23] The Franks went so far as to try to blind the Armenian Patriarch, Stephen, but the townspeople saved him by paying Baldwin a thousand dahekansi, gold coins of Armenia.

Matthew of Edessa doesn't seem to be telling the whole story, although he was in Edessa at the time. He implies that different factions within the city were telling lies about each other to Baldwin. Perhaps some were being accused of conspiring to return Richard to power. Whatever the cause, Baldwin's reaction seems to be over the top. Why loot and pillage one's own city? This is one of the many holes in our knowledge of the time. There is no other source for this event. In any case, Mathew states that after this episode Baldwin had no more problems with rebellious citizens.

The winter of 1109 was bitterly cold. Animals and birds died in the fields. Matthew, with his usual apocalyptic flourish, adds, "Moreover, black snow fell upon Persia, which was a frightful omen directed against the Persians, but something which their savants were unable to understand."[24]

Once spring came and the ground thawed, in early 1110, Baldwin and Jocelyn tried again to take the town of Harran. It was a sought-after prize.

Only fourteen miles southeast of Edessa, Harran had been continuously inhabited for over six thousand years. It was another Syrian town associated with the biblical Abraham. One of the mosques contained a rock that Abraham was supposed to have leaned upon when he visited Harran.[25] The town was securely walled, with an adjoining suburb that was also walled. It contained a number of baths filled from cisterns and a canal that had been dug from a nearby river. The inhabitants were mainly Hanbalite Sunni Muslims, followers of a ninth-century legal expert, and there were four important schools of Islamic law there.[26]

Of course, few armies, if any, have ever besieged a town for access to its university, and the attraction of Harran was mainly monetary. A twelfth-century visitor noted that the bazaars were full of luxury goods and "roofed with wood so that people there are constantly in the shade. You cross these *suqs* as if you were walking through a huge house."[27] It was not only wealth but the canal bringing fresh water and boats from the river that made Harran a useful acquisition for the promotion of lucrative trade.

In short, Harran had money and Baldwin needed a lot of it.

It may also be that being captured outside Harran still rankled Count Baldwin and he wanted to finish what he had started five years before. But he was doomed to failure. The Turks beat him back to Edessa again.[28]

There is no mention of Morfia or Melisende at this time in any of the chronicles. Their whereabouts were not of interest to the men composing a record of military activity. I believe that it is probable that they were with Baldwin when he took up his lordship of the county again. I also suspect that it was during the summer following his release, 1109, that Melisende's next sister, Alice, was born.[29] Of course, as with Melisende, there is no surviving record of her birth date. The girls spent their childhood in Edessa while their father spent his time either defending his lands or fighting with his cousin, King Baldwin I, as the Franks slowly expanded their influence.

Over the next few years the Crusader States added more territory, mostly along the Mediterranean coast. Baldwin and Jocelyn left their lands to assist in the conquest of Tripoli in June 1109. They were at the taking of Beirut in May 1110 and Sidon in December 1110, although Sidon had managed heretofore to keep the Franks at bay with hefty bribes.[30] At some point, Jocelyn married an Armenian woman, the sister of a lord named Leon.[31] Since his territory of Tel Bashir had a large Armenian population, this was a good tactical move. It is very likely that he relied on Morfia to help welcome his bride, whose name is unrecorded. Morfia must have been pleased to have a woman who spoke her language in the family.

Even though the Crusaders were focused on the rich coastal cities, Edessa was never a tranquil backwater. It was seen as the buffer between the Muslims of Persia (Iraq and Iran) and the ongoing Latin settlement of the Holy Land. Baldwin may have answered the call of his king to help take the coastal cities, but he had more than enough to keep him busy defending his own region.

Mawdud was still in power in Mosul and had also been granted Harran, which he had given to Najim al-Din Il-Ghazi, another Turk and the brother of Baldwin's first captor, Suqman, to govern.[32] In early May 1110, with the Franks busy at Beirut, Mawdud was determined to finally overrun Edessa. He managed, for once, to convince Tughtigin, the atabeg of Damascus, and several other Muslim leaders to join with him.[33] Tughtigin, a former slave warrior, had probably been born into a pagan Turkic tribe and either captured on a raid or bought as a slave while young.[34] This institution of slave warriors, known as *mameluks,* was unknown in Europe. Likely looking boys were taken as slaves, converted to Islam, and raised as soldiers, often becoming the bodyguard of their master. Many of them, like Tughtigin, were freed as adults and became important leaders in both the Near East and Egypt. Now Tughtigin controlled an army of his own.

Black snow, drought, locusts, and invasion were the seasons of the Crusader States. Even when there was the promise of a good harvest, raiders would often appear to destroy or steal the crops. It became a major duty for the knights and soldiers to come with the peasants to guard the fields while the fruit and grain were being brought in. If the warriors were called to fight, the peasants were on their own.

The Muslim army of Mawdud arrived at Edessa just as the planting season began, surrounding the city and cutting off supplies and access to the fields. They laid waste to the countryside and killed or enslaved the peasants, mostly Syrian and Armenian Christians—those who had not fled.[35] Matthew of Edessa, who was in the city then, gives a graphic description.

> "[T]he emir Mawdud arrived at the head of a countless number of troops which were spread over the vast plain of Edessa. His army surrounded the city on every side, being dispersed over every mountain and hill in the area. The whole east gathered under Mawdud's banner. . . . For one hundred days Edessa was put in dire straits; and everyone, exhausted by the incessant assaults, endured much suffering. Soon the townspeople began to suffer from famine because leaving or entering the city was prevented. . . . Moreover, the orchards outside the city were completely destroyed and all the monasteries found on the mountains were razed to their very foundations."[36]

Ibn al-Qalansi, who may also have been on the expedition in Mawdud's army, adds, "The city was short of provisions and the inhabitants reached the verge of destruction."[37]

Baldwin of Edessa may have been back in Edessa by then, although Jocelyn remained at the siege of Beirut.[38] King Baldwin I heard of his cousin's plight but refused to leave Beirut until the city capitulated. When Beirut fell to him on April 27, 1111, the king assembled his forces, including Baldwin of Edessa's old enemy, Tancred of Antioch, to come to the aid of Edessa. While there were intricate strategies unfolding, one can't really compare the politics of the time with chess, for the sides never stayed the same. The white knight could fight with the black knight for a time, then work with him, and then be lured back to the white army. This time, Tancred followed the king and supported Baldwin of Edessa, but that didn't imply that he wouldn't make another attempt to conquer Edessa in the future.

When he learned that the Franks were approaching, Mawdud lifted the siege and brought his army south to meet King Baldwin I's forces, at Harran, of course. The town itself was not attacked, but the land around it was destroyed just as the fruit trees were in blossom and the grain was sprouting.

The scholars, merchants, bakers, and bath attendants, along with the rest of the people of Harran, could not have been happy to see another battle on their doorstep. The town was fortified but did not have a large garrison. It was mainly a small Muslim town of farmers, traders, and students. Did it matter to them if their taxes went to the Franks or the Turks? It seemed that whoever governed them, the fields outside their homes were destined to host the battles of foreigners.

The diversion created by the Crusader army that brought Mawdud to Harran allowed the people of Edessa to evacuate the city, leaving only a garrison of Armenians to protect it, fortified with the provisions sent by the king.[39]

Edessa was spared, but the ensuing battle at Harran was a victory for the Muslim army. Matthew of Edessa writes, "Mawdud . . . filled the land from the gates of Edessa to the Euphrates River with blood."[40] The Armenian rear guard and the villagers who had followed the Franks' army in the hope of protection suffered most. Many were caught on the wrong side of the Euphrates and either killed or taken as slaves.[41]

Mawdud and his compatriots went to Harran, where they divided the spoils, after which they returned to their homes. The countryside around Edessa was devastated. Towns were destroyed and most of the people gone. The city had been saved, but for what? The replanted apricot and peach trees wouldn't bear fruit for years. It was too late in the season to replant grain, even if enough seed could be found. The winter would be a hard one for the Edessenes.

Count Baldwin and the people began to slowly rebuild, starting with the fortifications. For Melisende this continual uncertainty must have seemed normal. In her short life she had been either witness to sieges and destruction or forced to flee before them. How much did any of the children living in the midst of this understand? Did they take the life for granted or were they haunted by nightmares of soldiers, of being stolen from their parents and sold as slaves? Gilo of Paris recounts seeing one girl led away with other slaves, her hands tied, as she looked back longingly at her hysterical mother.[42] They had all seen such things happen, including Melisende.

This wrenching separation was repeated a thousand times over the years. A later story tells of a Christian woman who entered the camp of the emir Saladin. Her infant child had been stolen during the night by Muslim thieves. "She spent the whole of the night pleading for help in loud lamentations." Finally a dragoman was found to translate. Learning of her plight, Saladin found the man who had bought the baby from the man who stole it, paid his price, and returned it to the mother, "who took it, wept mightily and hugged it to her bosom, while people watched her and wept also." The baby was three months old and hadn't eaten since it had been taken the day before.[43]

The story comes from a Muslim source that is meant to show the kindness of Saladin. To me the story demonstrates what a mother would do to recover a kidnapped child. The baby was probably a boy, taken, as Tughtigin had been, to be raised as a Mameluk in the army of his master.

Did people think it would never happen to them, or was the possibility of invasion and capture a constant dread for parents and children? When the armies were sighted, everyone must have been terrified.

King Baldwin I returned to the coast to attempt to take the town of Sidon, this time aided by fresh reinforcements under Sigurd Jorsalafarer, joint king of Norway with his brother, Eystein. Sigurd had already fought for the Spanish Reconquista and had continued on by sea to the Holy Land to fulfill his pilgrimage vow. He was greeted with joy by the battle-weary Franks. His ships allowed the Franks to blockade the town from the sea as well as land. This prevented forces from coming from Egypt to reinforce Sidon's armies.[44] As with many of those who came to fight, these northern Crusaders seem to have been motivated by the desire to save their souls and make the sites of the deeds of the first disciples Christian again. The succession of events during the conquest of the Holy Land was seen as evidence of divine assistance.

The Muslim rulers of Sidon, seeing that there was little hope, made a deal with King Baldwin I. They paid him tribute in return for safe passage for all those who wished to leave Sidon to take refuge in Damascus. Thoughtfully, the city dwellers left the peasants behind, "because of their usefulness in cultivating the land."[45] This is rarely mentioned but the fact is that in most places crops continued to be planted and harvested. Barring natural disasters and invading armies, the small farmers persisted in their necessary occupation. In this case it was mentioned specifically that the peasants were tied to the land, but it is probable that this arrangement was often taken for granted.

Sidon was taken by King Baldwin I in early December 1111. The Norwegians, having accomplished their mission, went to Constantinople, where they gave their ships to the emperor. Then they returned home. Most of the Crusaders and pilgrims of this era did the same. Those who decided to stay were the exception. After the first wave of Crusaders who established holdings, settlers often came because family members who were already in the Holy Land encouraged them to. Sometimes the pilgrims made the journey on the promise of land or an advantageous marriage. Others were truly pious Christians who wanted to live and die in the places sanctified by Jesus and the Apostles. Throughout the two hundred years of the Crusader States, these pilgrims would be a mixed blessing. Some brought income and news from home. A few, like King Sigurd and his men, gave desperately needed military aid. Others arrived indigent and ill, needing charity and care. All too many pilgrims had no idea of the dangers outside of the fortified cities. They insisted upon visiting holy sites, particularly the Jordan River, where Jesus had been baptized, despite the fact that it was a favorite place for ambushes. In the years to come, special provisions had to be created for the protection of the many who were poor, sick, or just hopelessly naive. One particular group that addressed this problem would become the Order of the Templars, which Baldwin of Le Bourq supported wholeheartedly after he became king.

FOUR

THE FRONTIER COUNTY

EDESSA, 1111–1118

NEARLY FIFTEEN YEARS OF BEING TRAMPLED BY VARI-
ous armies seems to have left much of Edessa a wasteland. The forty thousand bezants that the county was supposed to produce a year had dwindled
by the time Baldwin returned. Periodic famine added to the suffering. In
1109, "the Tigris rose great and the roads were made impassable. The winter
and summer crops were inundated."[1] Some people were able to live on beans
and dates, but others had only grass and mulberries.[2]

As is noticeable through much of history, the very rich were barely affected by the misery of the populace. Ibn al-Athir reports that at the same
time that people were making grass soup in the countryside around Baghdad
the daughter of Sultan Malik-shah was married with a lavish ceremony and
that her dowry was one hundred thousand dinars.[3] Too often, the response
to a diminution in taxable resources led rulers to increase their efforts to
conquer rich neighbors rather than curtail their own lifestyles.

In 1111, Edessa was in the midst of a depression that seemed impossible
to climb out of. From Mosul, Mawdud made periodic raids, destroying what
crops there were and making trade impossible. It appears that Baldwin and

his family were spending more time at Jocelyn's estate at Tel Bashir than in Edessa. They may have decided that it was easier to defend than the city. When Mawdud attacked Edessa again in early 1112, it was not Count Baldwin, but Jocelyn, "the invincible soldier of Christ," who eventually rode in and saved the day.[4] Jocelyn arrived at the last minute, when the Edessenes had lost all hope of rescue, and drove away Mawdud's army.

Just before Jocelyn's arrival, in desperation, some of the men of the city had come to Emir Mawdud and offered to surrender. Matthew of Edessa, a patriotic Edessene to the core, excuses them, saying that, "since these men suffered from the effects of the famine, being in such dire straits, they were not really aware of what they were doing."[5]

Jocelyn, who had seen the ways in which the citizens acted independently when it suited their interests, was not convinced that the men had acted out of starvation. Consequently, he punished the people of Edessa. Ringleaders were "massacred, burned and tortured; now all this was not pleasing in the eyes of God," Matthew points out.[6] When Matthew writes that God is unhappy, the reader has to prepare for something apocalyptic to occur. And soon it would. Matthew is very good at ominous foreshadowing.

Between his perfidious subjects and the continued famine around Edessa, Baldwin must have felt that his dreams of lordship were unraveling. To make things worse, Jocelyn's land around Tel Bashir was flourishing.[7] Farther west than the outpost of Edessa, Tel Bashir was protected from the worst of the raids from Mawdud and the many Muslim and Armenian freebooters.

Adding to these depredations, Baldwin may have begun to wonder if God intended him to establish a dynasty in the Holy Land when Morfia gave birth to a third daughter, Hodierna.[8]

Whatever the underlying reasons, sometime early in 1113, Baldwin and Jocelyn had a major falling out. William of Tyre, writing long after the event, says that Jocelyn's servants taunted Baldwin's, telling them that the count of Edessa was unfit to rule and should sell his lordship to Jocelyn and return to France.[9] When this was repeated to Baldwin, it was said, he furiously sent for his cousin, who came to Edessa without a suspicion of danger.

When Jocelyn arrived, Baldwin immediately had him locked up. Whatever Jocelyn said in his own defense was apparently not good enough for Baldwin, who took back Tel Bashir and every other honor he had given Jocelyn.

Melisende must have been heartbroken. She had spent more time with Jocelyn than with her own father. This was another sudden upset in her life. Already, at the age of eight, she had learned that there was nothing constant.

There has to be more to the story than reported. Baldwin may have been envious of Jocelyn's military and financial success, but this was his first cousin, the man who had offered himself as a hostage so that Baldwin could be freed from captivity in Mosul. They had been allies and friends for years.

Whatever the reasons for the breakup, as soon as he had convinced his cousin to release him, Jocelyn took his Armenian wife and went to Jerusalem, where King Baldwin I, who was cousin to both men, was happy to give him the lordship of Tiberias and Galilee to replace the land Baldwin of Edessa had taken.[10] Jocelyn was certainly at the king's court in the fall of 1115, when he witnessed a charter.[11] It appears that the former lord of Tel Bashir settled in comfortably in his new situation and it was probably in Tiberius that he received something else his cousin didn't have, a son. This child, Jocelyn II, would be a steadfast friend to Melisende for all her life.

Back in Edessa things were not getting any better. Baldwin had lost any trust he might have had in the citizens of Edessa. He might have remembered that the first Baldwin had won the city as a result of a coup engineered by the people of the town. His attempts to accommodate the Armenian majority ended. Rather than be exposed to a possible insurrection, Morfia and the girls stayed in Tel Bashir, which Baldwin now controlled.[12]

Some time after Jocelyn departed, in early 1114, Mawdud of Mosul and his army reappeared. He based himself at Harran, of course, which was still Muslim, and prepared to invade Baldwin's land again. What happened next only appears in reports by Matthew of Edessa, but it seems to fit in with the count's growing mistrust of his people.

Matthew says that some "evil-thinking" Franks came to Baldwin to tell him of a plot on the part of the Armenians and Syrians to hand Edessa over to the Turks. "Baldwin believed these false slanders issuing from their wicked and evil mouths,"[13] Matthew tells us, adding that Baldwin believed the lies, for "because of the perverseness of their character, these Franks regarded all other peoples as basically malicious and evil."[14]

As a result of this calumny, Matthew continues, "On one Sunday . . . at dinnertime, a horrible and disastrous calamity fell upon Edessa."[15] He goes on to tell how Baldwin sent another vassal, Payens of Saruj, and his men without warning to evict all the citizens from Edessa because of their supposed treason.

The soldiers were none too gentle about it. Forced to abandon their homes with no provisions, the people of Edessa fled to the nearby town of Samosata. Matthew was likely one of the refugees. His lamentations are epic. "So the illustrious metropolis of Edessa remained deserted like a widowed woman, who once was a mother to all people and has gathered around herself the populations dispersed from other lands."[16] The poor monk is beside himself with anger and grief. The enemy is coming, their lord has abandoned them, and even God ignores their pleas.

Then something inexplicable occurred. Instead of taking advantage of the abandoned city, entering and looting it, Mawdud turned and headed south to pillage the kingdom of Jerusalem. Matthew sees this as a sign of God's love for Edessa. He adds that Baldwin, ashamed of his treatment of the Edessenes, ordered everyone home three days later, and all was apparently forgiven on both sides.[17]

If the accounts of Matthew of Edessa were all we had to rely on for the history of the Crusader States, one would assume that inexplicable things such as this happened all the time. But Matthew felt that the coming apocalypse needed to be predicted in every event, so it's possible that this altercation between Baldwin and the Edessenes did not happen exactly as described.

On his way south to raid the territory around Jerusalem, Mawdud of Mosul decided to stop in Damascus. He may have wanted to ask the Emir Tughtigin for reinforcements against King Baldwin I. Ibn al-Qalanisi insists that the two men were great friends and that Tughtigin showed Mawdud much honor during his visit.[18] The Frank Fulcher of Chartres agrees with

Ibn al-Qalanisi.[19] But Matthew was of the opinion that Tughtigin didn't trust his guest, believing that Mawdud saw Damascus as a prize as great as Jerusalem and wanted to add it to his territory.[20] Perhaps Matthew's suspicious nature was working overtime.

Or perhaps not.

All three men agree that, in February or early March 1114, a member of the Batini sect (called Assassins in the West), disguised as a guard, attacked Emir Mawdud as he walked in a religious procession in Damascus as part of the observance of the holy month of Ramadan. The assassin stabbed him at least three times. Mawdud's attendants drew their weapons and killed the assailant, but were too late to save Mawdud of Mosul. He was taken to the house of Tughtigin, where they tried to get him to break the Ramadan fast and have some water in his agony. He refused, saying, "I am determined to be fasting when I meet God."[21]

The murderer was unknown to anyone and his body was unceremoniously thrown in the fire. No one is certain who hired him, although Tughtigin of Damascus was suspected by more men than Matthew.[22] It was said that King Baldwin I wrote a letter of condolence to Tughtigin. He is supposed to have told the emir, "A people [the Batini] that has killed its main prop on its holy day in its house of worship truly deserves that God should destroy it."[23] If there is any truth to this story, it would indicate that Baldwin was learning about the beliefs and customs of the Muslims. But the king must have been pleased that this thorn in the side of Edessa was gone.

Ibn al-Qalanisi tried to eulogize Mawdud but had to admit that "his conduct in government was at first tyrannical and his treatment of the citizens of Mosul unpraiseworthy."[24] He adds that Mawdud repented shortly before his death and became a devout and observant Muslim so that "he died the death of a blessed martyr."[25]

Mawdud was buried and the world moved on. From Baghdad, the sultan sent a new emir to Mosul, Rukn al-Dawla al-Bursuqi.[26] Bursuqi would pick up the fight where Mawdud had left off.

Each of the chroniclers I cite has access to different information, as well as their own bias. The stories about Mawdud, Baldwin, and the struggle for Edessa encapsulate the challenge faced by the historian in trying to understand the events of the past. Some of the tales were written by participants or observers, while other chronicles were compiled much later, the authors relying on readings of now lost material or others' emotional memories. There are many times when an event is mentioned by only one person because it only mattered to the group he or she was writing for. Anna Komnene wanted to glorify her father, Alexis. Matthew cared about Edessa and the Armenians. Michael the Syrian notes minor details of happenings in his home town of Melitene. Ibn al-Qalansi is interested in the world of the Seljuk Turks and Damascus. Fulcher of Chartres was confessor to King Baldwin I and so follows his exploits. Many times more than one man will mention that a city was taken or a battle lost and we can assume that this indeed happened. But all of the chroniclers had to speculate on the motivations of the participants. Did Tughtigin hire the assassin? Was Mawdud planning to take over Damascus? What did Jocelyn do to make Baldwin of Edessa his enemy?

We can't know for certain. That doesn't mean that the chronicles are of no use. They have a great deal to say about how the writers themselves tried to make sense of their world and about what mattered to them. Since, for the most part, the voices of the people have long been stilled, these few opinionated, sometimes faulty commentaries are treasures.

In December 1113, another change occurred in the dynamics of the region. Ridwan, emir of Aleppo, died.[27] He had alternately fought and made treaties with the Franks, particularly the princes of Antioch, and his death, along with that of Mawdud of Mosul, made it necessary for all the players on the enormous chessboard of the Near East to rearrange the pieces and renegotiate alliances.

The following year was unusually tranquil. For once farmers harvested the crops without seeing them crushed and burned by armies. But the fragile peace was suddenly broken, not by the hand of man but a blow of nature. Hitting rich and poor, Muslim and Christian alike, this event traumatized the entire northern part of the Crusader and the Muslim States. For once, the apocalyptic ranting of Matthew of Edessa doesn't seem out of place.

It was the middle of the night on Sunday, November 27, 1114, the feast of the Discovery of the Cross. Matthew's report is that of an eyewitness. "Now, while we were in a deep sleep, a horrible, crackling, and reverberating sound was heard, and all of creation resounded from the noise. A severe concussion was felt, and the plains and mountains shook with a frightful echoing sound, while tremendous rocks were cleft and hills were split open."[28]

An earthquake of incredible force had hit the land from Antioch to Mosul. Edessa may have been close to the epicenter. Melisende and her family must have been among the terrified people thrown from their beds by the shaking.

> In this way, like a churned-up sea, all living creatures quaked and trembled with fear at the might of the Lord God; for all the plains and mountains resounded like the clanging of bronze, shaking and moving to and fro like trees struck by a high wind.[29]

Matthew was not alone in assuming that the Last Day had finally arrived. In Antioch, a cleric named Walter was also shaken abruptly awake. He "felt, saw, heard the collapse of walls. . . . More, indeed were caught in their sleep by the collapse, so that one part of the wall remained but they were nowhere to be seen."[30] Walter adds that everyone, "Latins, Greeks, Syrians, Armenians, strangers and pilgrims" each believed the disaster was because of his or her personal sins.[31]

Ever eager to make his point, Matthew says that the earthquake only destroyed the towns and monasteries of the Franks as punishment for their treatment of the Armenians.[32] Of course, he was mistaken about this. The earthquake was not selective, although there doesn't seem to have been much damage in Muslim Damascus. "The earth shook . . . and the people were anxious, but as the tremors ceased, their souls were restored . . . to tranquility."[33] Aleppo was also spared the destruction reported elsewhere, but Kemal ad-Din, a later historian, says that the Muslim fortress of Azaz was destroyed along with the towns of El-Athrib and Zardana. Harran, the site of so much warfare, was also badly damaged.[34] Archeologists have found evidence of the walls that collapsed there.[35] The town of Marash, north of Edessa, was swallowed up by the quake. "It was turned upside-down, that is, its foundations were sticking up and the buildings were all below. It became the tomb of the citizens."[36]

In Antioch, the aftershocks seem to have been particularly strong. People were afraid to return to even undamaged homes. The terror increased when they learned about the destruction of Marash and other towns. Like modern victims of earthquakes, the Antiochenes "adopted tents for homes, in the streets, in the square, in gardens, in thickets, with other dwellings abandoned."[37]

Meetings were held at once in the cities to decide which of the defensive walls should be rebuilt first.[38] Despite this urgency, there seems to have been a tacit truce in the wake of the disaster. I have not found any mention of warfare in the north in the months after the earthquake. With town walls no more than piles of stone, it would have been an opportune chance for the usual enemies to attack, yet none of the chroniclers mention this happening.

And then, as the stunned populace was beginning to dig out, it began to snow.[39]

Building materials were limited mostly to stone and brick. Survivors, working through freezing temperatures, would have had to pile the stones up again and just hope for the best, even though they lived in an area prone to earthquakes. It must have been a terrible winter for all.

Earthquake, drought, war, and insurrection, this is the world that Melisende and her sisters were born into. Even though they were part of the upper class, their life couldn't have had the same formality that it would have if they had lived in Baghdad or Constantinople or Paris or Rome. The economic difference between the count and his followers or the local merchants was not great. A good year could make a man of lesser rank richer than his lord, as had happened with Jocelyn. Baldwin had the power to take back the land that he had given Jocelyn from his territory, but Baldwin was also vulnerable. He could lose everything in the course of a battle or because he had offended the king. The first generation of Crusaders didn't have the benefit of hundreds of years of rule. Land in Europe that had been granted by a long dead king in return for service by an ancestor was often treated as an independent ownership by the descendants, but what rulers in Jerusalem had taken so recently in conquest could be snatched back in a moment and given to another.

For the new settlers, disaster could come slowly, as months without rain, or abruptly, as locusts and earthquakes. Invasion could come from former friends as well as long-time enemies.

But there were also religious festivals and celebrations. The liturgical calendar contained many feast days with processions and special meals. Along with the horrors of war and nature there were also times of joy. When the roads were safe, merchants would come through with brightly colored silks, aromatic spices, and exotic crafts.

Unlike her father, Melisende grew up in a pluralistic society. She wouldn't have thought it strange to live next to a family that celebrated Easter and Christmas at different times than she did. She would have known the stories of saints never heard of in the west. She would have heard of Passover and Ramadan, even if she didn't observe them. The shrine to Abraham at Harran was visited by Muslims, Jews, and Christians of many sects. While each group considered all the others heretics and infidels, it would have been impossible for her to think that everyone believed as she did, or to see the others around her as inherently evil.

It wasn't an idyllic world by any means. Everyone was categorized by religion and ethnicity. Within each group were subgroups with slightly differing beliefs and various geographic origins. But Melisende grew up knowing these divisions. She understood the rules, when to keep them, and how to break them. More than her father or even her mother, she belonged.

The importance of this wasn't evident while she was the daughter of the count of Edessa, a frontier colony dotted with villages that owed her father no particular allegiance, unless he gave them protection. As far as we know, she didn't even have the security of local family. Melisende's grandfather, Gabriel of Melitine, had left nothing to his children. His property had been taken along with his life. There was no guarantee that the same wouldn't happen to her, or worse.

In the spring of 1118, Baldwin of Edessa decided to go to Jerusalem to celebrate Easter at the site of the Crucifixion. He left his family behind, perhaps promising presents for good behavior in his absence. With his knights and companions, Baldwin set off on the 250-mile journey.

Baldwin, count of Edessa, would never return.

FIVE

OH, JERUSALEM!

EDESSA AND JERUSALEM,
1118–1125

IF NOT FOR ITS RELIGIOUS CONNOTATIONS, JERUSA-
lem would not have held much interest to the European invaders. Fulcher of
Chartres states bluntly, "The city of Jerusalem is situated in a mountainous
region, which is devoid of trees, streams and springs, excepting only the Pool
of Siloam, which is a bowshot from the city."[1] It was a stark contrast to the
lush fields around the coastal towns or the orchards surrounding the cities
on the banks of the Tigris and Euphrates. Jerusalem was on a trade route but
had little in the way of natural resources to offer settlers. Most of its water
came from cisterns, and wood for cooking and building had to be imported
from the countryside.

It was the Jerusalem of the mind that drove the motley group of pilgrims to cross the mountains, rivers, and deserts. Their belief in ultimate
salvation kept them going through bandit attacks, starvation, disease, and
terror. Many died on the way; some elected to stay in the Holy Land, often in
religious houses. Most returned to their families, who were often astonished
that they had survived the journey. One story tells of a woman who went to
Jerusalem, leaving her husband behind. On her return, she discovered that

he'd married again. She took her case to the abbot of the monastery at Vézelay, who ordered that her husband take her back.[2] No one commented on the fact that the woman had gone on the pilgrimage without her husband. While married people were expected to get the permission of their spouses before leaving, a pilgrimage vow was sacred, taking precedence over even the vows of matrimony.[3]

Therefore, it must have been religious zeal that made it the ultimate goal of the first Crusaders to free Jerusalem from the rule of the Seljuk Turks, who had taken it from the Egyptian Fatimids in 1071. The Seljuk Turks, newly converted to Sunni Islam, had strict beliefs of their own about the holiness of Jerusalem to their faith. They had forbidden Christian pilgrims from entering the city, just as the Christians would later banish them.

By the time the Crusaders arrived in 1099, the Shi'ite Fatimids of Egypt had retaken Jerusalem and pilgrims were welcome again. In many ways the Crusader's conquest was unnecessary to those wishing to worship at Christian sites without being harassed. But no one mentioned this at the time.

It took over a year for the Crusader armies to fight their way to Jerusalem. By then many of the lay pilgrims had either died, given up and returned, or had the sense to remain in Antioch or one of the other captured cities while the way was being cleared for them and so avoid the worst of the bloodshed.

The city fell to the Crusaders on July 15, 1099. Eyewitnesses reported: "So frightful was the massacre throughout the city, so terrible the shedding of blood, that even the victors experienced sensations of horror and loathing."[4] "So many were slain that our men were covered in blood to the ankle."[5] "Who could know the number of thousands who fell, when their remains were scattered everywhere you trod."[6] Even though some of the Muslim and Jewish inhabitants of Jerusalem did survive the conquest to be ransomed, by all accounts it was still a bloodbath.

Bodies and body parts were taken outside the city and burnt. At the height of summer, the smell must have been toxic. The knight who wrote the "Deeds of the Franks" was there and says that the bodies were dragged by surviving Saracens out of the city "because of the fearful stench."[7] Fulcher of Chartres states that this was done to collect any gold coins the Muslims and Jews might have swallowed, but I suspect that health concerns were dominant in the minds of the conquerors.[8] When Fulcher arrived from Edessa five months later, on the winter solstice, he could still smell the rotting corpses.[9]

Oddly, Ibn al-Athir only mentions the siege and conquest of Jerusalem in passing, noting that a number of Muslims negotiated for safe conduct in return for surrendering the fortress of the Tower of David. "The Franks kept faith with them and they departed at night for Ascalon," he adds.[10] There are also records of Jews in Egypt ransoming their co-religionists taken in Jerusalem and a letter from a woman who resettled in Tyre who had been allowed to leave Jerusalem with possessions including a box of books among her household goods.[11] It is certain that some escaped the carnage, but Jerusalem was nearly emptied of people and most of its buildings lay in ruins.

Several chroniclers note that not only the knights but common soldiers staked out houses for themselves and looted them.[12] Fulcher, especially, tells his readers that, "In this way many poor people became wealthy."[13] He implies that those who did not have the faith to join in the Crusade had lost out on earthly as well as heavenly rewards. But, he hints, it's not too late. Part of Fulcher's reason for writing the account of the taking of Jerusalem was to encourage settlement from the west. He often stresses the depopulation of the kingdom and the wealth that might be gained by those prepared to relocate.[14]

Nineteen years after the city was taken, in 1118, when Baldwin of Edessa arrived to celebrate Easter, Jerusalem was still desolate from war and neglect. King Baldwin I had used it largely as a base for further conquest, even removing the lead from the roof of what they believed to be the Temple of Solomon (the Al-Aqsa Mosque) to make weapons.[15] The Muslim and Jewish populations that had survived were forbidden to live in Jerusalem, although they could enter for the purpose of trade. Many of the exiles went to Tyre, Ascalon, Tripoli, or Damascus, all still under Muslim rule. Some settled with relatives as far as Cairo.[16] In the countryside, Muslim villages remained largely unharmed, as did those of Syrian Christians.

Perhaps the reason Baldwin of Edessa came to Jerusalem for Easter was from a desire to spend Holy Week at the site of the resurrection. None of the chroniclers give a satisfactory explanation for his journey at that particular time. William of Tyre only says that he wanted to visit the king and pray at the holy shrines.[17]

Baldwin of Edessa apparently didn't know that the king wasn't in Jerusalem. King Baldwin I had taken advantage of the Lenten season to attack the town of al-Farama' in Egypt. His army was able to plunder the area but could not capture the town, so they decided to go home for Easter. On the way back the knights skewered fish from the Nile on their lances for dinner. The next day King Baldwin I fell ill from the fish or, more likely, the recurrence of the effects of an earlier battle injury. As he was unable to ride, his men constructed a litter to take him back to Jerusalem. At the town of Laris (Al-'Arish), about fifty miles from al-Farama', the king died. "They took out his intestines, salted them and laid them in the coffin and hurried on to Jerusalem."[18]

Baldwin of Edessa was either in the city or near it when the funeral cortege arrived. It passed through the valley of Josaphat on Palm Sunday, April 7, 1118, where the soldiers with Baldwin's coffin met the religious procession of the Christians from the city led by the Patriarch, carrying palm fronds down from the Mount of Olives. The stunned citizens led the body along the road Jesus had taken and through the Golden Gate, which was only opened for special occasions. It was a fitting funeral for the man who had laid the foundations for a Christian kingdom. The king was buried on Golgotha, near the Church of the Holy Sepulcher, next to his brother, Godfrey.[19]

I've tried to imagine how someone could make the journey of over three hundred miles from Egypt to Edessa and tell Baldwin of Edessa of the death of his cousin in time for him to travel the two hundred and fifty miles to Jerusalem to meet the funeral procession. It doesn't seem possible. So I have to concede that it was simply a strange coincidence that the count appeared just when a new king had to be chosen.

Although King Baldwin I had been married three times—once possibly bigamously, depending on whom one asked—he had no children.[20] His closest relative was his older brother Eustace, count of Boulogne, who had gone home after fulfilling his vows of pilgrimage. At this point the story, as often happens, gets a bit murky. There are different stories about what happened next and the order of events.

Since it was Easter week, there were a number of nobles and bishops of the kingdom present in the city. Arnulf, the Latin Patriarch, assembled them to choose a new king. When Godfrey died, Arnulf had hoped that Jerusalem would be turned over to him as representative of the church rather than have Jerusalem pass to Godfrey's brother Baldwin. From the beginning there had been a debate about having a secular ruler for a city that had been consecrated by the deeds of Jesus. But, with the countryside still in turmoil and enemies all around, military needs won out over spiritual. The Patriarch's well-known lack of chastity may have kept him from reopening the question when Baldwin I died. The gathering of the leaders of the kingdom began the debate as to who should be chosen to be the next king.

The election by the nobility was a consternation to Arabs such as Usamah, an Arab nobleman of the time, who commented scornfully that even knights were allowed into the decision-making process.[21] The Latin states were possibly more inclusive than European courts in this, but the concept of the absolute monarch had not been adopted by Europeans yet. Kings were expected to seek counsel before major decisions, although they usually had the final say. If they did not have the support of most their vassals, kings rarely went against the majority.

In this case, there was no clear leader so all voices were heard.

Among the lords present was Jocelyn, now ruler of Tiberius and Galilee. The others were aware of how Jocelyn had been deprived of Tel Bashir and most of them believed that Count Baldwin of Edessa had been unjust in his treatment of his cousin. Therefore, when Jocelyn spoke in the count's favor and the Patriarch agreed, most of the others were convinced that Baldwin would make a good king. "The words of the proverb, 'All praise from an enemy is true' also recurred to their minds."[22]

Melisende's father was elected king of Jerusalem on Easter Sunday, April 14, 1118. At least, this is what William of Tyre believed, writing sixty years later and in the employ of Baldwin's grandson, Amalric. However, Matthew of Edessa, who was much more familiar with Baldwin, tells a slightly different story, one that was current among some of the ruling elite at the time.

According to Matthew, King Baldwin's dying wish had been for the count of Edessa only to be regent for the kingdom until messengers could be sent to Boulogne to offer the crown to Eustace. "So, in accordance with the dead king's wishes, they conferred the regency of Jerusalem upon Baldwin. However, he refused, for he sought after the royal throne itself."[23] Baldwin agreed to wait a year for his coronation, but, if Eustace hadn't arrived by then, he insisted that he be anointed king.[24]

Whatever Baldwin's dying wish may have been, when it appeared that Baldwin of Edessa would be the next king a dissenting party set out for Europe to inform Eustace of his brother's death. It's not clear whether they left before Baldwin was elected or after, but, upon their arrival, they convinced Eustace to return with them. The party had gone as far as Apulia in Italy when word came that Baldwin had been anointed. The anointing of a ruler was done by a bishop or archbishop and considered sacred. Eustace, no longer young and busy with his own county, seems to have been quite happy to return to Boulogne and leave the governance of Jerusalem to Baldwin of Edessa.[25]

It was often said that Count Baldwin of Edessa was a relative of Eustace, Godfrey, and King Baldwin I. However, there isn't any proof of this. If they were connected, it was a fairly distant relationship. This may have been stressed simply because it was the custom that lordship was passed down in a family and, as we shall see, the new King Baldwin was intent on his family retaining the crown.[26]

William of Tyre gives a rare description of the new king of Jerusalem, which he must have gained from those who had known him. Baldwin of Edessa was "tall of stature, of striking appearance and agreeable features. His thin blond hair was streaked with white. His beard, though thin, reached to his breast. His complexion was vivid and ruddy for his time of life."[27] Baldwin may have been anywhere from forty to sixty at the time of his coronation, but William was likely drawing on the memories of those who had seen him later in life. It's interesting that he was bearded, as the Muslim chroniclers all mention that the Franks were clean-shaven. Anna Komnene had had to look closely to decide the color of Bohemond's beard as he was not only clean-shaven but very blond. Was the beard a personal quirk of Baldwin's or had he adopted some eastern tastes in his time in the Holy Land?

Matthew of Edessa would have known what Baldwin looked like but superficial matters did not concern him. He was more interested in spiritual qualities: "a valiant man and a warrior, exemplary in conduct, an enemy of sin, and by nature humble and modest; however, these good qualities were offset by his ingenious avariciousness in seizing and accumulating the wealth of others, his insatiable love of money and his deep lack of generosity."[28]

Matthew seemed relieved to see the last of Baldwin in Edessa.

Once it was settled that Baldwin would rule Jerusalem, the new king sent Jocelyn to Edessa for Morfia and her daughters, Melisende, Alice, and Hodierna.[29] Jocelyn's advocacy for his cousin must have restored their former friendship.

We don't know if Morfia had been to Jerusalem before or how she felt about leaving her home and moving south to become the queen of a people whose language was not her own. By this time she would have learned some French, but she must have had mixed feelings and a little fear about the sudden change in her life. Then there was the problem of succession. The kingdom of Jerusalem required a militant king. Even if redoubtable women like Countess Matilda of Tuscany, a powerful ruler of this era, rode with her armies into battle, an elected king of a land constantly at war needed a son to carry on his line and lead the armies

And Morfia produced only daughters. She might have wondered if she would reach Jerusalem only to be cast aside as Baldwin I's Armenian wife, Arda, had been. Against her wishes, Arda was now a nun in the convent of Saint Anne.[30] Morfia may well have gone to see her predecessor upon her arrival in the hope of sympathy and advice. Saint Anne's was nearby and upper-class woman would often visit to spend a few hours or days in spiritual retreat, or simply to visit the nuns.

The Convent of St. Anne, Jerusalem. Photograph courtesy of Denys Pringle.

But even if Morfia was elated to learn that she was now queen of Jeru-salem, the reality of creating a royal court there must have made her heart sink. The city was still much in the condition described by William of Tyre just after the conquest. "[T]he inhabitants were few and scattered, and the ruinous state of the walls left every place exposed to the enemy. Thieves made stealthy inroads by night. . . . The result was that some . . . abandoned the holdings which they had won and began to return to their own land."[31] Toward the end of his reign, King Baldwin I had realized that "the Holy City, Beloved of God, was almost destitute of inhabitants."[32] Syrian and Ar-menian Christians were permitted to live there but so far, few had settled. King Baldwin I had sent word to Syrians living in the Transjordan, between the Jordan River and Arabia, an area often raided by Muslin freebooters, of-fering benefits to the Christians if they would move to Jerusalem. Many took him up on the offer, arriving with their families, livestock, and skills to take up residence in the former Jewish quarter of the city. But there were still too few full-time residents for Jerusalem to prosper.

The Syrians had barely settled in the city when Baldwin of Edessa became king. Morfia found many empty homes with shattered doors and hanging shutters. Streets were filled with filth. Few shops existed where one could buy fresh meat or vegetables. The only sellers of ribbons, rings, cloth, leather, and a hundred other essentials were peddlers from surrounding villages or merchants passing through. Almost nothing was being made in Jerusalem, even nineteen years after the conquest.

The one thing that Jerusalem did have in abundance was pilgrims. Since the third century, Christians had been making their way to visit the places where Jesus had lived, preached, died, and rose from the dead. The most famous of the pilgrims was Helena, the mother of Constantine the Great (c. 274–337). Around the year 326, Helena went on a voyage of discovery in the Holy Land. With the help of local guides, she uncovered and restored the site of the birth of Jesus in Bethlehem, the place of his ascension into heaven at the Mount of Olives, and the cave of the Holy Sepulchre, where he had been buried.[33] Tradition also said that she had discovered the remains of the True Cross. Just to be certain that her guides weren't lying to her, Helena had a convenient dead man touched with the cross, upon which he leapt back to life.[34] Bits of this miraculous find were scattered across Europe and Constantinople but one piece allegedly survived in Jerusalem and was found lying in a silver case in the corner of the ruins of the church of the Holy Sepulchre by the first Crusaders when they took the city.[35] The True Cross became the talisman of all the Latin States. It accompanied the kings into battle. Eventually, it was given into the keeping of the Knights Templar.

Guides were happy to show the newcomers the sites where the first martyr, Stephen, was stoned to death; the exact spot where Jesus was scourged; the house of Herod; the house of Simeon, where Jesus lived for a time; along with the wooden bath that he washed in.[36] Since Christianity was predicated on the belief that Jesus was the messiah foretold in the Old Testament, the pilgrims were also shown sites of events from the time of Abraham and Joseph that lay beneath the Christian monuments in Jerusalem, as Judaism formed the foundation of Christianity.

The first task for the new queen was to organize the cleaning and rebuilding of Jerusalem to make it welcoming to the thousands of visitors who were pouring in, believing that the route to the city was now safely in Christian hands.

So Morfia, her daughters, and their *familia,* a group made up of servants, retainers, advisors, and friends, set up housekeeping in a half-vacant city that needed serious infrastructure work and was inhabited by some Europeans, some Syrians, many transient tourists, and one other important group—the clergy.

Being the focal point of so many sects of Christianity, the churches and monasteries in Jerusalem were plentiful. The governance of the kingdom of Jerusalem was secondary to the business of religion.

The Church of the Holy Sepulchre, first built by Constantine in the early fourth century, had been inhabited by Christians almost continually since, despite alterations. The only time the church was in danger was when it was closed and partially razed in 1009 when the renegade Fatimid Caliph al-Hakim ordered all Christian buildings and shrines destroyed. "The Holy Sepulchre was then largely dismantled, only parts of the Rotunda, remains of some walls and architectural fragments remaining."[37] By treaty, the Byzantines were allowed to restore it after the death of the caliph but the work had not been completed. In the early years of the Latin Kingdom, no further construction was done on it. The dome was open to the sky with only a framework of wood.[38]

Considering the importance of the church to Christendom at large, its neglect during the reign of King Baldwin I is a reflection of the lack of interest or ability on the part of the invaders to rebuild the structures of the city they had come to free. Most of Baldwin I's time was spent in conquering the coastal towns and securing the borders of his lands, not to mention arbitrating the quarrels of the lords of Antioch and Edessa.

It must have surprised the pilgrims to realize that the holiest place in the Holy Land wasn't better maintained. Or perhaps most of them were too mesmerized by the sacredness of the space to notice. It wasn't until after Melisende became queen of Jerusalem that the building that we see today was finished. Her influence is still evident in many of the streets and churches of Jerusalem.

The unfinished round church, supported by columns, with its several chapels, was still enough to inspire reverence in those who visited. Close by was the separate church of the Calvary. "Within the door . . . is Mount Calvary, where the Lord was crucified. Below is Golgotha, where the Lord's blood fell upon the rock. There was Adam's head and there Abraham made his sacrifice."[39] The legend that Adam was buried under Golgotha was widespread. It was believed that the blood from the crucifixion dripped down through cracks in the stone and onto the skull of the first man to sin. This was Adam's baptism and at that moment he was resurrected and went to heaven, forgiven at last.[40]

There was a third major church used by the Latins, and today it is the building most people associate with contemporary Jerusalem. The Christian pilgrims called it the Templum Domini, the Lord's Temple. Despite the fact that the Jewish temple had been destroyed by the Romans in 79 C.E., some people believed that the beautiful domed structure, covered with mosaics inside and marble outside, was the original temple.[41] However, most knew that the building they saw had been constructed by Muslims, who called it Qubbat al-Sakrah, the Dome of the Rock. The shrine was built around the top of Mount Moriah, where Abraham was said to have offered his son Isaac as a sacrifice. It was also the scene of the Prophet Muhammad's Night Journey, from which he ascended to heaven in a vision.

One reason many of these sites had not been destroyed in the centuries of Muslim rule was that Islam and Christianity draw upon the same stories. Abraham, Isaac, Jacob, and Jesus are all venerated in Islam. Muhammad's Night Journey to the Dome of the Rock only completed the sanctification of the city in Muslim eyes.

The Dome of the Rock escaped destruction by the Crusaders because of their convenient identification of it with the pre-Islamic temple. Not everyone seems to have understood the significance of the rock. As Fulcher comments, "this rock, because it disfigured the Temple of the Lord, was afterwards covered over and paved with marble. Now an altar is placed above it and there the clergy have fitted up a choir. All the Saracens held the Temple of the Lord in great veneration."[42] The newcomers also painted the walls with Christian scenes and removed the gleaming copper on the dome, but little else was altered.

The building chosen as the king's "palace" was the Al-Aqsa mosque, built on remains that were thought to be the Temple of Solomon, but that actually dated to the time of Herod. Fulcher knew that the building was not Solomon's but assumed that the foundations of the original were somewhere beneath. "This one," he explains, "because of our poverty, could not be maintained in the condition in which we found it. Wherefore it is already in large part destroyed."[43]

This ruined mosque was where Morfia was expected to create a home and a place for the king and his retainers to meet. The roof leaked. Not all the floors were sound. No attempt had been made to decorate the walls. Did she even have money to begin repairs? At least it was summer so she had a few months before the autumn rains and chill began. Melisende was about fourteen at this point, Alice around nine, and the third sister, Hodierna, four or five. The younger girls might have thought the change was exciting, with new places to explore. But anyone who has been or known a girl of fourteen will know that puberty is not the time for radical life upheavals, not with all the internal ones going on. It could not have been an easy time for the new princess Melisende.

Also, more than her sisters, Melisende had seen what her mother had endured and had shared much of it with her. The clerical chroniclers don't mention if Morfia and her daughters were close, if the children were hugged a lot, or how they interacted with their father, who was often absent for months, or years if he was in captivity. So we can only look at the conditions around them, the archaeological remains, and the few remaining records, and try to imagine their lives.

In Jerusalem, there were two other important Christian religious establishments. The first was the convent of Saint Anne, built by the crusaders for women who wished to spend their lives in prayer at the place where the mother of the Virgin Mary had lived and where Mary herself was thought to have been born. There had been an early Byzantine church on the spot that was razed in the obliteration of Christian buildings by Caliph al-Hakim in

1009. The building found by the crusaders in 1099 was a newer one. It was then being used as a school of Shafi'i, one of the four branches of Islamic law practiced by the Sunni. The crusaders had converted it into the convent by 1104.[44] The number of noblewomen who had come to Jerusalem intending to take the veil and die there was a major factor in the swiftness of the work: it was the donations of the nuns and their families that provided the funds.

The second was the hospital of St. John, the most important religious establishment to the welfare of the city. This served as both a place for pilgrims to stay during their visit and a refuge for the sick and aged. This was part of the church of Saint Mary Latin, close to the Church of the Holy Sepulchre. There had been a foundation in Jerusalem to care for Christian pilgrims from the west as early as 870 C.E., and it was said that the original one was started by Charlemagne.[45]

Through the centuries the ability of the monks to live and worship in the city and the safety of pilgrims wanting to enter Jerusalem varied according to the attitudes of the Muslim rulers. There were periods when all but a few Christians were forbidden to enter the city for any reason. The shelters were closed and the monks dispersed several times, the most recent had been during the short occupation of the city by the Seljuk Turks at the end of the eleventh century.

While Jerusalem had traditionally always had a place for pilgrims, the hospice of Saint John that the crusaders found had actually been started by Benedictine monks coming from the trading city of Amalfi on the southern coast of Italy in about 1060. They built a monastery as well as houses for sick and poor pilgrims, one for men, dedicated to John the Baptist, and another for women, dedicated to Mary Magdalene.[46]

The importance of the hospital was immediately understood by the new Latin rulers of Jerusalem. In one of his earliest charters in 1099, Godfrey of Bouillon, uncrowned ruler of the kingdom, gave the hospital the village of Hessilia and the tithes from two ovens in the city.[47] This gift was confirmed and added to when his brother, Baldwin I, became king. The housing and care of pilgrims were paramount to the economy of Jerusalem. Melisende would follow this tradition.

The monks, known as the Hospitallers, would soon have a military role to play in the kingdom. But in 1118, when Morfia arrived, the hospital of St. John was still solely a hospital or *xenodochum,* a Greek term for a place that welcomes and cares for strangers. The abbot of the hospital was a man named Gerard, whose past and even nationality we don't know. He had kept the hospital secure and functioning through the occupation of the Seljuk Turks and then the Egyptian Fatimids. He survived the taking of Jerusalem along with his monks and those under their care. In the Hospitaller records, he is known as "the Blessed Gerard."[48]

At this point in King Baldwin II's rule the city contained a small contingent of Westerners, many of them in the clergy. Most were French speaking, but not all. There was also the new group of Syrians, mostly farmers and craftspeople. Morfia and her daughters would have been able to talk with them and bargain with expertise.

One other group soon formed an important section of Jerusalem. There had been an Armenian presence in the city since at least the fourth century, mostly composed of merchants. There is a legend that the head of the Armenian community in Jerusalem predicted that Arab armies would one day conquer the country and so "travelled to Mecca and received from the Prophet Mohammed an edict that safeguarded the life [*sic*] and property of the Armenians living in Jerusalem and recognized their church's rights over all religious sanctuaries under its control."[49] When the Caliph Umar conquered Jerusalem in 638, it was said that the Armenians handed him the edict and he honored it.[50] The Greek Orthodox inhabitants doubted the story and got their own permission from the caliph to live unmolested. However, since any written evidence had long since vanished, if it ever existed, the two sects struggled for religious dominance until the arrival of the Latin Christians, who settled the matter by taking over the custody of all the sites themselves.

By 1099 there were few Armenians in Jerusalem and the small community was scattered about the city. While it's difficult to be certain, the Armenian presence appears to have increased considerably after the arrival of Morfia. Many of the Armenian settlers arrived from the area north of

Edessa, such as Melitine, that had been taken over by Turks and was now caught in the struggle between Byzantium on one side and Damascus on the other. It's possible that they relocated to Jerusalem because of the turmoil in the north, and knowing that they would receive a welcome from their queen would have been an added incentive. At this time the church of Saint James, which is still the center of the Armenian Quarter, was either appropriated from the Georgian Christians, a minority sect from the Caucasus, or expanded to accommodate the Armenian faithful. This church was built on the designated site of the beheading of Saint James the Apostle by Herod Agrippa in 44 c.e.[51]

One of the early pilgrims to Crusader Jerusalem describes the Armenians: "These have some slight skill in arms, and differ in many respects from the Latins and Greeks. They hold their forty days' fast at the time of Christ's nativity; they celebrate Christ's Nativity on the day of the Apparition [January 6] and do many other things contrary to the rules of the Church. They have a language of their own and there is an irreconcilable hatred between them and the Greeks."[52]

There were also Jacobite and Nestorian Christians. At this time, the Arabic-speaking Christian Syrians would have been the most able to communicate with Muslim Syrians in the nearby towns. It would be strange if none of the Latins learned the language, at least enough to shop, order goods, and curse each other. Remember, although the new arrivals are called "Franks" by the Easterners and some historians, this is for convenience. In Jerusalem there were "Germans, Spaniards, Gauls, Italians and the other nations which Europe produces."[53] The Italians were few as they tended to settle in the coastal cities rather than Jerusalem, but there was no uniform European speech for the new arrivals or the pilgrims to use.

So, this is the city that, in the hot, dusty summer of 1118, Melisende settled in, the city she would one day rule.

After seeing that his family had a roof, however leaky, over their heads, the new king Baldwin II left almost immediately. There was trouble brewing in Antioch again.

SIX

THE FIELD OF BLOOD

ASCALON, ANTIOCH, AND JERUSALEM, 1119

BALDWIN DIDN'T STAY LONG IN JERUSALEM, SO HE may not have realized how bad the living conditions were. He left behind a pregnant wife who had not yet been crowned queen. Her authority over her subjects, especially the Europeans, may not have been secure. It must have been dreadful to know that everyone was watching her stomach grow and praying that there would finally be a boy. Their fourth daughter, Yvette, was born late in 1119. Did Morfia have enough faith in Baldwin to trust that he wouldn't manufacture an excuse to divorce her? Despite the different cultures, religions, and language, there seems to have been genuine affection between Baldwin and Morfia. But could the marriage survive the lack of a male heir?

Baldwin doesn't seem to have spent his time worrying about this. He may have been more concerned about his legacy in terms of territory. His first expedition as king was an attack on the Fatimid city of Ascalon. The Latins had long wanted to take control of this city on the southern coast. It had a good port and was well fortified. The Egyptian caliphs used it as a base from which to attack the Christians as well as the Sunni Arabs, Turks, and Kurds. But now something happened that the rulers of Jerusalem hadn't expected.

The atabeg of Damascus, Tughtigin, heard that Al-Afdal of Egypt was planning a major incursion into the Kingdom of Jerusalem, with the goal of recapturing it for Islam. Now, although these two had been enemies for many years, Tughtigin came to the aid of Egypt. William of Tyre tells us, "He followed unfrequented routes, in order not to encounter our army, crossed the Jordan, and entered the camp of the Egyptians."[1] Instead of launching an attack on an unsuspecting foe at Ascalon, Baldwin was surprised by a united force of Sunni and Shi'ite forces before the king came near the city he intended to attack.

Al-Athir, writing, like William, several decades after the event, heard the story a bit differently. He says that Tughtigin had been preparing to attack Baldwin I when he learned of the king's death. Emissaries from Baldwin II came to the emir in Damascus "asking for a truce."[2]

There were often truces between the Muslim towns and the Latin ones. In almost all cases, the Turks paid a tribute to keep the Latins from invading.[3] Although this didn't stop raids from both sides, it did allow a modicum of security. Tughtigin agreed to the truce if Baldwin would stop taking part of the yearly crop from the fields around Damascus. Baldwin refused. At that point, the atabeg grew angry. He cut off the talks, pillaged the lordship of Tiberias, and then went on to meet the Egyptians at Ascalon and attack the common enemy.[4]

According to Al-Athir, the Muslims hadn't been as surreptitious as they had thought in their plans. Somehow, on the way to Ascalon, Baldwin got wind of the upcoming joint attack and sent to Antioch and Tripoli for reinforcements. With his army, he camped on the plain before Ascalon hoping that Roger of Antioch and Pons of Tripoli would arrive before the Damascene army did.[5]

So here are the forces of Islam and the forces of Christ facing each other, prepared for the ultimate battle. And what happened? Nothing. The armies stood in place from July through September trying to stare each other down. Then for no explainable reason, except the strange one offered by Fulcher, "because each side greatly feared the other and because they preferred to live rather than to die,"[6] they mutually decided to retire to Cairo, Antioch, Damascus, Tripoli, and Jerusalem respectively. There must be more to the story than this. Perhaps there was dissension among the members of both armies. Tancred and Baldwin were not on friendly terms and Tughtigin and the caliph of Egypt were normally on opposite sides. But to position two armies and not use them was unheard of.

In the meantime, a relieved peasantry was, for once, able to harvest their crops without having the fields trampled or the olive and fruit trees destroyed (although they still had to battle locusts and grasshoppers). To them the stalemate must have seemed like a miracle.

This alliance between the Shi'ite and Sunni rulers lasted only a few months, but it was the beginning of a more organized resistance to the Crusader States that would culminate sixty-seven years later with the conquest of the city of Jerusalem by the Sunni Saladin, who also defeated the Shi'ite Fatimid government in Cairo. Saladin brought the various independent emirs to heel to drive the Franks out of the holy city.

As has been said, when the Westerners arrived in the East in 1098, they joined in the mix of Greeks, Fatimid Egyptians, Arabs, Armenians, Jews, Syrians, Georgians, Persians, and Turks. Only the Greeks, Jews, and Syrians had been in the area more than four hundred years. The Arabs arrived in the seventh century, bringing their new faith. The Turks and Armenians were relative newcomers who had been in the area less than a hundred years. The Turks were as alien to the Near East as the Europeans. Despite their conversion to Islam, their language and customs were different from those of the Arab and Syrian inhabitants. Turkish society was tribal and their women had more rights than Arab women did. Like the Europeans, Turkish women were not veiled.[7] The Arab aristocrats, such as Usamah, looked down on them and few made any attempt to learn Turkish, even after the Seljuks had taken Baghdad and Damascus.[8] Both the Turks and Franks either learned Arabic or were forced to rely on translators.

In the scrabble for land and power, religion took a back seat when alliances were formed. When Tancred and his Muslim allies fought Baldwin and his Muslim allies, they were following the pattern they found already in place. In 1115 this was repeated when Roger of Antioch, Tancred's nephew and successor, joined with Il-Ghazi, emir of Aleppo, and Tughtigin of Damascus to defeat the sultan of Baghdad at the battle of Danith.[9] It was said that Roger and Il-Ghazi had become close friends during their time together, although it didn't stop Roger from demanding the tribute due each year from Aleppo.[10]

But slowly, the idea of the jihad was growing among the Muslims, particularly the Turks.

The concept, often misunderstood to mean "holy war," has been part of Islam since the beginning. "Jihad" actually means "struggle," and there are two forms it might take. The greater jihad is the internal struggle to submit to the laws of Islam. The lesser jihad is a struggle against the unbelieving world. The particulars of the jihad were established after the death of Muhammad and not all the Muslim schools of law interpret them in the same way. However, much is based on a line in the Qur'an: "To war [in the sacred month of peace] is bad, but to turn aside from the cause of God, and to have no faith in him, or in the sacred Temple, and to drive out its people, is worse in the sight of God, is worse than bloodshed. . . . But those who believe . . . and fight in the cause of God, may hope for God's mercy."[11]

The lesser jihad had been marginalized in the years after the major Arab conquests, but was still being exercised sporadically. The Turks had been defeated and converted through jihad.[12] The idea of joining with Christians to fight other Muslims was foreign to the original concept of jihad, but the practice had become common as the Latin States made alliances with Muslim ones such as Aleppo and Mosul. It took some time before the battle against the infidel would take precedence over internal struggles for political power.

The first glimmerings of this jihad were brought to the gates of Antioch in the summer of 1119: "An intensifying of the Muslim jihad spirit was to return as a result of the coming of the Crusaders."[13] That spirit was about to be roused in the battle known to Westerners as the "Field of Blood."

Roger of Salerno, son of Richard, who had tried to keep Edessa for himself, and husband of Baldwin II's sister Cecelia, was regent of Antioch for the child Bohemond II, who was living with his mother in Italy. Roger certainly hoped that the young Bohemond would stay in Europe when he came of age. Just like his uncle, Tancred, Roger considered Antioch his. His coinage had an image of Saint George slaying the dragon on one side and "Roger, prince of Antioch" on the other.[14]

Roger's relationship with the nearby city of Aleppo was always in flux. He and the current emir of the city, Il-Ghazi, may have been friends who had combined their forces to fight against the sultan in Baghdad, but they also spent considerable time raiding each other's land. There are few natural barriers between the two cities and the lands were ripe for plundering, especially at harvest time.

The princes of Antioch had previously made treaties with the emirs of Aleppo and not only received tribute from the city but also collected tolls from the pilgrims going to Mecca.[15] Once, the citizens of Aleppo appealed for help from the Antiochenes against Il-Ghazi, who had established an unpopular representative at the town of Bales. "Soon, part of the army of Aleppo, with a detachment of Franks, besieged Bales; the arrival of Il-Ghazi and his Turkmen obliged the Aleppenes and the Franks to withdraw."[16] This was another example of townsmen who had a sense of collective identity and rights. Like the citizens of Edessa, they did not submit passively to tyrants.

But the endemic raids and attempts to increase territory were wearing on all sides. Part of the reason for the constant warfare was the determination of some of the European conquerors to create a Latin Christian state that encompassed Baghdad or even Constantinople, under the guidance of the Roman pontiff. The Seljuk Turkish lords had much the same plan for themselves, with authority residing in Baghdad.

Najim al-Din Il-Ghazi ibn Artuk, emir of Aleppo, was at least in his forties at this time, perhaps older. One of the sons of the Seljuk leader Artuk, Il-Ghazi had been entwined with the Franks since their arrival. For a short time, Il-Ghazi had been joint ruler of Seljuk Jerusalem, with his brother,

Sukman.[17] The men had lost the city to the Fatimids in 1096, as related above.[18] The Artuk family had retreated to Damascus. Later, Il-Ghazi was made prefect of Baghdad, where he battled "urban gangs," groups of young men, inspired by poverty, lack of work, and religion who pillaged the outskirts of Baghdad and were a continual trial to the sultan and the people.[19] Eventually, he became the emir of Mardin and, finally, Aleppo.

Ibn al-Qalanisi says that Il-Ghazi was a man who couldn't handle wine. When he drank "he habitually remained for several days in a state of intoxication, without recovering his senses sufficiently to take control or to be consulted on any matter or decision."[20] In 1115, it was said, Il-Ghazi was besieging the stronghold of Khir-Khan, emir of Hims. Hearing that the emir of Aleppo was in a drunken stupor, Khir-Khan raided his camp and captured Il-Ghazi. When the atabeg of Damascus, Tughtigin, heard of this, he forced Khir-Khan to release his captive, but Il-Ghazi's reputation was stained forever.[21] How much of this is accurate is hard to say. Thomas Asbridge, who has made a particular study of this event, points out that Il-Ghazi was also accused of celebrating a particular victory by drinking to excess but that he seemed to function quite well in the following days.[22] Walter the Chancellor, who was living in Antioch at the time, also says that Il-Ghazi often drank until he passed out.[23] One can assume that Il-Ghazi was known to drink wine, despite the religious prohibition against alcohol; how much he imbibed is open to speculation.

The minor clashes between opposing neighbors inevitably escalated into a major explosion. For Il-Ghazi, Roger's siege of the town of 'Azaz, in Il-Ghazi's territory, was the spark that set it off. The town had no special meaning to the emir, but for Il-Ghazi this was one attack too many.

All the treaties interspersed with skirmishes between Antioch and Aleppo finally came to a head in the winter of 1118. Il-Ghazi made the journey to Damascus to implore his old ally Tughtigin to send troops for a holy war against Roger of Antioch. He also sent out messages to the other Turkman tribes "inviting them to carry out their obligation of *jihad*."[24] Having just returned from the aborted mission to Ascalon with troops still ready for battle, Tughtigin was ready to listen.

Learning of the combined force being prepared against him, Roger of Antioch sent word to King Baldwin II to assemble his men to meet the gathering army and defeat the Turks. Baldwin was at that moment in the vicinity of Damascus fighting a part of Tughtigin's army. He had been in the area for most of the time since his return from Ascalon. Upon hearing that his opponent was planning a major attack, Baldwin set off for Antioch with Pons, the count of Tripoli. Jocelyn probably was also with him at this time, not yet having received his land in Edessa back.[25]

Il-Ghazi was supposed to be waiting for Tughtigin and other emirs near Aleppo before starting out, but provisions were low. He learned through his spies that Roger, over-confident, had also grown tired of waiting for reinforcements. Il-Ghazi sent out carrier pigeons with messages to discover how near the prince of Antioch was to his camp.[26]

Roger had with him about seven hundred mounted knights, including an Armenian contingent under Prince Leon, whose sister had married Jocelyn. He also had a large number of foot soldiers along with all the support people: bearers, cooks, tent raisers, laundresses, etc. For some reason, the night before the battle, Roger sent many of these along with the heavier goods to the citadel of Arttah for safety.[27] This wasn't a usual occurrence. For every fighting man there had to be people to carry the luggage, tend to the mules, get the camp ready, clean the bloodstains out of tunics, cook the meals, and stitch wounds and set bones. All of these were essential except at the actual time of battle. So it was odd that Roger sent all the noncombatants away when he wasn't expecting to fight imminently.

The army of Antioch settled for the night in a valley "with steep, wooded sides."[28] The next morning, they woke up to find themselves facing Il-Ghazi's army with no way out except through it.

The Franks and Armenians charged first and were decimated. Even for those accustomed to battle, it was unusually brutal. "[T]he Muslims charged down upon them and encompassed them on all sides with blows of swords and hails of arrows. . . . and not one hour of the day of Saturday, seventeenth First Rabi' 513 had passed ere the Franks were on the ground, one prostrate mass, horsemen and footmen alike."[29] Al-Qalanisi adds that the horses were so full of arrows that they "looked like hedgehogs."[30] When the Muslims made a pyre of the bodies they found, "in the half-burned corpse of one knight, forty spear tips."[31]

Among the dead was Roger of Antioch.

The Field of Blood soon assumed epic status. Both the Muslim and Christian chroniclers recount legends about the battle. William of Tyre states that, "In the midst of the combat . . . a terrible whirlwind came forth out of the north. . . . As it writhed along, it swept with it such clouds of dust that the men of both armies were blinded and could not fight."[32] It was this whirlwind that cost the Franks the battle, he asserts. No other chronicler mentions it.

Fulcher, who was in Jerusalem at the time, has a more prosaic reason for why God didn't give victory to the Antiochenes. Roger's private life was dissolute and his treatment of Cecelia unworthy of his rank. "The prince himself shamefully committed adultery with many others while living with his own wife."[33] Fulcher also felt that Roger was squandering the inheritance of the child Bohemond on libertine living. There is a trace of smugness in the priest's insistence that Roger got what he deserved.

If God brought defeat to the Franks, he also was responsible for Il-Ghazi's victory. A hundred years later, Kemal ad-Din tells the story of a Frankish prisoner who had been captured that day by a Muslim foot soldier. Brought before Il-Ghazi, the knight is taunted. "Aren't you ashamed to be taken by a commoner, you all covered in iron armor?" To which the knight replied, "He didn't take me prisoner; . . . it was a huge man, taller and stronger than I, who put me in his power. He was dressed in green and rode a green horse."[34]

This may seem to be the knight's way of denying that any human could take him, but to Kemal ad-Din, if not Il-Ghazi, it was a sign that a spirit of a descendent of the Prophet had come to aid the Muslim host. The Shi'ite belief that the inhabitants of heaven are dressed in green had spread in Syria by the thirteenth century when Kemal ad-Din wrote. Since Il-Ghazi was a Sunni Turk, it's unlikely that the story would have meant much to him, but it shows how this battle, fought seventy years before Saladin fought Richard the Lionheart, was seen as a precursor of the great jihad that was to come. A Muslim poet, Al-'Azimi, wrote:

The Koran rejoiced when you brought it victory
The Gospel wept for the loss of its followers.[35]

Baldwin arrived a few days later, bringing the fragment of the True Cross and reinforcements, which Roger clearly should have waited for. Fulcher states that the king pursued Il-Ghazi seeking vengeance. When the Franks found the emir, they attacked, carrying the cross into battle, "fighting around it constantly and gallantly and not deserting it."[36] The Christians won, or at least Il-Ghazi withdrew.

Among the Arabs taking part in this battle was a young boy of noble birth, leading his first command of twenty or so men. He was only on the fringe of the fight and was forced back with the others, but for him it was a day of glory. Years later, Usamah ibn-Munqidh would describe it in his memoirs. "Though a tyro in warfare, and never before that day having taken part in a battle, I, with a mare under me, as swift as a bird, went on, now pursuing them and plying them with my lance, now taking cover from them."[37]

Usamah was a cultivated nobleman from the town of Shaizir, near Aleppo. At the end of his long life he wrote his autobiography, colored by memory and ego, showing a vivid portrait of the life of a man of privilege. Usamah disdained almost everyone not of his Arab breeding, but he interacted with the Franks, even dining with some who had Muslim cooks and going hunting with others.

The elation of his first battle is so clear in his description. It shows how much this was a warrior society on both sides among the upper classes. Perhaps the dream of peace was only held by monks and peasants.

This string of battles had left the fields in the area ruined and uncultivated. A small amount of wheat cost a dinar, more than most people saw in a year.[38] Towns were deserted. Shortly before the Field of Blood, the people living north and west of Aleppo had made a truce with the Franks in their area—not the great lords, just the local officers. Before the battle, the nobles of Aleppo had made sure that the fields were planted and that the peasants were "furnished with the necessary resources."[39] This is a rare comment about the people who suffered the most as a result of continual warfare. It's not certain that the peasants were able to save their crops after the fighting, nor if the truce was continued.

The shock waves from the Field of Blood rippled across Europe. While pilgrims had been arriving in the Holy Land since the conquest, some to lend their swords for a time, some only to worship, there had been no outpouring of military volunteers. News of this ignominious Christian defeat caused fighting men throughout the continent to take the cross and vow to replenish the army of God. The enormity of the disaster is also reflected in the letters sent from the Crusader States to Pope Calixtus II and to Domenico Michiel, the doge of Venice, asking for help. The pope sent out a formal letter to all Christians but especially to the Venetians, calling for them to join in the defense of the Latin Kingdoms. Hundreds responded and a Venetian fleet set out in August 1122.[40]

Baldwin II had been king less than four months and had fought for almost all of it. Now he was obliged to go to Antioch and provide for his sister Cecelia, who, if Roger had been the philanderer Fulcher made him out to be, was probably not grief stricken. Still, she may have wondered what would become of her. Roger, for all his pretensions, had only been steward of Antioch. They had no children. Was she to be given in another political marriage or encouraged to join a convent? Either was possible.

Reading the chronicles, it's easy to see how the idea arose that women, particularly noble women, were no more than pawns to be thrown to the wolves in order to form alliances. We know nothing more of Cecelia, except a tantalizing and obscure reference in an 1126 charter to a donation made to the monastery of Our Lady of Josaphat near Jerusalem. In it Cecelia, "lady of Tarsus and sister of the king of Jerusalem," gives the monks villages in the area of Mamistra, north of Antioch, and a large field.[41] Roger had captured Tarsus, so the area might have been Cecelia's dower, land that was hers by right from her marriage. She also might have remarried a lord of Tarsus who also died. We don't have the information. However, it is clear from this that Cecelia is living on her own, not in a convent, and has property that she can alienate. The only other person mentioned in the charter is Prince Bohemond II, who by 1126 had arrived in Antioch. He was her overlord and had to give his approval of the donation just as he would have had she been a male vassal.

While it is slim evidence, it does appear that Cecelia was in charge of something in Tarsus. Sometimes a pawn can win. But in the aftermath of the Field of Blood, it must have seemed unlikely.

Baldwin stayed in Antioch for several weeks. He not only took care of his sister, but also would not leave, Fulcher tells us, "until he granted out the lands of deceased nobles in legal form to the living; until he had united widows, of whom he found many, to husbands in pious affection [!] and until he had reorganized much in need of restitution."[42] Fulcher puts his own spin on what must have been a series of alliances based on financial considerations. Baldwin couldn't force the widows to remarry but it's possible that many of them made their own arrangements. When property was involved, sentiment was of secondary importance.

Fulcher was saying that things were a mess in Antioch. The population was then made up of Greeks, Syrians, Armenians, Jews, and a new influx of Italian traders. The Latin Church wasn't powerful enough to exercise complete control and Baldwin didn't trust the Greek or Syrian Patriarchs to govern. He might have handed authority to Jocelyn, but that would have given too much power to the cousin he had so recently exiled. At this point, Jocelyn wasn't lord of Edessa, but he soon would be. For him to have Antioch, too, was asking for a family takeover.

The chroniclers don't dwell on the grief of the widows and orphans or mention the many who had no property and therefore didn't rate having the king find new husbands for them. Most of the records concerning Antioch have vanished, so we can only guess how the citizens of the city survived. In that society, when six months of peace was cause for comment, it is a good guess that much of the labor, skilled and unskilled, was being done by women, young boys, and, possibly, Muslim slaves. But by 1120, most of the Latin citizens had, like Melisende, been born in the East. It was the only home they knew and so they coped, not having another homeland to return to.

The death of Roger without an heir also meant that a new ruler had to be chosen for Antioch. Thoughts turned west again to the son of Bohemond, who was not only related to the Norman rulers of Italy and Sicily, but was also the grandson of the king of France.

The leaders of Antioch made Baldwin II regent of the county, until Prince Bohemond was of age to govern. This young man was acquiring an almost messianic reputation among the Antiochenes. They acted as if they believed that when the prince came, all would be well again.[43] Tancred and Roger had spent much of their rule fighting Turks, Greeks, and other Latins. They had been popular when they brought spoils of war back to the city, but it appears that the Latin Patriarch, Bernard, was the main civil authority. It was the Patriarch who had announced in 1115 that those who returned alive from an upcoming battle, should gather at a council in which, under the guidance of the Antiochene church, civil suits would be heard and decided.[44] Bernard was from Valence in central France and had been among the clergy that accompanied the First Crusade. He had been chosen Patriarch of Antioch in 1100. While he had only moral authority over the military actions of the princes, he seems to have administrated the daily operations of Antioch and was known to have directed the defense of the city in emergencies.[45] But he could not be expected to govern the mixed population permanently. This would not only be objectionable to the eastern Christians but set a bad precedent of theocratic rule.

Fulcher states that Baldwin II became king of Antioch, but that is the old priest's flight of fancy. Baldwin was never more than regent and he probably entrusted Bernard with legal power. Still, when speaking of Baldwin II's being chosen regent in Antioch, Fulcher says wonderingly, "The Lord has made others the possessor of one kingdom but Baldwin of two. Without fraud, without the shedding of blood, without litigation, but peacefully by divine will, he acquired them."[46] A miracle indeed!

Antioch was to be a problem for Baldwin for the rest of his life.

SEVEN

KEEPING THE HOME FIRES BURNING

JERUSALEM, 1119–1125

IT WAS HIGH SUMMER IN JERUSALEM. THE HEAT WAS accentuated for Morfia, who had just given birth. Her new home, the king's "palace," was a ruin that had been built as a mosque. She was surrounded by Franks. She had more in common with the Syrian craftspeople now settling in the abandoned streets, planting gardens, and reopening the shops, than she did with the men who had been left to govern the kingdom while her husband was fighting Il-Ghazi in the north or laying siege to Muslim towns on the coast.

Who had Baldwin II left behind to run things? The chancellor under Baldwin I was Pagan, a common name at that time, especially in southern France and Italy. Where he came from is not certain. It's also not clear if at that time he was in Jerusalem or with Baldwin II. Most of the fighting men had left with the king, along with Everard, bishop of Caesarea, and the True Cross. Who did Morfia turn to?

Melisende was of an age when most princesses were already married. She was presumably fluent in French, Armenian, and probably Arabic, the three cultures she had lived among. She was also the heir presumptive of the kingdom unless a new sibling should turn out to be a boy. As translator for her mother, she could have had a part in forming relations with the Patriarch of Jerusalem, Warmund, with the monks of the Hospital, and the canons of the Church of the Holy Sepulchre. These were the people who could give Morfia the best information on the situation in the city and the nearby countryside. But the new queen had to be constantly on her guard. The prelates also might be eager to subvert her authority. There was a contingent among the clergy who still felt that the holy city should not have a secular ruler. It was not too late for them to establish a theocracy in Jerusalem, given an opportunity.

Patriarch Warmund of Jerusalem was the younger son of a lord of Picquigny in the north of France. He had been elected Patriarch in 1118 and seemed more amenable to working with the crown than his predecessors, who were among those who thought that the holy city of Jerusalem should be governed by the Latin Church.[1] He was also of better character—or more discreet—than Arnulf, Patriarch until 1118. Even the pope, Pascal II, knew that Arnulf had had an affair with the wife of a local lord and fathered a daughter with a Muslim slave woman.[2] A successor of more saintly disposition than the former Patriarch might manage to become ruler of Jerusalem, if he so desired

The summer of 1119 was important for more than battles. In Hebron, south of Jerusalem on the West Bank, a canon at a priory affiliated with the Church of the Holy Sepulchre discovered the long-lost tomb of the biblical patriarchs Abraham, Jacob, and Isaac. This event was reported more excitedly by Muslim chroniclers than Christian. Ibn al-Qalansi says, "they [the Patriarchs] were all together in a cave in the land of Jerusalem, . . . they were as if alive, no part of their bodies having decayed, and no bones rotted, and that suspended over them were lamps of gold and silver. . . . This is the story precisely as it was told, but God is more knowing of the truth than any other."[3]

The story has been preserved in French sources from Avranches and Tournai along with others in Europe. The particulars vary somewhat, but the gist in the Western versions is that one day, the prior at Hebron went to

Jerusalem to confer with Patriarch Warmund, and in his absence, one of the canons snuck into the chapel for a nap. He noticed air flowing from a crack in the flagstones and became curious. Calling others to help, they excavated and found the tombs along with a room full of vats containing bones.[4]

There had been a long-established belief that the patriarchs had been buried somewhere in the area, but the canons had found no evidence of it when they built the priory. This discovery was greeted with delight, as the church had, up until then, no good biblical site to bring in the pilgrims. Even better for the financial security of the priory, this was a place that Jewish, Muslim, and Christian pilgrims wanted to see. The Jewish traveler Rabbi Jacob Ha-Cohen mentioned his visit there in the middle of the twelfth century, writing that he disguised himself as a gentile to enter the tombs. Jacob dismissed the church built over the cave with disdain and did not believe that the graves shown were those of Abraham, Isaac, and Jacob. He was certain that they were hidden in another cave nearby.[5] By the time of Rabbi Jacob's visit, the monks had added the tombs of the matriarchs Sarah, Rebecca, and Leah. Perhaps someone had remembered that the Bible said Sarah was buried next to Abraham.[6]

About fifty years after this, the Spanish-Jewish traveler Benjamin of Tudela visited the site and found a thriving tourist business. He says that there were six tombs in the church of St. Abraham that were shown to Christian pilgrims. "The custodians tell the pilgrims that these are the tombs of the Patriarchs, for which information the pilgrims give them money."[7] But Benjamin was too canny for that. "If a Jew comes," he continues, "and gives a special reward," he is then led down through two empty caves until he finds the real tombs with a lamp that burns day and night.[8] Hebron became one of the important pilgrimage destinations. Muslims taking the Hadj to Mecca would visit the tombs on the way. Even the great Jewish sage and philosopher Maimonides prayed at the tombs of the patriarchs when he came from his home in Egypt to visit the Holy Land.[9]

In the twelfth century the caves were open to all faiths. The year the caves were discovered, the Muslim Hamza ben Assad el-Tamimi visited the tombs on his way to Mecca for the Hadj, and had no trouble being admitted.[10] Jews, Christians, and Muslims were all allowed access. However, this situation did not survive into the modern world. Under Ottoman rule, in the 1880s, when a scholar wrote of the tombs, he could only quote from earlier pilgrims for, "today it is surrounded with barriers that keep the archeologists out with a most jealous fanaticism."[11] In the twenty-first century the tombs are more accessible, but still a bone of contention between Israelis and Palestinians.

The fact that all faiths were welcome wasn't just a desire for money, and it certainly wasn't born out of religious toleration. The canons had built their church over the traditional site of the tombs as a sign to all that Latin Christians were divinely chosen over other sects. Only they had been able to uncover the graves of the patriarchs. Building monuments to this idea, and inviting all religions to witness them, was their way of vindicating the Latin settlement in the Holy Land. A later version of the discovery has Abraham first appearing to the French monk while he's in France. In a series of visions, Abraham shows the monk the way to his final resting place in several episodes until the rather dim and constantly sleepy monk finds the tomb.[12] This variation on the original story emphasized even more strongly that God was on the side of the French.

This rededication of sacred places was happening all over the Latin Kingdoms. Just as the Arab Muslim invaders of the sixth century had destroyed or adapted Christian churches and the first Christians had destroyed or adapted pagan temples, the Crusaders marked their territory with Latin churches. While they made few changes to such iconic structures as the beautiful Dome of the Rock, it was important to them that a cross was now at the top of the dome.[13] The rock itself had been covered with a metal grille and an altar placed over it to hide the Islamic object of veneration.

The canons at Hebron sent invitations for the grand opening of the shrine to Jerusalem. It is likely that Warmund attended, and, since Baldwin was still sorting matters out in Antioch, Morfia went, as well, accompanied by her older daughters. Appearances at religious occasions were an important part of her royal duties.

That summer, Morfia may have had her first experience with two holidays that were specific to Jerusalem. The first, Crusader independence day, fell on July 15, the anniversary of Jerusalem's fall to the Latins.[14] It was known as the Feast of the Liberation of Jerusalem. Starting the day before, processions wound from the Church of the Holy Sepulchre to the Temple of the Lord, then outside the city through the Golden Gate opened especially for the event, to the burial site of those who fell "liberating" Jerusalem. After prayers for the dead, the people continued around Jerusalem, ending at the place where the Crusaders first breached the walls and entered the city.[15] The other feast, June 16, was the traditional date of the return of the True Cross from its "Babylonian captivity" in Persia in 628 C.E.[16] Having holidays that were particular to the kingdom was an important part of the formation of a society unique to Frankish Jerusalem.

Already it was becoming difficult to tell the natives from the newcomers. The wool clothing common in chilly northern Europe had been exchanged for loose cotton or linen robes that fell to the ground, covered by tunics that came to the knees. Silk was also fashionable among the rich. European women already wore head scarves, at least in public, and some may have adopted the Muslim veil as protection from the sun.[17] Morfia might well have also had robes made from silk embroidered with gold thread, a specialty of Damascus.[18]

Frankish men had also begun to wear the long tunic in the home, especially in the long, hot summers. Turbans became popular, both as fashion and because of the fierce sun. Whether Morfia ever convinced her husband to wear one is unknown.

Pilgrims were astounded at the behavior and dress of the second-generation Franks. Their language was even acquiring a different accent, laced with foreign words. Soon they would be known in the West as "poulains" or "pullani." This is a term used for colts, and why it came to be a term for the Latins in the East, I'm not sure, but both the natives and the new Westerners made a clear distinction between those born in the East and newcomers. Melisende's generation was not just a hybrid but a new culture. I believe that it was the influence of women like Morfia that created a bridge for the newcomers to cross, easing the way for them to become part of the land they had conquered.

Another local event in 1119 would be crucial to Melisende's future. Sometime earlier a knight from Champagne, Hugh de Payens, had come on pilgrimage to Jerusalem and then found himself at loose ends. He didn't want to go home, wishing instead to serve God in the Holy Land, but didn't think he had it in him to become a monk. With his friend Godfrey of St. Omer and a few other knights of the same mind, he formed a band of armed guards whose purpose was to protect the many other pilgrims who were prey to roving bands of brigands. Soon another warlike pilgrim, Fulk, count of Anjou, would meet Hugh and his men. The knights and their cause impressed him greatly. A few years later, Hugh would see Fulk again when the knight came to Europe to acquire new recruits and official recognition for what had become a quasi-religious military order. Eventually, they would be known as the Knights of the Temple of Solomon—the Templars.[19]

Slowly, through the hot summer, with the fields nearby plagued by grasshoppers, making the price of grain high, and with mice eating up the stores, Morfia began to settle in to life in the city that Western maps called the navel of the world. What her daily life was like is not recorded. She and her daughters were certainly obliged to be a part of the commemoration of Latin church feasts, although there is no indication that she ever converted from the Greek Orthodox faith she had been raised in.

By December 1119, Baldwin had returned to Jerusalem. On Christmas day, December 25, 1119, Baldwin and Morfia were solemnly crowned in the church of the Nativity in Bethlehem.[20] The tall, blond, Latin Christian man from northern France and the slight, dark, Armenian, Greek Orthodox woman now ruled one of the most diverse and contentious kingdoms in the world.

With enemies inside the kingdom and out, how long could they last?

EIGHT

FORGING A KINGDOM

JERUSALEM, 1125–1129

WHILE BALDWIN WAS MANAGING TO KEEP THE HU-
man enemies away from the kingdom, Jerusalem was suffering from an invasion he couldn't defeat with a sword. Locusts and mice had been destroying
the crops for four years throughout the land, leading to widespread hunger.
"It seemed as if the whole world lacked bread."[1] The population felt that
these plagues from earth and sky could only be caused by divine wrath.

Patriarch Warmund and Gerard of the Church of the Holy Sepulchre
sent a begging letter to the archbishop of Santiago de Compostela, Diego,
hoping for funds. They mentioned the locusts, grasshoppers, and mice, and
added drought to their woes. "We throw ourselves at your feet, weeping co-
piously, and implore you to come to our aid."[2]

It appears that help wasn't forthcoming, so more drastic measures had
to be taken.

On January 16, 1119, along with Patriarch Warmund, Baldwin gathered
the nobility, bishops, and abbots of the kingdom to a council at the town of
Nablus, in Samaria, north of Jerusalem. Nablus at that time was one of the
wealthier towns of the kingdom. In fact, it was so wealthy that the viscount
was obliged to send more armed men to the king's service than the city of

Jerusalem did.[3] Baldwin may have decided on it as a meeting place simply because there was still enough food there to feed those who attended, along with their retinues.

It was apparent to everyone at the meeting that God was not happy with His people. The stated purpose of the meeting was the moral reform of the citizens of the kingdom of Jerusalem, with the hope that God would then show them mercy. There is a record of the council, along with the laws enacted, almost all of them covering sexual indiscretions.

The account begins by saying that, because of the grievous sins of the people, the kingdom was being afflicted not only with the mice and locusts but with attacks by the Saracens such that pilgrims were unable to complete their journeys. Therefore Warmund and Baldwin, along with the notables assembled, intended to make laws that would put the people on the straight and narrow and turn them from their "sinful delight."[4] The example of the destruction of Roger of Antioch and his army was mentioned, with the unspoken reminder that he had always been ready for sinful delight.[5]

So much emphasis is put on salacious acts that one might be forgiven for missing the fact that the first two *capitula,* or chapters, gave the Church, in the person of Warmund, tithes that the King Baldwin I had forgotten to share with the Patriarch. The neglect of support for the upkeep of churches and monasteries was a great sin, worse than sexual misconduct, because it showed a lack of respect for God. This was seen as the root of all the other failings that the laity had fallen into. "And for this offense, I beg pardon." Baldwin II concludes in the first *capitulum.*[6] "Don't mention it," Warmund answers in the second. "I accept gladly."[7]

That very important matter being taken care of, the men got down to the real sins that needed correcting. They make interesting reading. One wonders if the law makers were drawing on recent scandals or picking interesting peccadillos that they had heard as gossip. The first deals with what a man should do if he suspects his wife of adultery but can't prove it. The laws escalate to what a man should do if he catches his wife and lover in the act. Interestingly, since both in Europe and the Muslim world, the husband is allowed to kill them both, the punishment listed here is almost mild. The wife is to have her nose cut off and the man is to be castrated, unless the husband takes pity on them. In that case they are exiled overseas.[8] The husband who exacted the maximum punishment would still not be allowed to remarry as long as his wife remained alive, as adultery was not given as a reason for divorce.[9] Since Baldwin I had forced his wife, Arda, into the convent under the pretext that she had been raped while in captivity, this ruling seems unusual. But it may have been the actions of the early lords that provided the reason for some of the laws.

The next couple of laws are variations on the theme of adultery. After that there are four admonitions against sodomy. The active partner is to be burnt alive. This is the strongest punishment for homosexual conduct I've run across in the twelfth century. Hans Eberhard Mayer, a twentieth-century Crusade historian, suggests that this particular law was in reaction to the behavior of King Baldwin I, who may well have been homosexual.[10] William of Tyre has an oblique reference that can be read as such: "he [Baldwin I] is said to have struggled in vain against the lustful sins of the flesh. Yet so circumspectly did he conduct himself in the indulgence of these vices that he was a stumbling block to no one . . . in fact, a thing rare in such cases, only a few of his personal attendants were aware of his licentious habits."[11]

There are other hints about Baldwin I's sexuality in the chronicles, but most of the writers overlook or even excuse Baldwin I's lack of interest in women. Their acceptance of the king's sexuality might be due to his discretion, as well as the fact that he was a strong man who took and held cities and sorted out the squabbles of the other lords. The focus on sodomy at the council may have indicated that people believed the natural disasters were the result of Baldwin's sins, but I think it is more likely that the prudish Latins were shocked, or perhaps tempted, by the Muslim's treatment of slave boys. There may have been other reasons, events the records of which have been lost. Any kind of sex outside of marriage was forbidden, of course, although that didn't stop it from happening.

My argument for this point of view is that the next two capitula absolve the passive participant of the act of sodomy if he or she is a child (the word *infans* is used to indicate a child, and the term can be either feminine or masculine) or if he is raped.[12]

The next four laws address cultural transgressions. From these, one can sense the council's fear that as the minority in an alien land, they could be swallowed up by the natives. There are laws against fraternization, sexual or otherwise, with Saracens. A Christian woman can't marry a Muslim man; nor can a Christian man have sex with his Muslim slave girl. Muslims aren't allowed to dress like Franks. This seems odd to me, because it appears that, due to the climate, more Franks were dressing like natives. But it does indicate that it was becoming difficult to tell the difference, after only one generation of intermarriage between European and Oriental Christians. The Franks had no physical way of telling a Muslim man from an Eastern Christian man. On the other hand, most Muslim women covered their faces in public, unlike European women, a stark difference that shocked Arab commentators.[13]

The final group of laws pertains to theft, which means that murder as a sin is left completely unaddressed by the council. As a matter of fact, capitulum number twenty states that a cleric may take up arms for the defense of himself or his community without blame.[14] This is a startling statement that runs counter to every clerical rule in the West. In Western society, monks and priests were to be protected, just as women, children, and the elderly were, for they were not allowed to fight. This strict observance had already been ignored in the conquest of the Holy Land. Bishops led armies and used weapons. Even Fulcher seems to have picked up a sword when faced with the choice of fight or flight.[15] This is another example of how the culture of the Europeans was adapting to the circumstances of life in the East.

It's not clear how often the laws of Nablus were invoked. There are no records of people being burned for gay behavior and there doesn't seem to have been a sudden rise in noseless women. Perhaps the threatened punishments were enough to make people more careful not to get caught. That may have been sufficient for the Almighty, for Fulcher states that the next year, 1121, was "peaceful, prosperous and rich in fruits of all kinds."[16]

To prevent backsliding, of which there was a lot, copies of the laws were distributed widely over the next decades. They were still common in the 1180s when William of Tyre was writing. "Anyone who desires to read these articles," he says, "may easily find them in the archives of many churches."[17]

The concerns of the council indicate both a fear of the native population and the acknowledgement that not everyone shared that fear. It also hints that the Latins weren't as certain of God's favor as they had been in the first flush of conquest.

Immediately after the council, Baldwin returned to Jerusalem. There he issued a decree that the tolls on merchants entering the city of Jerusalem would be lifted. "Moreover, to the Syrians, Greeks, Armenians, and all men of whatever nation, even to the Saracens, he gave the free privilege of carrying into the Holy City without tax, wheat, barley, and any kind of pulse."[18] This included lentils, fava beans, and chickpeas. The text also makes it clear that the Muslim traders are not to be molested.[19] This decree is witnessed by most of the nobles and religious leaders of the kingdom, more than those who signed at Nablus. Morality was important in this religious state, but getting the economy going was essential.

The famine of 1120 that precipitated the council was not confined to Jerusalem of course. Arab writers chastised Il-Ghazi of Aleppo for not following up on his defeat of Roger of Antioch by laying siege to the city. The emir did try but decided that he didn't have enough provisions, especially since the Patriarch of Antioch was rumored to have laid in enough provisions to survive several months. There had been little rain in Aleppo, either. The drought was particularly bad in Baghdad, so much so that many of the peasants left their homes in search of better land. In consequence, the emir al-Mustarshid bi-Allah "cancelled every unjust demand in the fief that was specific to him" in an effort to decrease the labor drain.[20] Il-Ghazi also abolished tolls for bringing food into Aleppo for sale as well as other taxes and he also waived the tax on gold thread, perhaps in an effort to keep the makers of brocade and gold cloth from emigrating, as well. The practice of taxing goods being bought and sold in the city was illegal under Muslim law but many rulers ignored this.[21]

Il-Ghazi, who now controlled both Aleppo and the town of Mardin, was in a similar situation. There had been a hail storm that "killed the cattle and destroyed the crops and trees."[22] Aleppo had more natural resources than the city of Jerusalem, but war and natural disasters had worn down the population.

For once, money was trickling down to the craftsmen and farmers.

Melisende was now learning her first lessons in government. It's not known if she was at the council of Nablus, but it's possible. She was certainly in Jerusalem to see the stream of grain, apricot, date, sugar cane, and bean merchants flood into the market places. She saw that the strength of a kingdom is in the strength of its people. They have to have food and work to earn it. When she became queen, one of her first projects was the building of a covered central market in Jerusalem, like those in Aleppo and Harran, for the convenience of both buyers and sellers.[23]

Another event that Melisende was certainly aware of was the growth of the group of knights, led by Hugh de Payens and Godfrey of St. Omer, who had pledged themselves to protect the pilgrims on whom Jerusalem had based its economic fortunes. At this early stage, it was said that there were only nine men, but that was likely a later myth.[24] In the years since they had been founded, their numbers had steadily grown, so the number was likely higher. These knights were already proving a godsend to pilgrims.

In 1120, this band of fighting men was not an organized religious order. They had no habit, nor rule to live by. It is possible that at some point early in their existence they allied themselves with the Patriarch and became canons regular. William of Tyre says so, but it doesn't make sense to me.[25] Canons regular live in a cloister attached to a cathedral. The knights seem not to have had any single place to live when they began.

Actually, a lot about the early days of the Templars is murky, confused by legend, myth, and a lack of primary documents. My take on them has already been stated elsewhere, but since then, I've thought more about the particulars of the origin of the order.[26]

I don't think they were canons. Few, if any, of the knights read Latin, necessary to the recitation of the hours of prayer. The men may have looked to Patriarch Warmund for spiritual guidance, but it seems more likely that they would have had more to do with St. John's hospital than any other religious establishment. At the hospital the monks cared for sick, elderly, and wounded pilgrims, and there the knights would have heard firsthand accounts of the hardships travelers suffered trying to get to popular sites from the life of Jesus, such as the River Jordan. They might have offered to guide pilgrims who had arrived in Jerusalem safely to the river and other sacred places.

Another reason I assume there were more than nine men is that William states that the knights had no place to live. Housing was still easy to find in Jerusalem, especially fixer-uppers. Nine men would have had no trouble finding shelter, even with servants. But if there were, say, thirty knights, it might have been more difficult.

However many there were, these knightly protectors were looking for a place in which they could establish themselves, their retainers, and their horses. William states that "the king granted them temporary dwelling in his own palace on the north side by the Temple of the Lord."[27]

The palace was, of course, the Al-Aqsa mosque, built on what was reputed to be the ancient Temple of Solomon. It was perfect for them, with lots of space and an area for stables beneath. They moved in at once.

The king may have done the granting, but I see Morfia's hand in this. Morfia would have been familiar with organizations for worn and ailing pilgrims and the good they did. At his fortress of Tel Bashir, where she had spent so much time, Jocelyn had established a smaller such hospice.[28] Knowing this, it was natural that she would want to be a patron to the selfless knights.

On a more pragmatic note, the mosque was not appropriate for a royal palace. Morfia was trying to raise four young girls and maintain some sort of court while massive renovations were being done. She may well have suggested to Hugh that he and his men could move in cheaply in return for

The Tower of David, Jerusalem. Photograph courtesy of Denys Pringle.

taking over the work. Morfia, meanwhile, had her eye on the nearby tower of David: a solid, well-fortified structure with a roof that didn't leak.[29]

So King Baldwin and his family moved to the tower and the knights took over the job of making the Temple livable. In a short time, they became known as the Knights of the Temple of Solomon.

Melisende and Alice, who was about eleven in 1120, might well have passed the time watching the Templars train. The area of the Temple Mount was small and the princesses don't seem to have been sequestered, although they were probably chaperoned. There is no way the girls could have missed seeing and meeting a new party of warrior pilgrims who came from France in the spring of 1120 in response to the call sent out after the defeat of Roger of Antioch.

Among them was the stocky, red-headed Count of Anjou, Fulk V. The count came from a long line of independent-minded people and had spent most of his life fighting, usually for his overlord, Louis VI of France, known as "Louis the Fat."[30] Fulk, then in his thirties, had decided to take a break from warfare in France and make the pilgrimage to Jerusalem. He fell in with the Templars and may have stayed with them during his visit. A man of his position and reputation would certainly have been entertained at the king's court, whether Baldwin were there or not. It isn't likely that Melisende would have dined with them, although, at around fifteen, she was reaching the age where she would be expected to have some social duties. But she must have known who he was and perhaps spoken to him. He seems to have stayed in the Holy Land for several months but was back in France fighting for King Louis by 1122.[31]

The fact that she had seen the man and had a chance to take his measure would matter a great deal in a few years, when a committee would be sent to Anjou to ask the widowed count to marry the girl he may have only vaguely remembered and become king of Jerusalem.

NINE

QUEEN IN TRAINING

JERUSALEM, 1128

BALDWIN AND MORFIA MAY STILL HAVE HOPED FOR A son but, at the moment, Melisende was next in line for the throne. The customs that kept women from inheriting were not yet established. Failing a male heir, daughters could and did govern. Melisende knew that she needed to be prepared to take over on her father's death. Between disease and warfare, this could come at any time.

One sign that Baldwin was aware of this possibility was that he had as yet made no effort to arrange a marriage for her. This was unusual in that both male and female children in noble families were often betrothed before they could walk. Sybille of Anjou, whom we shall meet again, was betrothed to William, son of Henry I of England, when she was four or five.[1] King Henry's daughter Matilda, was sent to Germany at the age of eight, to learn the language and customs of her future husband, the Holy Roman Emperor Henry V.[2]

But neither of those women were the presumptive heirs of their kingdom, although, with the death of her brother William, Matilda would soon be. Her struggle for the throne of England was still in the future. However, if Melisende were to be queen, she would need a husband who was able to handle the warfare and bickering both within the kingdom and without. He would also need to have some status of his own, but not be so important that he would make Jerusalem merely an appendage to his own estates.

This dilemma must have cost both Morfia and Baldwin sleepless nights.

The education of upper-class women at this time has not been well documented. However, by this age, Melisende would have learned to read and write, at least in French. Whether she could read the different alphabets of Armenian and Arabic is harder to guess, but doubtless she spoke both languages. By the time they moved to Jerusalem, Baldwin might have decided that his daughters needed a Latin tutor, to enable them to understand the language of the mass and the common tongue of the Roman clergy.

The most important lessons Melisende was absorbing were practical. Even though only Christians were allowed to settle in the city of Jerusalem, the prohibition didn't extend to the countryside, nor to the towns in the kingdom. In some ways, Jerusalem was a world away from the many villages that surrounded it.

While some towns were devastated by the armies fighting around and through them, most, like Harran in the north, picked up the pieces and carried on. The people of the countryside around Jerusalem in 1120 would have been made up of Syrian Muslims and Syrian Christians, indistinguishable except for religion, since they were both of the same ethnicity. These were mainly farmers. The Arab and then Turkish invaders tended to treat them as part of the landscape, as did the Franks.

A Spanish Arab traveler, Ibn Jubayr, passing through a few years later on his way to Mecca, observed them with perplexity. "[T]he inhabitants were all Muslims," he says. "living comfortably with the Franks. God help us from such temptation!"[3] Ibn Jubayr was only in the Kingdom of Jerusalem for a few days and had no way of knowing how the Muslim peasants interacted with their Christian neighbors, but to him it seemed that they were content with their Frankish masters. Ibn Jubayr also mentions a village that was divided down the middle, separating the Christians from the Muslims. "They apportion their crops equally, and their animals are mingled together, and yet no wrong takes place between them because of it."[4]

To this assemblage were added Western Christians who had been foot soldiers, followed the armies, or arrived as pilgrims. Some of them must have married local women without worrying overmuch about their religion. Other locals settled on abandoned land or even created new towns under the auspices of a local ruler, often ecclesiastical.

A rare charter, issued by Melisende in 1150, gives names to these peasants. Melisende is confirming a gift of the proceeds from the village of Bethsurie. Among the inhabitants are both Muslims (Selman, son of Maadi; Selim; Hasem; Nasen; Mahmut; and several others) and Syrians (*Suriani*) (Cosmas, Samuel, Ibanna, Meferreg, and Gerges).[5] We know nothing more about these people except that they all lived in close proximity and paid taxes to Melisende before the canons of the Holy Sepulchre took over collection duties.

Franks also built their own towns, receiving special incentives to do so. In under-populated areas, lords could be lured into a bidding war for settlers. As inducement to relocate to the town appropriately named "Nova Villa" (Newtown), northwest of Jerusalem, citizens were given a plot of land to build a house on along with land for a garden and trees, and the right to use the communal flour mill and ovens.[6] In return, they had to pay taxes of a quarter of their grain and vegetables and a fifth of the wine grapes and olives. These tithes were delivered to the representative of the canons and kept in a vault in the village until they were picked up.[7] Almost every village had one of these storage vaults for tithes, as excavations have shown.[8]

The farmers, shepherds, and olive growers also expected protection. Most towns had a fortified tower, often part of the local church, in which the people could take shelter if they were attacked. In the town of Magna Mahumeria, not far from Jerusalem, the women and children survived by barricading themselves in the tower during a Muslim raid in 1123.[9]

Depending on the size of the village, the inhabitants would also be expected to send foot soldiers to fight in the Lord's army for a set time.

Melisende would have traveled through these towns, stopping for the night or a meal. She would not only have gotten to know some of the people but also would have been a living example to them of the integration possible between the natives and the new comers. Most of her companions would have been Franks, some already adapted to local customs, but others would not have had any idea of what the native people were saying or doing. Melisende's understanding of the local population would help her and her foreign husband considerably as rulers later on.

Melisende would have found some differences from Edessa in the makeup of the areas within the Kingdom of Jerusalem. When she arrived from the north, the Armenian population was just beginning to migrate south to the area and they mostly settled in what is still the Armenian quarter.

There was a greater variety of Christians in Jerusalem. The theological differences among them were not always clear to lay people, and Melisende might have found it difficult to understand why some were accepted by the Latin clerics as fellow Christians and others considered heretics.

A European pilgrim gave an explanation of these differences for those back home. He may have come from a German-speaking area for he begins by describing the Franks: "They are warlike men, practiced in arms, are bareheaded and are the only one of all these races who shave their beards."[10] Greeks are cunning men who say that "the Holy Ghost doth not proceed from the Father and the Son, but from the Father alone. They also use leaven in the Host; . . . and have an alphabet of their own."[11]

He continues, Syrians are "useless in war," and have roughly the same faith as the Greeks but trim their beards and use the Arabic alphabet. Armenians celebrate their holy feasts at the wrong times and hate the Greeks. Georgians have long hair and beards and "wear hats a cubit high."[12] They are almost like the Greeks but have their own alphabet, too. Finally, the Nestorians are heretics, "saying that the Blessed Mary was only the mother of a man. . . . They use the Chaldean alphabet."[13]

Another pilgrim adds, "Of the diverse kinds of pagans [are] the Jews, Sadducees, Samaritans, Assassins and Bedouins."[14]

Melisende would have heard tales of the Assassins, called Batini by the Turks and Arabs. They called themselves Nizari, after the name of their first imam. They lived mainly in the north and rarely had anything to do with the Crusaders at this point, although Melisende's family would have a personal encounter with them much later. The Samaritans still lived in the same area they had when Jesus met them, physically indistinguishable from the Syrian Christians and Muslims. As for what the pilgrim called "Sadducees," he may have meant the Karite Jews, a sect that denies the validity of the Talmud. They came from Iraq and Persia but their beliefs spread to the east, including Syria, Egypt, and Muslim Spain. Karites were and are considered heretical by the majority of Jews.[15] There is no mention in the records of Melisende encountering them.

The Bedouin would have been new to Melisende, although she may have heard of them from travelers. No one knows when these tribes first appeared in the Sinai and Negev deserts, where many still live, but there is a report that they aided the Byzantine general Heraclius in fighting against the invading Muslim armies in the Negev and Egypt in the seventh century.[16] Not one people but a loose confederation of extended families, the Bedouin did their best to stay autonomous, herding camels, sheep, or cattle from one grazing place to another. Muslims on pilgrimage to Mecca paid them protection money. Ibn al-Athir tells how one of the Bedouin tribes, the Zughb, attacked a party of Persians going from Mecca to Medina who refused to pay the Bedouin price. The pilgrims' property was promptly stolen and they were left in the desert to die. The Bedouin were no more respecters of the Hadj than the Christian brigands who ambushed pilgrims to Jerusalem.[17]

Bedouin often crossed Crusader territory to let their animals graze outside of Damascus by arrangement with the emir, and more than once they became the prey of the Franks. As soon as Baldwin's cousin, Jocelyn, officially became lord of Edessa he raided the nearest Bedouin camp, eager to get as many sheep and goats as he could, along with the treasure stored in their tents. Not allowing religious qualms to keep him and his friends from easy booty, Jocelyn attacked on Easter Sunday, 1120. The Bedouin, however, had had long practice in guarding their possessions. Jocelyn's party was routed. Albert of Aachen states unsympathetically, "I think . . . they were given into the hands of the enemy because they were greedy for plunder on so very holy a day."[18]

Jocelyn's raid was deplorable not just because he fought on a holy day. He was breaking a truce and inviting retribution. However, Baldwin was forced to threaten the Bedouin just to save face. Luckily they preferred to pay him off rather than fight.[19] The custom of bribing an enemy to go away was well established and accepted with little loss of honor.

Observing the complexity of her father's duties, Melisende could see just how much authority and diplomacy were needed to hold a kingdom together. She also might have noticed that diplomacy often worked better than a head-on confrontation. As queen, she would attempt to negotiate treaties rather than fight. But, as was clear from Jocelyn's unilateral decision to plunder the Bedouin, the hardest part would be controlling her own subjects.

Baldwin must have done well at keeping the lands around Jerusalem safe, or perhaps the Templars' patrols discouraged banditry. The serious battles moved back to the north and for the next twenty years there was no major invasion of the area around Jerusalem. It's not the chroniclers who tell us this; they always followed the armies, at least on the page. It's the modern archaeologists who have discovered the remains of the new towns built by western settlers in the area around Jerusalem and found that the buildings are arranged for easy access to the fields, not clustered behind stone walls in fear of enemies. Fulcher does add, in an aside, that 1121 and 1122 were good years, with abundant harvests and peace. "At that time, neither Parthia [Iraq and Iran] nor Babylonia [Egypt] undertook any wars."[20]

In the same paragraph where he extols peace and prosperity, Fulcher also mentions that Count Jocelyn was captured in a "crafty ambush"[21] by Balak ibn Bahram, a nephew of Il-Ghazi, who imprisoned the count in the fortress of Khartbirt, north of Edessa.[22] With Jocelyn was a cousin, Galeran, the lord of Bira, also Baldwin I's cousin, and an unnamed nephew.[23] At first, Baldwin let his cousin handle his own release, but, eventually, the king had to intervene and pay the ransom.

Fulcher was not overly concerned about Jocelyn's misfortune. In his entry for the year 1122, he was more excited about learning of the Concordant of Worms, a treaty between the Holy Roman Emperor Henry V and Pope Calixtus, which ended a decades-old rift punctuated by warfare and anti-popes.[24] The Latin States had long been a bastion of support for the papacy, which brought the popes some prestige. But the split between the popes and emperors had kept vassals of the emperor from coming to the aid of the Crusader States, which were chronically short of manpower. German-speaking pilgrims had been discouraged by the lack of hostels where their language was known. A hospice had been founded in Jerusalem in 1118 by German monks but there were few others. Even the military orders were largely made up of French or Italians. The Teutonic knights were founded in 1190 to encourage the influx of men from the north.[25]

Although he spent much of his time coping with the power vacuum in Antioch, and then, during Jocelyn's captivity, Edessa, Baldwin still dreamed of expanding the kingdom into Muslim territory. He now had the means and the time to look outward, since the land he already held was peaceful and productive.

In 1123, or perhaps even earlier, he began to make arrangements to gather a strong enough force to conquer the important port city of Tyre. For this he took advantage of the crusade oath made by the doge of Venice after the Field of Blood to make him provide ships and men to attack from the sea and, most importantly, fend off the Egyptian naval force.[26] Tyre was an ancient city, mentioned by classical Greek and Roman writers as well as the Bible. Built on an island just off the coast, south of Beirut, it seemed impossible to take, and, without the Venetian naval force, it would have been.

It seemed logical to Baldwin and his advisors that Tyre should become part of the kingdom. It was part of Roman and biblical history, traditionally subject to great empires. As such, they may have believed it was their duty to return it to the Roman fold. Tyre was also rich. The dye known as Tyrian purple had been manufactured there since before records had been kept or the Bible written. Made from the mucus of crushed murex snails, it was so expensive that at one time cloth stained with it had only been worn by kings. The Venetians were particularly eager to share in the production and trade of Tyrian dye. Tyre also had a flourishing glassware industry in which the Jewish community was particularly active.[27]

The fields on the mainland of Tyre were lush, watered by an artesian spring. They produced grain and fruit and sugar cane. Sugar was a rare commodity in Europe. Refined and molded into hard cones, it was shipped everywhere in the Mediterranean and sold for a high profit. The crop had been introduced to Tyre sometime after the Muslims had conquered Iraq. The Arabs then brought the first canes to plant in the humid coastal areas. The earliest mention of crops of sugar in the Near East is in the tenth century, when it was grown on small plots solely for the use of the nobility.[28] By the twelfth century, it was a major industry. Honey had been the main sweetener for centuries in the West. When sugar was introduced, it was used more for medicinal purposes than for food, which made it all the more precious.[29]

Tyre was theoretically subject to the Shi'ite caliphs of Egypt, but Tughtigin, emir of Damascus, had rights to a third of the profits of the town, in return for military protection.[30] This unusual Sunni-Shi'ite alliance had been the result of Baldwin I's siege of Tyre in 1111. The citizens had been not been able to get reinforcements from Egypt and were forced to apply to Damascus for help.[31] Inexorably, the European invaders were forcing old enemies to come together against them.

The siege of Tyre began in April 1124. In spite of his plans and the arrival of the Venetian fleet, King Baldwin II wasn't there. Once again, he was in the hands of the Muslims. But this time his imprisonment wasn't the result of a battle but a botched attempt to free Jocelyn. Once again, Morfia had to endure the possible loss of her husband. This time, however, she was more experienced in diplomacy and more confident of her position. She took an active role in negotiating for his release.

The tale of Baldwin's imprisonment and release is straight out of a thriller. It began with Jocelyn's capture in September 1122 by Balak ibn Bahram, the nephew of Il-Ghazi, emir of Aleppo. Jocelyn offered to pay for his own release and that of his fellow captives and also return Muslim prisoners that he was holding. Balak wasn't interested. He had only a small holding north of Edessa and felt that the best way to increase it was to get rid of the Christian menace to his south. He demanded that Jocelyn hand over the county of Edessa in return for his freedom. Jocelyn refused.

Stymied, Balak even took his prisoners to the gates of Edessa and threatened to kill them if those inside refused to surrender. Jocelyn forbade them to do so and reportedly told Balak, "We [Franks], are like camels bearing burdens in our holding of our fortresses. If one camel dies, the packs are passed to another." If he died, Jocelyn implied, another lord would be found.[32] The city wouldn't capitulate. Jocelyn II was still a child at the time, but his father preferred death to losing his son's legacy.

Infuriated, Balak took the men back to their prison.

Two months later, Il-Ghazi, after over twenty years of on-again, off-again relations with the Westerners, crowned by the defeat of Roger of Antioch, went out to participate in one more skirmish near Aleppo. Even though the old emir's health was failing, he fought with his usual force. Afterward, he set out to return to his favored town of Mardin but, like Baldwin I before him, he never arrived. He died on 1 Ramadan, 516 A.H. (November 3, 1122).[33] The only contemporary who goes into detail about his death is Walter, the chancellor of Antioch, who said, "his filthy soul issued forth from his anus along with a flux of dung from his body, and it was dragged away by the claws of infernal scorpions to tumble into the halls of deepest hell."[34] This may have been wishful thinking on Walter's part. He was never a fan of Il-Ghazi. No one else, including the Muslim chroniclers, said what illness he suffered from, so it's only my guess that it may have involved his liver.

Il-Ghazi's successor in Aleppo, who was busy consolidating his power, made a truce with Baldwin II, who finally decided in mid-April 1123 that he had time to try to rescue his cousin from Balak's prison. What he didn't know was that Balak was out and about in Jocelyn's territory, raiding the fields and taking more captives. Baldwin only had a small party with him when he camped for the night near a river in a place called Shenchrig. Once his tent was up, the king decided to do some falconry to get a few birds for dinner. Just as he was ready to loose his bird into the sky, Balak's army made a surprise attack. As a result, Baldwin joined his cousins in prison.[35] Balak must have thought he had been given a miracle when he captured the king so easily, or at least a sign that his fortunes were improving.

If Balak thought that capturing the king of Jerusalem would cause chaos and immediate surrender, he soon learned that Jocelyn's statement was true of Baldwin, as well. The burden of Jerusalem, Antioch, and now, Edessa was just moved to another camel. Fulcher gives an eye-witness account of the deliberations following the news that the king had been taken. "After this news reached us at Jerusalem all came to an assembly in the city of Acre to take counsel. . . . They chose as the guardian and leader of the land one Eustace, a stout man of honest character."[36] This was Eustace Grenier, lord of Caesarea and Sidon. He was a Fleming and had long been a supporter of the kings, often witnessing royal charters. Eustace was married to Emma, niece of the scandalous Patriarch Arnulf.[37] Emma's parents aren't known, but, upon her marriage, her uncle gave her, from church property, the tithes of a town worth five thousand gold bezants a year.[38]

As soon as he had been chosen viceroy, Eustace went back to Jerusalem to consult with Morfia and Patriarch Warmund about freeing the king.

Less than a month later, the Venetian fleet arrived and the siege of Tyre began as scheduled.

It was amazing that, with the prince of Antioch dead and the king of Jerusalem and count of Edessa imprisoned, the Crusader States could continue functioning so well. In some ways, things went better than usual because, as is the tendency of humans, the lords of the region put aside their usual bickering and came together in a crisis. At least most of them did. The Flemish chronicler Galbert of Bruges reports that a minority group sent word to Charles the Good, count of Flanders, offering the crown to him. Their main complaint was not that Baldwin might not return but that the king was tight-fisted with money, refusing to spread it among his vassals.[39] Charles turned them down.

Kharphut, the fortress where Baldwin and Jocelyn were being held, was over one hundred miles north of Edessa in the center of Turkish territory. This made a full-scale attack almost impossible, especially since most of the fighting men were now involved in the siege of Tyre as Baldwin had intended. It seemed that the king and the count, along with various relatives, were not likely to be rescued any time soon. But they steadfastly refused to cede their lands to Balak.

Ransom doesn't seem to have been discussed up to this point. Morfia must have been doing all she could to arrange for Baldwin's freedom. She had every reason to fear that Melisende, at her young age, could become a queen in name only or even set aside for a man elected by the nobles, if her father never returned

Since no one stepped forward to mount a rescue of the king, Morfia took matters into her own hands. Along with a Frank, Godfrey Almuin, the queen contacted Armenian soldiers. Together they laid a plot to get past the gates and into the castle.

Fifteen Armenian soldiers disguised as local peasants, first spent several days watching the comings and goings at the fortress. One day, they learned that Balak had gone to Aleppo. They had already noticed that the guards were lax in their responsibilities, dozing or leaving only a few men on duty. One morning, the Armenians approached the main gate, arguing with each other over a supposed complaint between two of them. The men demanded that the person in charge adjudicate the quarrel.[40]

After they were let into the fortress, the Armenians attacked and killed the guards. With Balak gone, the captain of the guards "was giving a banquet to the officers, wine was passing and they were merry."[41] The officers never finished their party. The Armenians "rushed on the diners and killed them all."[42]

Matthew says that they freed the king, Jocelyn, Galeran, and many other prisoners, including soldiers and women.

Instead of getting on a fast horse and heading back to Jerusalem, Baldwin took over the fortress, deciding that it was too great a prize to ignore. Jocelyn did leave, sending back his ring to let Baldwin know he had made it through enemy lines and would return with help.[43]

When Balak heard that his prisoners had escaped, he made a forced march north and began a siege of his own fortress.

Meanwhile, Jocelyn was trying to make his way through enemy territory. He and three companions traveled by night, hiding in caves and underbrush by day. Finally after several tense days, they came to the Euphrates River. Jocelyn looked at it in panic. There was no ferry or ford. They had to cross to the other side to reach Christian territory. But Jocelyn had never learned to swim! His friends came up with an idea. They inflated two wineskins that they had first obligingly emptied, tied them with ropes, and "guided by an experienced swimmer on either side, through God's will, he reached the other side safely."[44]

Jocelyn's adventures on his way home weren't over yet. He then was found by an Armenian peasant family who discovered and recognized him. Offering to help, they decided to dress him as one of their own and guide him back to his home. The count and his men accepted with gratitude. Jocelyn's understanding of peasant life was apparently better than that of most noblemen. When the man offered to slaughter a piglet for his dinner Jocelyn told him, "No, you don't normally eat a whole pig; don't give your neighbors cause for suspicion."[45]

He may have known about commoners' eating habits, but Jocelyn showed total incompetence when, to keep up the ruse, the man gave him a toddler girl to carry. This didn't work. Jocelyn wasn't familiar with the handling of babies and the child didn't like being toted about by a clumsy stranger. She cried, whined, and wiggled until he gave up and returned her to her family.[46]

At last the party of peasants, with the count in disguise, reached Tel Bashir. Jocelyn's Armenian wife had died a few years previously. His second wife, Marie, greeted him with joy, along with his son, Jocelyn II, and his new daughter, Stephanie.[47] Jocelyn rewarded the peasant handsomely, spent a little time recovering, and then headed first for Antioch and then to Jerusalem in order to raise an army to get Baldwin and the others out of Kharphut and safely home.

As Jocelyn, Eustace Grenier, constable of Jerusalem, and the armies were preparing for the long march north, word came that Balak had succeeded in retaking Kharphut. He had brought one of the towers down by tunneling beneath it and lighting a fire to destroy the wooden supports that the engineers had set up. Once he was in charge again, Balak killed everyone except

Baldwin and a few other valuable hostages. Incensed at the actions of the Armenians, who were his vassals, Balak tortured those he found inside the castle and eventually had them flayed alive.[48] Morfia's adherents paid a high price for their loyalty to her.

Upon learning of this Jocelyn reasoned that there was no chance of freeing the king by force. The armies turned back.[49]

Melisende was now in her late teens and fully aware of her father's situation. She and her mother now had to find a way to ransom Baldwin or he would never return. Apart from the emotional worry this caused, their own status had to be considered. If Baldwin died, the best they could hope for was that Melisende would be put on the marriage market, much as Morfia had been, and sold to the highest bidder.

It was essential for Melisende's future that Baldwin be freed.

Balak now had the king under even tighter security in an even more remote fortress. Feeling confident that his guards would not make the same mistake as before, he returned to the vicinity of Aleppo, where he laid siege to the Muslim town of Manbij. He bombarded the citadel town with catapults. In desperation, the town sent a messenger to Jocelyn and Geoffrey the Monk, lord of Marash, who had taken care of Edessa while Jocelyn was absent. The men came at once to lift the siege, perhaps hoping that they could capture Balak and make a trade for Baldwin.

In the course of the battle outside Manbij, Balak was killed. The Franks rejoiced and Jocelyn had the emir's head cut off and taken on tour to Antioch, Jerusalem, and Aleppo so that everyone could be certain that Baldwin's captor was really dead.[50] Oddly, Matthew of Edessa adds to this report that Armenians in Balak's lands mourned him, for "he had dealt compassionately" with them.[51] The Syrian chronicler adds that "Balak would impale a Turk for taking a bit of meat from a poor man and he would not let any harm to Christians, even by word."[52] If these Christian writers could praise Balak so, he must have been a complex personality. But the more accounts I read, the more it becomes clear that few on any side were one-dimensional heroes or villains.

This victory over Balak did not help Baldwin any more than the death of Jokermish had during his first captivity. He was transferred, along with all Balak's other property, to yet another prison, this time in Aleppo, by his new captor, Bursuqi.

At this point Morfia traveled north to consult with Jocelyn. Messengers were sent back and forth between Edessa and Aleppo. At last the king's ransom was set at 100,000 dahekans, an enormous sum.[53] Baldwin couldn't raise that amount. In order to secure his immediate release, Bursuqi demanded that Baldwin provide him with hostages of equal value.

The price of Baldwin's freedom was the children of the Frankish nobility, including his own youngest daughter, Yvette. The child was four or five at the time and Morfia must have been sick at the thought of handing her over to the enemy. But she couldn't ask others to do what she wouldn't. So she took Yvette to Aleppo and gave her as hostage. With Yvette went Jocelyn's son, Jocelyn II. He would have been around ten. Another dozen children became collateral for Baldwin. When the children were safely delivered to their captors, Baldwin was released in September 1124.

It is a popular myth that people at this time didn't love their children; so many died as babies or in their first few years that it wasn't worth investing emotion on them, the saying goes. This is not true, as anyone who really thought about it would realize. Children were treasured as much as they are today. The fact that so many died in infancy only made each one more precious. Giving a child as a pledge almost always guaranteed the good behavior of the parents.[54] This practice of exchanging children as hostages had long been accepted among Western and Eastern peoples. Records of this type of exchange can be found as early as the fifth century. At the age of eight, the Goth Theodoric was given by his father to the Roman Emperor in Constantinople as a hostage. Theodoric spent ten years in captivity and emerged having learned enough about the Empire to eventually conquer Rome.[55]

Generally, the children were well treated, although it still must have been traumatic for them.

The only story I know about a child who was abandoned in captivity is that of William Marshal, who, in 1152, at roughly the same age as Yvette, was held hostage by King Stephen of England for the good behavior of William's father, John. When John reneged on his promise, Stephen threatened to hang the boy. John is supposed to have sent back this message. "Kill him if you like, I still have the hammer and anvil to make more and better sons."[56] Stephen didn't have the heart to do it and William was eventually set free. John's callousness horrified both friends and enemies, although some did criticize Stephen for being too soft-hearted. If hostages were not executed when the pledge was broken, the custom would have no value.

In this case it's likely that the children were treated better than the adult hostages. Jocelyn had been kept in chains, which he brought back to lay at the Church of the Holy Sepulchre in Jerusalem in thanks for his deliverance, much as Bohemond had earlier made an offering of chains to the church of St. Leonard in France after he gained his freedom.[57]

Galeran and Bar-Noul, who were captured with Baldwin II, were not ransomed and were eventually executed.[58] It's not known if anyone even tried to set them free. Michael adds that the lord of Mardin, Hossam ad-Din, didn't wish to kill them but feared that Bursuqi of Aleppo would be angry if the men weren't massacred. Ironically, after the men had been executed, word came that Bursuqi had been assassinated while at his prayers. When he heard this, "Hossam ad-Din regretted having killed the Franks."[59]

Galeran died unmarried. He left his property to his widowed sister-in-law, Alice of Corbeil. She eventually gave it to the monastery of Josaphat, where Galeran's brother was abbot.[60]

Yvette's fate was another matter. Baldwin was desperate to get his child back. But how was he to raise the money? The drought had returned so tithes were low. Tyre had not yet fallen, although the siege continued. While he was considering options, he learned that Timurtash, son of Il-Ghazi and the new ruler of Aleppo, had taken the children and returned to his father's favorite city of Mardin. The emir did this, according to Ibn al-Athir, because, "he saw that Syria was a frequent battle-ground with the Franks and he was a man who loved a calm and easy life."[61] The poor man was obviously born into the wrong family.

Timurtash had made a wise move in distancing himself from Jerusalem. Upon learning of the transfer, Baldwin may have panicked, fearing that, like he had been, Yvette would be taken too far into Muslim territory to recover.

The king wasted no time in strategy but attacked a number of prosperous villages in the area of Damascus in his frantic attempt to raise the ransom. He "seized, ruined and destroyed three of the richest and returned home with as much booty as he could carry."[62] With the proceeds of these raids and donations (willing or not) from the people of the kingdom, Yvette and the other children were liberated a few months later.[63]

About ten years after her captivity Yvette entered the convent of St. Anne. Her reasons for becoming a nun were never given. She may have felt a sincere calling. Or she may have been tainted by the possibility that she had been raped in captivity. This was the reason that Baldwin I had given for putting his Armenian wife, Arda, in that same convent after she had briefly been held by Saracen pirates. But there is no hint that the children were mistreated in any way. Many of the hostages, like Yvette and Jocelyn, had one native parent so they and their custodians would have resembled each other. The children would have spoken some Arabic and been familiar with the customs and food. I suspect that Morfia would have sent a Syrian or Armenian nanny to care for her child, if possible. They weren't entering an alien world, frightening as it might have been to be taken from their homes and given to the enemy.

It was common sense for both sides to treat noncombatant hostages well. Muslim women and children were also sent as pledges or taken in raids and held for ransom. The more important they were, the less likely they would be harmed. It was a complex set of rules, but understood by all. That didn't mean that families wouldn't move heaven and earth to get their relatives back.

There is another theory about Yvette's entry into the convent. Since Yvette was the only child born after Baldwin became king, some believe she would have had a better claim to inherit the throne than Melisende. Under this theory, Melisende forced Yvette to become a nun in order to preserve her own power.[64] It's a feeble idea at best; there is no suggestion of it during Melisende's lifetime and the sisters seem to have had a loving relationship. What it does indicate is a prejudice against Melisende by some historians that has affected how she and her reign are perceived. It's only by examining the sparse records and reading between the lines of the chroniclers that a more balanced picture forms.

Another case in which chroniclers exaggerate or skip information on anything beyond military events is the account of the siege of Tyre. During Baldwin's captivity, the siege of the island city had continued, under the combined leadership of the doge of Venice, Patriarch Warmund of Jerusalem, Count Pons of Tripoli, and William de Buris, who had succeeded Eustace Grenier as constable of Jerusalem at the latter's death. Due to the lack of wood in the Holy Land, the Venetians had brought equipment for building siege engines, such as catapults and rolling towers to shoot arrows from.[65] Most of the Venetian soldiers intended to return home, but in some cases the ships themselves were cannibalized in order to build towers or shore up tunnels dug by sappers to bring down the stone walls of fortresses.[66] Tyre was worth sending back to Venice for more ships.

With the city weakened, William says that the rulers of Tyre convened a meeting and the elders and governors laid out the situation to the people. The population contained some Christians but mostly Muslims and Jews, some of whom were refugees from Jerusalem. They had businesses and property in Tyre and had no intention of losing it all again. By unanimous consent, they agreed to surrender.[67]

The Venetian attitude toward war and commerce was apparent at Tyre. When the city finally surrendered, instead of wholesale slaughter, there was market haggling. Tughtigin, emir of Damascus, had taken over lordship of Tyre from the Egyptians, who had given up trying to break the Venetian blockade. He offered bribes to the Latins in order to convince them to allow citizens to take their belongings with them and leave the city empty for the conquerors. The Latin soldiers, being paid mostly in whatever they could loot, didn't like the idea of having no plunder at all and told their leaders as much. Counter offers were made. After much back and forth, the Tyrians were allowed to leave with as much as they could carry, abandoning large pieces and most livestock.[68] The exodus began on July 8, 1124, but it seems that many of the citizens received assurances that they would not be molested by the new lords and so decided to stay with their shops and houses.[69] Most of the others migrated to the area around Damascus, where they judged they would be protected.

William continues his tale to add that although the rank and file of the army were still furious that they would be deprived of their traditional prizes, especially of people and horses, "The saner will of the more prominent men prevailed."[70]

For once, it actually did. Al-Athir says that the refugees left unmolested, "and only the weak, who were incapable of moving, were left behind."[71] Fulcher adds that, "those of the Muslims who chose to remain in the city did so in peace, according to the agreement."[72] Among the large number of the inhabitants of Tyre who decided to stay was a fairly substantial Jewish population. This included several Talmudic scholars, including the head of the community of Palestine, and three synagogues.[73] The Jewish merchants living there may have been both competition for and collaborators with the Venetians. Jews also were active in glass making, for which Tyre was famous.[74] Long after the Christian take-over, the Jewish community of Tyre thrived. In the 1160s the leader of the community was an emigrant from Egypt, Rabbenu Ephraim. He was known as a scholar and sage, and his wisdom was praised by the famous scholar Maimonides. The Jewish community of Tyre was even rich enough to contribute money to ransom Jews taken captive in other places.[75]

In many ways, the taking of Tyre was more important than the taking of Jerusalem. Al-Athir, writing a hundred years later, still mourned its loss. "May God restore it to Islam and assuage the hearts of the Muslims!" he lamented.[76] Tyre survived as a Latin Christian city until it fell to the Egyptian Mameluks in 1291. Even though Baldwin wasn't there for the fall of the city to the Crusaders, it was the major achievement of his reign. The deal he made with the Venetians guaranteed trade with Europe and more pilgrims to Jerusalem. It also diminished the danger of invasion from Egypt.

Baldwin still had Antioch to worry about. The city was too far away for him to continually keep an eye on things. Even though his cousin Jocelyn had twice redeemed him from captivity and had remained loyal during their estrangement, Baldwin still didn't want one man to control both Antioch and Edessa. But there was one possible solution for the problem: the appearance of the mysterious rightful heir, Bohemond II. The question was, would he come?

In 1126 Bohemond II was sixteen or seventeen years old. Years before, when he was nine, he had been offered the lordship of Antioch by a council that met in the city just after the death of Roger at the Field of Blood, with the provision that the boy bring an army to defend the country, honor the property of the local lords, and marry Alice, Baldwin's second daughter. Alice was also about nine at the time.[77]

Bohemond II's mother, Constance of France, very likely had had reservations about sending, or even bringing, her only child to a wild corner of the world, where the life expectancy of a ruler was short. It's not clear if Bohemond I intended Antioch to be his son's inheritance; he had land in Taranto, Italy, that had escaped his brother's grasp. Constance may have wanted to wait to see if any better offers were forthcoming from anywhere. As regent for her son, she took an active role in preserving his inheritance in Taranto. It was no easy task. Bohemond II's relative Roger of Sicily considered himself a rival for any inheritance, especially of their mutual cousin, William, duke of Apulia, if he should die without heirs.[78]

In the end, Constance may have decided to take the land in Italy. However, she died when Bohemond II was in his late teens and Bohemond decided to seek his future in the Holy Land. In September 1126, Bohemond set sail from Taranto to take up his duties as prince of Antioch. Some say that he made a pact with Duke William that if either should die without children, the other would inherit.[79] This was disputed by Roger when William died a year later. Roger declared himself duke of Apulia, and when Pope Honorius disagreed with this, Roger led an army to Rome to convince the pope to change him mind. Bohemond seems not to have challenged his cousin's takeover, settling instead for being prince of Antioch.

When the news came that Bohemond was on his way, the whole country went mad with anticipation. Rumors flew through the land like the doves of Edessa, only to be quickly proven false. Fulcher tells of some recent arrivals from the West, "two-faced and gluttonous," who said that Bohemond had landed, causing many to rush down to the dock to welcome him. But the ship that arrived had only brought the prince's "falcons, fowlers and dogs, which he had sent on ahead."[80]

Bohemond had such fame by then that I imagine even the disembarking of his hunting equipment brought excitement to the citizens of Antioch.

At last the flotilla was sighted. True to his promise, Bohemond had brought twenty-two ships full of arms and soldiers. Baldwin and his family were already in Antioch, awaiting him eagerly. They and the people of the city met him with a great procession and cheering. Baldwin's heart must have leapt at the sight of the ships. And Alice's heart must have leapt at the sight of Bohemond. "He was a beardless youth of twenty years [sic], but a valiant and mighty warrior, tall with a lion-like face and blond hair."[81]

Bohemond and Baldwin had a little chat, perhaps about the use of the reinforcements against Aleppo with a few words on being good to the king's little girl. Then the prince and the princess were introduced and wed.

Soon afterward, Bohemond was formally invested with the principate of Antioch. Seated on a throne and wearing a robe of office, he received oaths of fealty from the nobles of the land. Once this was accomplished, Baldwin returned to Jerusalem.[82]

Bohemond and Alice were left on their own, and Alice was soon pregnant.[83]

The fact that Baldwin had promised his second daughter to the prince of Antioch as early as 1119, before his youngest child was born, indicates that he suspected Melisende would be his heir. Her marriage required much thought and consultation. It wouldn't do for her to marry a vassal who might put his own holding ahead of the needs of Jerusalem. She needed someone strong, seasoned in battle, and able to give orders. She needed a man who would bring an army with him.

Melisende was over twenty now. She had no illusions about marrying a handsome young prince as Alice had.

The search was already under way when on October 30, probably in 1127, Morfia died.

There is no record of her passing or mention of her funeral. The day is known because of the custom of paying for masses or prayers to be said on the anniversary of a death for the soul of the deceased. She was buried at the monastery of St. Mary Josaphat, and the monks kept the date in their record of prayers. Morfia's husband and children provided for many years' worth of remembrance.[84]

Her cause of death is unknown. It might have been illness or accident. She may have even had a miscarriage. It is a tribute to her that Baldwin doesn't seem to have considered remarriage. The young woman from Melitine whose father had been happy to trade her to anyone in return for patronage and military aid had found wealth she couldn't have imagined. Her husband loved her, her children were devoted. There are few records of her life. But in order to have raised four strong-willed girls who stayed close, looking out for each other all their lives, she must have been a wonderful mother and wife. Morfia is barely a footnote to history, but, to her family, she was everything.

TEN

FINDING A KING

JERUSALEM AND ANJOU,
1127–1128

MATTHEW OF EDESSA STATES WITH APPARENT PUZ-
zlement that Baldwin was devoted to Morfia and grieved for her.[1] The king
was in his fifties when she died, certainly young enough to anticipate father-
ing more children. But instead of looking for a new wife, he set about putting his daughters in positions of power, drawing the other Latin States into
his family circle. The internecine arguments among the Latins were a stumbling block to presenting a united front to the Muslim leaders. Marrying his
sister, Cecelia, to Roger of Antioch and Roger's sister, Marie, to Jocelyn had
put an end to the squabbles between Antioch and Edessa. Perhaps, Baldwin
thought, his girls could also be peacemakers.

Alice's marriage to Bohemond was definitely a lucky coup. First of all,
Antioch was now somebody else's problem, a relief to Baldwin. But the
king was also aware that being the father-in-law of the prince meant that
he would have an excuse to interfere if necessary. The fact that he was now
connected to the ruling Capet family of France was also a plus, one that as
a younger son from an obscure town he couldn't have hoped for if he had
stayed home.

It may also have been ironically satisfying to have his daughter marry the son of the Norman brigand who had been a constant irritation to the king in his early years and who had refused to pay for his ransom. And, of course, this marriage might help to repair the damage caused when Baldwin I sent back his Norman Sicilian wife, who was the mother of Roger of Sicily. As well, in the continually cash-strapped Latin kingdoms, rich relatives were much to be desired and Sicily was richer and closer than France. Roger could only be grateful that Bohemond had come to Antioch and left Apulia for the taking. Baldwin may have hoped to remind Roger of this the next time Jerusalem needed funds.

In keeping with his dynastic schedule, Baldwin arranged for Melisende's next sister, Hodierna, now around thirteen years old, to be betrothed to Raymond, the son and heir of the count of Tripoli. Raymond was from the family of the counts of Saint-Gilles and Toulouse, who were powerful lords in Provençal and Languedoc. This marriage provided the double result of tying Tripoli to Jerusalem and forging a family connection with the southern magnets who were richer than the king of France. Provence was still independent of France and would be for another hundred years. The local families had already provided a number of recruits to Baldwin's army and even more to the Templars, whose ranks were growing.

Yvette seems to have been destined for the convent. She couldn't have been more than nine when Morfia died, so Baldwin may have been keeping her in reserve for a future marriage to an ally. But it would not be unusual for the youngest child to be intended for the Church. Alliances with God were even more important than those made with inconstant men and were considered just as beneficial.

That still left the problem of finding a husband for Melisende. The man needed to be a seasoned military leader but not connected to any of the Latin holdings. The relations among the lordships were already precarious. Making a lesser nobleman king could upset the balance. Also, the practice of marrying into local families hadn't persisted among the nobility of Jerusalem, despite the early weddings between crusaders and Armenian women. Instead they had intermarried among themselves so that Melisende was related, either by blood or marriage, to almost every eligible man of her class. Whoever Melisende married would have to be from the outside. He should have experience in ruling and be strong enough to keep peace among the crusading families as well as defend the kingdom against the Egyptians and Turks.

On the other hand, he couldn't be too powerful. Byzantium had any number of noblemen who would have been willing to marry the heiress to Jerusalem. Baldwin and his advisors didn't even consider them. There was danger in entering into any union with the Byzantine Empire. The emperor, Manuel, already had his eye on Antioch, which he considered part of his domain. Baldwin II had not come all the way from Flanders and fought for thirty years to hand his kingdom over to the Greeks.

It was a difficult balance to achieve. Melisende knew this; she was an adult and acutely aware of the situation. She was as determined as her father to keep the kingdom of Jerusalem from becoming a Byzantine fief. Nor did she intend for it to be used as a stepping stone for some foreign lord to consolidate power in his own hands.

Melisende was not a European, despite her mixed heritage. Her roots went deep into the land. Her ancestors had fought both Greeks and Arabs to make a place for themselves in Anatolia when they had been driven from their home in Armenia. Even Baldwin may not have realized the strength of her determination to keep her kingdom. Both of them knew that the kingship of Jerusalem had so far been decided by election, not inheritance, so the succession must be guaranteed from the start.

There is no record of who first suggested Fulk, count of Anjou. It could have been Hugh of Payens, the first grand master of the Templars. When Fulk came to Jerusalem in 1120, he was much taken with the efforts of Hugh and his fellow knights to provide protection for the pilgrims streaming in from the West who tended to be far too oblivious of the dangers on the road. Fulk had become a lay member of the Templars even before it became an official order. He had also given a yearly donation of thirty pounds to help maintain the knights.

A king with money and influence who was already a known friend was just what the struggling Templar order needed. A warrior, used to command, was what Jerusalem needed. An added advantage was that Fulk had few relatives among the families ruling the Latin States and therefore would not be likely to side with any in their internal quarrels on the basis of loyalty to kin.

Melisende must have seen Fulk when he first visited Jerusalem. In 1120, he had been about thirty. He was of medium height and had the Angevin red hair that his son Geoffrey and his grandson Henry would inherit.[2] To a fifteen-year-old girl he may have seemed exotic, even romantic. Or she may have thought him only another tiresome visitor from Europe. But at least he wasn't a completely blank slate. She even knew a lot of the scandals that were the Angevin heritage.

Fulk came from a tumultuous family on both sides. His ancestors had been counts of Anjou since the tenth century. Through military success and shrewd marriages they had also become counts of Maine and Vendôme.[3]

The counts were tough fighting men who stood for no nonsense, even from the Church. The women who married into this family were also independent. Fulk's mother, Bertrade, had left his father when Fulk was a child and run away with Philip I, king of France. The couple had lived together openly, despite the wrath of popes and the embarrassment of the families. Eventually, Bertrade and Philip were married by the bishop of Rouen, but remained under excommunication. As a result, any town they were staying in could not hold church services and the bells would begin ringing as they left, which Philip found highly entertaining.[4]

So Fulk had half-siblings who were children of the king of France. One of these, Cecelia, was an early settler in the Latin kingdoms. She had married first Tancred, regent of Antioch for Bohemond II, and then Pons, count of Tripoli.[5] Melisende almost certainly would have known her, as Cecelia was the mother of Hodierna's future husband.

Despite the betrayal by his mother with King Philip, Fulk fought on the side of the French kings against the English for most of his career.[6] He was a stalwart defender of the rights of Philip's son, King Louis VI, against the various barons who nibbled away at the edges of the small area that was then France.

At the time of his first pilgrimage to Jerusalem, Fulk's wife, Eremberga, was still alive. She died in 1126. Like Baldwin, Fulk hadn't rushed into a second marriage. Instead, he concentrated on finding spouses for his children. His elder daughter, Matilda of Anjou, had been married to William, the only son of Henry I of England. Fulk was delighted to have forged a link with his sometime enemy and secured the English crown for his descendants, or so he thought. But shortly after Fulk returned home in 1120, William drowned in the disaster of the *White Ship*, leaving Matilda a widow and King Henry with no male heir.

Matilda of Anjou chose not to remarry but to enter the convent of Fontevraux, near Tours. Fulk tried again to secure the English crown, marrying his second daughter, Sybille, to William Clito, King Henry's nephew and the most likely contender to succeed his uncle, who now only had one legitimate child, Matilda of England, currently the Holy Roman empress.

But Clito's fortunes fell and Fulk knew when to cut his losses. Sybille was conveniently divorced from Clito on the grounds that they were too closely related.[7] Eventually she was married to Thierry, count of Flanders, in 1134, several years after her father had gone to Jerusalem.[8] Sybille had the Angevin spirit. She maintained the county while Thierry went twice to Jerusalem. She directed a war against invading neighbors, only pausing to give birth. At last, in 1157, she made the pilgrimage to the Holy Land with her husband. She decided to remain there, retiring to the convent of Bethany near Jerusalem. From there she would play a role in the fortunes of her stepmother, Melisende, and more particularly, Melisende's sons and grandchildren.

Fulk's second son, Helias, was given the county of Maine and the daughter of a natural child of King Henry. So all of Fulk's children except his eldest son, Geoffrey, were settled. Fulk decided to make one more attempt at a legitimate English alliance. He seems to have had his heart set on adding Normandy and England to a grandson's inheritance.

This is the point, in early 1128, when the party arrived in Anjou from Jerusalem with the offer of Melisende's hand. The emissaries consisted of Fulk's old friends, the two Templars Hugh of Payens and Godfrey of St.

Omer, along with several noblemen and clerics of Jerusalem led by the king's constable, William de Buris, who had helped to keep the kingdom intact during Baldwin's captivity and led the siege of Tyre.[9]

There is no evidence that Fulk had considered seeking a crown for himself. His energy had been expended in consolidating his power in Europe through his children. When the envoys appeared, the count was in the process of negotiating once again with King Henry to marry Geoffrey to Henry's only remaining legitimate child, Matilda of England. She had been married to the Holy Roman emperor but he had died, leaving her childless.

Matilda was twenty-five and Geoffrey barely fifteen. Neither party was thrilled with the idea of the marriage but this was Fulk's last chance to fulfill his dream. King Henry's motives are not so clear. Anjou was a strategic county and the counts had been instrumental in turning the balance in conflicts over the years, but that hardly made Geoffrey worthy of the king's daughter. King Henry might have hoped that a young husband would increase Matilda's chances to conceive, and for both Fulk and Henry a male grandchild was the ultimate goal. It was a total misalliance; the couple loathed each other. They knew their duty, however, and the marriage did achieve the purpose. Despite their mutual antipathy, Geoffrey and Matilda managed to have three sons. The eldest, Henry, would succeed his grandfather as Henry II of England.

The sudden appearance, in the midst of these negotiations, of a party of men offering Fulk the crown of Jerusalem and a bride the same age as his younger daughter may have come as a shock. Or Fulk may have already sent hints to Jerusalem that he wouldn't mind a change of scene once he had his children settled. Whatever his reaction to the invitation, Fulk took his time making such a momentous decision.

His first concern was to see that Geoffrey and Matilda were officially married and that Matilda was firmly established as her father's heir. At the same time, he made a list of conditions that had to be met before he would agree to emigrate. First of all, he wanted solid assurances that Melisende would not be passed over for the throne of Jerusalem. He also insisted that he be crowned king in his own right, something he couldn't achieve for Geoffrey.[10]

The embassy was made up of men who were authorized to decide whether or not to agree to Fulk's demands. William de Buris, prince of Galilee, was Baldwin's most trusted advisor. Born in Normandy, William had been in the Latin states for nearly twenty years and had served the kings faithfully.[11] With him was Guy of Brisbarre, lord of Beirut, also a trusted advisor. The men brought relics as gifts along with the written offer.[12] Fulk would ultimately donate several to local monasteries before he left, to ensure that his soul would not be forgotten.

Hugh of Payens was happy to stop and add his voice to the request for Fulk to return to Jerusalem, but may not have had the authority to agree to anything in the king's name. The main reason for his journey was to drum up support and recruits for the Templars. He and his fellow Knight of the Temple, Godfrey, would continue on to Champagne where they received official support from the church for their order.[13]

Having reviewed all the possibilities that might keep Geoffrey and Matilda's (yet unborn) son from becoming king of England, Fulk was intensely cautious about committing himself to Jerusalem. He insisted that he have written assurance that he would be king and that no other claimants would suddenly appear. This was more than the emissaries could guarantee. Who knew who might decide that he had a right to Jerusalem? Guy of Brisbarre had to travel back to Jerusalem to consult with the king and Patriarch, returning to Anjou with all the promises Baldwin could give.[14]

Baldwin had conditions of his own. He and his counselors had decided on Fulk as the future king. But Baldwin was also determined that his daughter be a queen in her own name as well. In March 1129, Melisende began to witness charters issued by her father. In the first, her name appears at the head of the list, before the bishops and lords. It states that she is the heir of the king. Her status as next in line for the throne was established.[15]

Fulk received another reassurance when the archbishop of Tyre and the bishop of Ramla took advantage of a trip to Rome to have the pope, Honorius II, arbitrate an argument between them. They also asked Honorius about the choice of the next king. Prompted by their unified request for an endorsement of the count of Anjou, Honorius sent an official letter to

Baldwin commending Fulk to him. He also confirmed that Baldwin II was indeed the rightful king of Jerusalem. Baldwin made sure that Fulk received a copy.[16] That seemed to settle the question of unexpected claimants to the throne.

The negotiating went on for nearly a year. In the end Fulk decided to accept the invitation and come to Jerusalem. It was agreed that he would be presented to all as the future king. He and Melisende were to have the cities of Acre and Tyre to govern until Baldwin's death, at which time they would return to the kingdom.[17] Fulk may have believed that he was to be king in his own right, not by virtue of being Melisende's husband.[18] Since Baldwin had been elected king, this may not have been an unlikely supposition on Fulk's part. All the conditions he established before he agreed to come to Jerusalem indicate that he expected to be the final authority in Jerusalem.

He apparently didn't think to ask what Melisende had in mind.

Baldwin had promised that the marriage would be celebrated within fifty days of Fulk's arrival. Fulk reached Jerusalem in May 1129. He and Melisende were married that month.

Now that he was the husband of the heiress of Jerusalem, Fulk only had two duties. The first was to prove he could hold his own against Muslims and warring crusaders. The second was to ensure that the royal line would continue.

In 1130, Melisende gave birth to a boy, named Baldwin for his grandfather. The kingdom rejoiced and Fulk was treated as a savior.

Fulk must have felt that everything was going his way. He no longer had to imagine future greatness through grandchildren, although he wouldn't be adverse to it. He was now a powerful lord of a legendary kingdom. He had a young, docile, and fertile wife who, he believed, would leave all major decisions to him. The count of Anjou was ready to manage Jerusalem just as he had his lands in France.

He was soon to discover that Melisende had plans of her own.

ELEVEN

PREPARING TO PASS THE TORCH

JERUSALEM, 1130–1131

BALDWIN MUST HAVE BEEN ECSTATIC TO HAVE TWO new militant sons-in-law. Bohemond had already proven his worth by retaking the fortress of Kafartab, near Antioch, which had been lost in the give and take of battles. In a fit of youthful exuberance, the young prince ignored the traditions of taking captives or bribes and killed everyone there. William adds, "Such were the first fruits of his natural prowess."[1]

Baldwin may have been relieved that the new ruler of Antioch was able to defend his territory. But the people, especially the clergy of the city, weren't so pleased. Michael the Syrian reports that Bohemond was proud and wished to have his new subjects submit to him unquestioningly, not something the independent citizens of Antioch were accustomed to do.[2] Bernard, the Latin Patriarch of the city, was outraged that Bohemond had no intention of donating any of his recent booty to the Church. To punish Bohemond, Bernard closed all the churches, stopped the priests from saying masses or daily prayers, silenced the bells, and refused to give Latins a Christian burial.[3] Bohemond got the message and turned over a part of his loot in tithe.

For the most part, Bohemond was liked by the chroniclers. Most observers seem to have been bowled over by his looks and pedigree. We don't know what he and Alice thought of each other, but, considering the other noble marriages being made at this time, where one partner was much older than the other or there was no common language, they may have been more than content.

Sometime before 1130, Alice gave birth to a daughter, named Constance for Bohemond's mother. She would have been roughly the same age as Melisende's son Baldwin. The third generation of "Frankish" settlers was established.

AROUND THIS TIME THE CHRONICLER FULCHER OF Chartres died. He was one of the few people who kept track of his age, and so we know that he was sixty-eight at the time of his last entry in 1127. He had arrived with King Baldwin I and his two brothers and had outlived all three. Most of his chronicle reports battles, conquests, and defeats. He admits that "perhaps it will bore the hearers of my story if all things are reported which happened in the war."[4] Still, he felt that each encounter was necessary to understanding the land in which he spent the last thirty years of his life. Over the course of his entries we can see him adapting to existence in Jerusalem. He marveled at eclipses and shooting stars, and worried over the lack of rain and the plagues of locusts and grasshoppers. He seems never to have contemplated returning to his homeland.

Fulcher believed in a mixed society, a new world growing from the old in the Latin East. While he didn't countenance freedom of religion by any means, in his years among the Syrians he became more open to other forms of Christianity. His statement about his ideal society has been often quoted. "We who were Occidentals have now become Orientals. . . . Some have taken wives not only of their own people but Syrians or Armenians or even Saracens who have obtained the grace of baptism."[5]

The picture he gave was intended to encourage other Europeans to immigrate, and there was a grain of truth in it. His next paragraph is less quoted but, I believe, is an even better reflection of life in Jerusalem by the

1120s. "People use the eloquence and idioms of diverse languages in conversing back and forth. Words of different languages have become common property, known to each nationality."[6]

The Franks in the Near East could not have interacted perpetually through a few translators. Melisende was one of the early members of the nobility who spoke and understood the speech of the natives and the Franks. But those of her generation who had been born in Edessa, Antioch, Acre, Tiberias, Galilee, or Jerusalem could not have lived in a bubble of Western culture. There simply weren't enough Westerners. And, if the rich changed their speech and customs to accommodate the country in which they now lived, it's even more likely that the blacksmith or winemaker or farmer would as well, even if some villages were largely settled at first by Franks.[7]

There are those who equate the Latins in the Near East with the British in India and other colonies.[8] It doesn't seem to me to be the same situation. Most of the British in India or China were only there for a short time and their children were sent home to be educated. Many pilgrims to Jerusalem decided to stay, either as members of religious houses or in secular occupations. These immigrants had to adapt to the different languages, climate, food, and politics. Once the initial invasion was over, the new arrivals often sided with Muslim factions against other Muslims or other groups of Latin Christians with whom they had disputes. Very few of the children of the crusaders were sent back to Europe to be educated. The only one I know of is William of Tyre.[9] And, despite spending twenty years studying in Europe, William was still fluent in Arabic, which he must have learned as a child. He used Muslim sources in writing his history. He also translated the works of Arab historians. These have, sadly, been lost.[10]

Fulcher hoped that in another generation, the assimilation would be complete. It might have happened if not for a new force that had arisen in Baghdad and was now moving west toward Aleppo and across the Crusader States. This Muslim counteroffensive would be aided by another, disastrous invasion from Europe. But, in 1128, there was still reason to believe that the Kingdom of Jerusalem would last forever.

Matthew of Edessa also died about this time, disappointed at not having seen his longed-for apocalypse. Perhaps his gloom came from experience with the many tyrannical lords of Edessa, the sieges and skirmishes just outside the gates, or perhaps just his own depressed personality, but Matthew provided the flip side of Fulcher's story. He worried about his Armenian people and saw events from their point of view. He watched them ally themselves with the newcomers and suffer for it more than once. His chronicle was taken up by another cleric, Gregory, who provides some good information, but Gregory doesn't have the fire in the belly that Matthew did.

The loss of these two men leaves a gap in our knowledge. Much of what we know of the next two decades is found in William of Tyre, who wrote his history fifty years later. There are Arabic chroniclers who fill in the story somewhat. Ibn al-Qalanisi was living in Damascus for most of this time and focused on the emirs' interactions with the Latins. Al-Athir and Kemal ad-Din, like William, wrote many years later using material compiled by others, much of which has been lost, but they also help to corroborate William. The dashing nobleman Usamah ibn-Munqidh hasn't played a large role in the story yet, but he not only lived through much of the events to come but also took part in them. His book is more the memoir of an old soldier than an honest attempt to make an accurate record. For this reason, he's much more fun to read, but his accuracy is open to debate.

Michael, the Syrian Patriarch of Antioch, wrote in the 1170s. His work is useful for attitudes and some events but he was more concerned with the fate of his hometown of Melitine than with what was happening far south in Jerusalem.

Each of these men had their own points of view and opinions. And, unfortunately for social historians, they all seemed to be intensely interested in warfare.

BY SEPTEMBER 1129, BALDWIN WAS TAKING ADVANtage of his new son-in-law's skill as a warrior. The king had long desired to capture the city of Damascus and now he had a second in command who might make that possible. Fulk and Baldwin left Melisende in Jerusalem and headed up to Damascus.[11]

Melisende had hardly had time to get to know her new husband. But she may have already begun to realize that while her father had included her in councils, Fulk was doing his best to edge her out. Being left to govern on her own was the best thing that could have happened. As a married woman and confirmed future queen, she could use the time to consolidate her own power base. There's no way to know if she saw matters in this light, but it would have been a prudent move to find out who she could count on if Fulk ever attempted to limit her power. And when he would come to do exactly that, she would act swiftly and decisively, as if well prepared.

She knew that her father intended her to be a true ruler and not just a provider of male children. Even before Morfia's death he had begun to associate her as an equal grantor in his donations to churches and monasteries. In one made in early 1129, Baldwin donates property to the canons of the Holy Sepulchre. First among the witnesses is Melisende, who "praises and consents to this."[12] There are three things to note about this charter. The first is that Melisende is listed before archbishops, bishops, abbots, and all the lords present. The second is that her sisters aren't included. In Europe especially, donations often required the consent of all members of the family to avoid future lawsuits. This didn't always work, but the attempt was made.[13] Melisende, however, as heir to the throne, had a greater claim to royal property than her sisters. It was customary for all such gifts to be renewed by the next ruler when there was a change of leadership; Baldwin may have thought it was better that she agree to the donation from the start, a simplification that also clarified her status as heir to the throne to observers.

The third point is that the charter was not signed in Jerusalem, but the royal city of Acre, on the Mediterranean coast. Acre had often been used as a central meeting place for the kings to hold councils and would be the last stronghold of the Crusader States, taken by the Muslims only in 1291. If Melisende was with her father and not home with her younger two sisters, it's a strong possibility that she was also part of the king's council. How much she was listened to at that point is impossible to guess, but, later, it is clear her counsel was valued.

It may not have just been the fun of having an experienced warrior along that encouraged Baldwin to attack Damascus. The city had been having its own upheavals. The long-time atabeg, Tughtigin, had died on February 12, 1128. Al-Athir praises him as being a just ruler and one who waged *jihad* against the Franks.[14] This was not completely true. Tughtigin was willing to establish truces with the Christians and even join them against a common enemy. His eldest son, Taj al-Muluk Buri, succeeded him.

I have occasionally mentioned the Batini, who came to be known as the Assassins. They were a sect of Shi'ite Islam that had begun centuries before. Also known as Hasan-Ismaili and Nizari, they were a branch of Shi'a Islam who were waiting for the return of Ismail, a descendent of Muhammad in the seventh generation. They were certain that Ismail had not died, but merely gone into hiding until the time was right to make himself known.

The Assassins had a complex, often mystical, theology and, like most Shi'ites, believed that the Sunni majority had abandoned the roots of Islam. The Batini only began to flourish in the late eleventh century, when a scholar from Persia named Hasan-i-Sabbah converted to the sect and began to preach to the disaffected Muslims of northern Persia and Syria.[15] They had a large following among the poor and craftsmen in Damascus and Aleppo.

Tughtigin had hired assassins to murder enemies when he felt it necessary. The assassins were considered a useful, if unpleasant, part of society, at least by those who used their services. The assassins didn't see themselves as murderers for hire, though. According to their histories, volunteers were requested by the spiritual leaders of the sect to remove Sunni enemies.[16] They targeted specific men to kill and did not engage in wholesale slaughter. Guards of the Sunni leaders might also die, but not bystanders, nor women and children.

The new atabeg, Taj al-Muluk didn't share his father's tolerance for the Batini. By the time he assumed power, the area around Damascus and Aleppo had been proselytized by a Batini missionary named Bahram. "He lived in extreme concealment and secrecy, and continually disguised himself, so that he moved from city to city and castle to castle without anyone being aware of his identity."[17] Bahram's base in Syria was the town of Banyas, which he had been given by Tughtigin in return for services rendered to Aleppo. From there he sent out not murderers, but missionaries. In contrast to the Sunni emphasis on law, which many found dry and sterile, the Batini preached an emotional, militant Islam with mystical overtones and secrets known only to the elect. Bahram's followers found many converts in the towns and countryside.

Al-Qalanisi doesn't mince words in his opinion of the Batini converts. They are, "ignorant folk . . . and foolish peasantry from the villages and the rabble and the scum, persons without intelligence."[18] According to him, the vizier of Damascus, Abu 'Ali Tahir, allowed the Batini to rob travelers and conspired with the sect for his own ends. Al-Qalanisi considered them heretics of the worst sort and unfit to live.

Eventually, the missionary Bahram went too far, capturing and killing a man from a powerful family for no known reason. With the approval of Atabeg Taj al-Muluk, Bahram was surprised in his tent and cut to ribbons. This slowed the Batini for a while, but Bahram's successor continued to plot with the Damascene vizier, Abu 'Ali, to overthrow Taj al-Muluk. On September 4, 1129, Abu 'Ali was cornered while taking part in a procession in the Rose Pavilion at the palace of Damascus. He was killed and his body immediately thrown on a pyre in the "ash heap at the Iron Gate."[19]

The death of the vizir signaled a bloodbath in Damascus, equal to the massacre in the capture of Jerusalem thirty years before. A mob scoured the city hunting for Batini, killing all they found, including those who sought refuge with important friends. Some of the leaders of the sect were taken alive and then crucified on the battlements of the town, "at which the hearts of many of the Believers were comforted."[20]

Al-Qalinisi believed that this massacre was the impetus for Baldwin's decision to try his luck once again at taking Damascus. He was probably right. The combination of local civil unrest, a new atabeg, and Baldwin's eager reinforcements from the West must have been irresistible to the king. Added to that, Hugh de Payens had returned from France with a papal privilege legitimizing the Order of the Templars. He had also brought several hundred new recruits.[21]

Melisende was probably in Jerusalem when the fresh army left for Damascus. There is no doubt that she kept herself busy with the governance of the kingdom.

While Hodierna and Yvette would have had maids and tutors, Melisende was responsible for filling Morfia's role and preparing her sisters for their future lives. Soon Hodierna, now about fifteen, would become the countess of Tripoli. Unlike her older sisters, her future husband was a local man, the son of Pons of Toulouse and Tripoli, who had not always been on Baldwin's side in the chess game of the Levant. His mother was the sister of her new brother-in-law Fulk. Hodierna would have had many opportunities to meet her future husband. All the same, marrying into the family of the southern counts of Toulouse and St.-Gilles, she would have to learn how to find her way among a different set of customs and how to hold her own as mistress of a household. The Provençal language of the south would not have sounded the same as the northern French her father spoke. Hodierna and Raymond may have found it easier to speak Arabic together.

Yvette required less care on Melisende's part, although she probably hadn't yet entered the convent permanently. While very young girls might be sent to live with the nuns for instruction, most convents would not allow children to take vows. The age of discretion varied, but was usually about fifteen or sixteen. At the Paraclete, in Champagne, the rule stated that no one could become a permanent member of the order until they were eighteen.[22] Yvette was probably taking lessons at the convent of St. Anne. The nature of those lessons isn't certain. At the minimum she would have been taught some Latin along with reading and writing French and, possibly, Arabic. She would have had needlework to do as many of the vestments used in the church and worn by the bishops and patriarchs usually were made by nuns.

Melisende would have had little time to study. The date of her son's birth isn't known, but Fulk would probably have done his duty to provide an heir before he left with Baldwin for Damascus. She probably remained in Jerusalem while pregnant and for the first few months after the baby arrived, but that doesn't mean that she wasn't involved in the concerns of the kingdom.

The court of Jerusalem didn't have the ancient traditions and rituals of those of Constantinople or Baghdad. Even in Europe the lives of royalty weren't as sequestered as they became much later. Melisende as princess would have interacted with servants: cooks, bodyguards, stablemen, seamstresses, and many others. She didn't have to run down to the *Rue de Malquisinat* (street of bad cooking) for a take-away meal if her dinner burned.[23] Although, due to the lack of firewood in the area as well as the spartan living arrangements, many people survived on the soups and stews prepared in the shops every day. In this they followed the tradition of the first-century Romans; it was just another practical Mediterranean custom the newcomers had adopted.

Even if they didn't have to fetch their dinners, Melisende, her sisters, and their friends might well have wandered down to the shops that sold jewelry, perfumes, silks, and other personal items. The princesses might have ridden a donkey, easier to negotiate in the narrow, steep streets than a horse, or they may have walked, with a proper escort, of course. It would have been incumbent upon Melisende particularly to attend Mass, make offerings at the shrines, and listen to the reports of those in charge of the money-changers and tradesmen, builders, and pilgrims. She may have consulted with the latest Patriarch, Stephen, a new arrival from France who was also a distant relative.[24] She would also have interacted with the leaders of the Hospital, the Church of the Holy Sepulchre, the Temple of the Lord, and the myriad of smaller churches, including the Syrian and Armenian ones.

It's also possible that she would be called upon to settle legal disputes. While she wasn't the official head of the courts, at this point the legal system hadn't developed much complexity in Jerusalem. It would almost fifty years before the first parts of the *Assises de Jerusalem* would be compiled, a list of laws based partly on custom and partly on problems that had come up in the first years of the kingdom.[25]

Legal authorities varied according to religion. When two people of the same faith had an argument, they often went to their priest to decide

Covered Suq in Jerusalem from the time of Melisende. Photograph courtesy of Denys Pringle.

who was in the right. It was more difficult with people of different sects. In that case Melisende might have been considered a logical judge, by virtue of her rank and heritage. Noblewomen did decide nonviolent altercations, especially in their dower lands. The countesses of Champagne had rights of judgment in the town of Nogent. This meant that they collected any fines imposed, but when they were in the area, it also gave them the right to hear the complaints and pass judgment.[26]

Melisende may also have been making lists of things that needed doing once she was queen: what should be repaired, which new buildings should be added, better ways to organize the running of Jerusalem, ecclesiastical rights that needed to be clarified, and so on.

The army returned around Christmas time without having taken Damascus. William says that the main reason was "a violent rainstorm accompanied by fog. . . . The roads were rendered impassable."[27] He concludes, "At length, they [the army] realized that the tempest had been sent against them because of their sins."[28] William doesn't list any specific sins. Al-Qalanisi tells the story differently, not mentioning any rain, but saying that the Franks decamped in the middle of the night, leaving their possessions behind.[29]

Fulk's first military excursion had not turned out as he and his father-in-law had hoped.

TWELVE

TRAINING A KING

JERUSALEM, 1130

THE YEAR 1130 BEGAN WITH THE LEADERS OF THE
Crusader States still smarting from their defeat at Damascus. It seemed impossible that they could have failed. They had ignored old feuds to band
together. Fresh, enthusiastic new recruits had come from the West. It should
have worked. The only possible reason must have been that God was angry
with them, but for what? No one gives any answers to this conundrum. At
least this time there was no attempt to enforce draconian moral laws as there
had been in 1119. For the present, Prince Bohemond returned to Antioch,
Count Pons to Tripoli, and Baldwin and Fulk to Jerusalem. All the other
survivors retreated to their respective lands and castles.

In Damascus, "the people felt secure and went out to their farms and
dispersed to their own abodes and places of work, freed from sorrow and
anxiety."[1]

A side effect of the massacre of the Batini in Damascus was that the sect
realized that it couldn't hold on to the town of Banyas, which Tughtigin of
Damascus had given them in return for their aid in fighting off a Frankish
attack in 1125. Rather than let it fall to the Sunni Turks, they offered it to
the Franks. No doubt surprised by this sudden twist, Baldwin accepted.

Banyas became part of the Kingdom of Jerusalem.[2] The Batini retreated into the mountains north of Lebanon. They acquired several fortified towns, which they held for years against both Christian and Muslim attacks. They would continue in their special trade of assassination of selected Sunni enemies but don't seem to have sent any missionaries back into Syria.[3]

Life went on more peacefully for a time. Things were calm enough that Michael the Syrian was able to report on local non-military events. He states that in this year a local woman gave birth to quadruplets, three boys and a girl. Ten days later, the boys died "at the same instant." The girl survived.[4] Multiple births were very rare and even twins often could not survive more than a few days due to low birth weight and other complications. For some reason, the nobility of the Crusader States produced more healthy female babies than male. The high rate of male death in the wars added to this gender imbalance and meant that Melisende would not be the only woman to inherit lands the first Crusaders had settled. The throne of Jerusalem would be passed through the female line from the late twelfth century until the demise of the kingdom.

For the moment, Fulk was proving himself a model son-in-law. "During Baldwin's life," William of Tyre says, "he deferred to the king, fulfilled the duties of a son and faithfully attended to royal business."[5] The three words "during Baldwin's life" say much, but William was writing for Fulk's son, King Amalric, so he kept most of his comments about Fulk positive.

William does mention one quirk that made life difficult for those at court. Fulk had a terrible memory, "so fleeting that he seldom remembered faces or names, not even those of his own domestics." This proved a problem when someone whom Fulk had recently honored reappeared a few days later to introduce a friend, only to find that his patron had no memory of him.[6] The king must have needed someone with him much of the time to cover for him. Melisende would have been a good choice, since she already knew most of the people at court.

Despite the defeat at Damascus, things in Jerusalem seemed to be going well. With the lords back in their own lands, each of them could now attend to local matters. In Edessa, Jocelyn intervened in a dispute between a Syrian abbot and a man whom the abbot had excommunicated. The man had the support of the emir of the town where the abbey was located, one of several towns that were governed by Muslims who paid tribute to and expected aid from the count. The emir locked up the abbot in an effort to force him to lift the excommunication. Jocelyn sent word that the abbot was to be released or Jocelyn would devastate the countryside.[7] The emir obliged. It was business as usual in terms of local people cooperating on local matters, irrespective of faith. The emir did a favor for his Christian friend until the consequences proved too extreme. The wrath of the count was more worrisome than the problems of the friend.

The abbot was released, but, shortly after, as he was saying Mass, he seems to have had a heart attack. "He shook, his color changed and he passed out." He was put on his chair and the bishop finished the Mass.[8]

This would seem to have been a good time for a moral lesson, but Michael gives none. Perhaps he expected the reader to know that this was God's punishment for an unjust excommunication. Michael doesn't mention if the abbot survived. I would love to find another source for this. The interplay among people of different faiths in this story indicates that townspeople knew each other well enough to be aware of individual behavior and take sides regardless of religious sect.

Jocelyn kept busy with raids against the local Turks. That summer he ordered that a tower be undermined at a fortress near Aleppo, the better to capture it. Something went wrong with the logistics, however, and, when the tower fell, Jocelyn was buried under a shower of bricks. His men rushed to uncover him, fearing that he had been killed. Jocelyn was alive but was found to have a number of broken bones. He never healed completely from this and became a semi-invalid.[9]

In Jerusalem, Baldwin must have felt life had finally become tranquil. His dynasty was assured, at least for the moment, with his new namesake grandson. Fulk and Melisende were demonstrating their competence in governing. Alice seemed happy in Antioch. Hodierna would soon marry Raymond of Tripoli and Yvette would pray for them all. For the first time in over thirty years he was at war with no one.

He was particularly relieved to have the care of Antioch off his shoulders. Having to deal with crises so far north was getting to be too much for him.

Then, near the end of the year word came that Alice's husband, Bohemond, the long-awaited prince, had been killed in battle. The enthusiastic young ruler of Antioch had heard that a newcomer had arrived from the east. The Imad al-din Atabeg Zengi had been appointed by the caliph of Baghdad to govern Mosul in 1127. The next year he took over Aleppo. Seeking to expand his territory he was now raiding the countryside close to Antioch. Bohemond had not come up against Zengi before but the man's reputation for brutality, even toward his own followers, had reached Antioch. Bohemond rode out in an attempt to cut the atabeg off before he threatened the city. But Zengi's forces were too much for him and the prince and his men were surrounded and killed in a brief encounter not far from Antioch. Apparently, no one recognized Bohemond until it was too late. Otherwise, he would have been taken hostage, ransomed, and released, and the history of Antioch would have been greatly changed.

Bohemond was about twenty-one when he died. Usamah tells a story of meeting the prince when the Arab nobleman was in his youth. One day, Usamah and his friends were patrolling the area when they came across Bohemond's party camped by the Orontes. The young men charged at each other in a very minor melee that ended in a draw.[10] Bohemond must not have been wearing any special insignia on that day, either, for Usamah didn't learn who he was until later, but the old soldier remembered the event proudly when he came to write his memoirs.

When the news came of this disaster, Baldwin's heart must have sunk. He and Fulk rode at once for Antioch. When they arrived, they were astonished to find that the gates had been barred to them.

Baldwin's daughter Alice was not about to turn her city, her child, or herself over to the control of her father and brother-in-law.

The main source for what happened next is William of Tyre, who, from his account, seems to have born a grudge against Alice. He vilifies her in no uncertain terms, saying that she rebelled against her father and intended to deprive her daughter, Constance, of her inheritance and seize power for herself.[11] It does seem that Alice intended to rule Antioch, but it's not clear if she planned to be regent for Constance or, perhaps, marry again and have a son to inherit. Kemal ad-Din says that "at that time [December 1130] Antioch was governed by the wife of Bohemond, daughter of Baldwin. This princess conspired with several Frankish officers against her own father."[12]

But why did she decide to take charge of Antioch herself when she learned that her husband had been killed? And why did anyone obey her? Alice was barely twenty, if that. The people of Antioch must have seen a toughness and intelligence in her. There is no indication that she was being dictated to by others. And yet, there doesn't seem to be any reason why she would turn against her father. William's only explanation is that "an evil spirit led her to conceive of a wicked plan."[13] This is not helpful to the historian.

Even before Bohemond's death, Alice had established a place for herself in her dower town of Latakia. There is a record of a gift to the Hospitallers from Walter of Sourdeval from his lands in Latakia with the permission of Princess Alice. This was land that Walter's father had been given by Baldwin II and Bohemond I. Bohemond II is not mentioned. Walter was constable of Antioch but sided with Alice against Baldwin and became constable at the court she set up in Latakia.[14] Was Alice just being diligent in attending to her property or was the marriage not as happy as most assumed?

While he was cooling his heels outside Antioch, Baldwin had sent for Count Jocelyn, even though his health was precarious. The king may have thought that Alice would listen to the man who had so often given refuge to her and her sisters. But Jocelyn could not get Alice to reconsider, either. The gates remained closed.

Perhaps there had been an argument between Alice, her father, and his cousin and no one recorded it. But, I suspect another reason. Couldn't it just be possible that it was Fulk who worried Alice? Baldwin and Jocelyn were both at least in their fifties, not that old, but they had both endured imprisonment, illness, and innumerable battles, and might not last much longer, especially Jocelyn, considering the severity of his injuries from the accident.

Both Baldwin and Jocelyn were well known and respected by the people of Antioch who would normally be expected to overrule the princess and admit the king. Michael the Syrian doesn't mention Alice in his account of the incident, but says that it was the people of the city who barred the king and his men from entering.[15] The citizens were accustomed to help from Jerusalem and Edessa. After the death of Roger, they had even come to expect it. But, it appears that Alice and some of the citizens of Antioch were worried that there was danger in allowing Jerusalem back in control of the city.

William of Tyre accuses Alice of offering Constance in marriage to Zengi in return for an alliance and protection. None of the Muslim sources mention this and it isn't likely, although Zengi was certainly taking advantage of the chaos in Antioch to ravage the countryside.[16] This excuse sounds as if William was grasping at straws because he either didn't know the real reason or thought it impolitic to report. But what would make him think that the princess of Antioch would go to such extremes?

From her actions, Alice's main concern was the autonomy of the principate. But Baldwin had already proved that he wasn't interested in adding Antioch to the kingdom. Jocelyn didn't want it, either; he may have already realized that he didn't have long to live. The only new player on the field was Fulk of Anjou. It isn't absurd to suspect that Alice and Fulk weren't on the best of terms. Later interactions between them were adversarial to say the least. She may have feared that he was planning to create a unified state after the death of her father, incorporating Antioch into Jerusalem as his first wife's inheritance of Maine had been made part of his county of Anjou.

Whatever the reason, Alice's rebellion was soon over. Someone in the city decided that it would be better to open the gates. Alice and her supporters retreated to the citadel for a time but were convinced at last to surrender. In tears, Alice begged forgiveness. Baldwin wasn't happy with his defiant daughter. He sent her to live in Latakia and entrusted the governance of Antioch to various deputies under the authority of Jocelyn. William doesn't say if the two-year-old Constance was allowed to stay with her mother, but I would hope her father didn't separate the new widow from her child.

This was not the end of Alice. It was only the beginning.

Fortunately, Baldwin didn't know that. He returned to Jerusalem, where he suddenly fell ill. What the nature of his sickness was, we don't know, but it was mortal. Realizing that he was dying, Baldwin had himself taken to the Patriarch's palace. He summoned Melisende, Fulk, and baby Baldwin, and "To them . . . he committed the care of the kingdom, with full power."[17] He had himself dressed in the robe of a monk, and promised to take up the religious life if he should live, although he had no expectation of a miracle. Baldwin died on August 21, 1131. He was buried with great ceremony next to his predecessors at the foot of Mount Calvary.[18]

The northern Christian chronicles don't mention the death of Baldwin. Ibn al-Qalanisi does note his accomplishments, especially in escaping prisons. He adds, "His place was taken by the new Count-King, the Count of Anjou . . . but he was not sound in his judgment, nor was he successful in his administration."[19]

Not long after, Jocelyn also died on the battlefield, having been brought there on a litter to supervise the fight. His son, the half-Armenian Jocelyn II, succeeded him.

With their deaths, the era of the first lords of the Crusader States was over. It was time for the second generation, the New Syrians, who had been born and raised in the East, to take over.

THIRTEEN

TAMING A KING

JERUSALEM, 1131–1135

TWO WEEKS AFTER BALDWIN'S DEATH, MELISENDE
and Fulk were crowned and anointed joint rulers of the kingdom of Jerusalem, according to Baldwin's wishes. A picture of them, painted a few years
later, depicts them wearing royal robes and regalia in the Byzantine style.
How much this actually looks like Melisende is impossible to say. But it gives
a good idea of her size and coloring.

After the coronation, Fulk immediately ignored his promises to Baldwin
II about co-ruling with Melisende. Very few of his charters remain but, in
the first one, where he consents to a donation of property by William de
Buris, Melisende isn't mentioned.[1] Now, she may not have been available
when it was signed, but the next two charters, which date to 1134, have to do
with Alice and were issued at Antioch. Melisende doesn't seem to have been
consulted about either of the Antioch charters although the contents were
innocuous. Her name doesn't appear at all, even as a witness.[2] As joint ruler,
she should have given her consent to them. In these charters it is interesting
to note that the king had brought his own scribe, Elias, to write them.[3] Antioch had a chancery full of clerks. Was Fulk suspicious of their loyalty? He
also had to use his own seal to give his sanction to them, for Alice had taken

Melisende and Fulk from The Melisende Psalter, *made in her lifetime.* © *The British Library Board, Egerton 1139 f9v.*

the seal of the Principate of Antioch with her.[4] It appears that Fulk and his sister-in-law were preparing for a showdown.

In Fulk's endeavors in Antioch he definitely was acting on his own. In his later Antiochene charters, from 1134–1135, he doesn't even use the seal of Jerusalem. Historian Hans Eberhard Mayer suggests that this is a sign that there was already criticism of his rule and that he wasn't permitted by Melisende and her adherents to remove the seal from the kingdom.[5]

In an age when literacy, especially in Latin, was reserved for a few, the seal imprinted in wax on a document was the main way to prove its authenticity.

Fulk may not have been behaving maliciously. He had spent his life being in charge and probably assumed that was why he had been invited to become king. His first wife, Eremberga, was the only child and heiress of the county of Maine, north of Anjou. There is no suggestion that she preferred to control her inheritance herself. Fulk doesn't seem to have understood that his second wife was far different from the first.

It was a time of radical change throughout the land. Antioch, Edessa, and Damascus all had new leaders. Shams al-Maluk, the son of the last ruler of Damascus, divided his time between attacking Frankish towns and those of his brother and other Muslims.[6] Jocelyn II was establishing his authority in Edessa but there were rumblings from the Antiochenes when he tried to take over the stewardship of Antioch in his father's place. He quickly returned to his own land.[7]

The younger Jocelyn had a good relationship with his second cousins, Alice and Melisende. He had been held captive with Yvette and had certainly grown up around all four of the sisters. It's a shame that we mainly have William of Tyre's opinion of him, for William was as little fond of Jocelyn as he was of Alice.

William's first story about the new count of Edessa deals with the death of Jocelyn I. He tells the reader that the dying count wanted his son to attack the sultan of Iconium, who was besieging one of the fortresses of Edessa. Jocelyn II pointed out to him that their informants had said that the sultan had a much larger force than they did. Angered at his son's cowardice,

Jocelyn had the litter prepared and set out to his death. William assures us that, when the sultan heard the count was coming, "he beat a hasty retreat."[8]

Fortunately, Michael the Syrian also recorded the events around Jocelyn's death, casting his son in a better light. In this account, Jocelyn II is part of the force coming with his father to meet the sultan. Before the two armies met, Jocelyn died. Learning of this, the sultan called off his men and sent his condolences, telling the Edessenes, "Take care of your affairs; choose a new ruler according to your custom and govern your land in peace. You have nothing to fear from me."[9]

It would be nice to have a third account. Both of these stories seem to have been somewhat embellished. Michael does seem to be more even-handed about Jocelyn II, but the only fact we can be sure of is that Jocelyn I died and the battle did not take place.

William, later Archbishop of Tyre, was born in Jerusalem around 1130 and left to study in Europe when he was about sixteen. Although he was too young to remember most of the events in the early 1130s, he must have heard gossip of those times swirling around him on his return. For his history, he interviewed many people who had been eyewitnesses of the events William would record. But his informants each had their own interpretations of those events. He may well have acquired his dislike of Jocelyn II from supporters of Fulk. William probably saw the count of Edessa when Jocelyn visited Jerusalem during William's childhood, and William leaves a thorough physical description of him.

"Though small of stature, Jocelyn was stout of limb and very robust. His skin and hair were dark, his face broad and covered with scars from the disease called smallpox. He had bulging eyes and a prominent nose. Although of a generous disposition and distinguished for military prowess, he was given to excessive revelry and drunkenness."[10]

William has more criticism of Jocelyn, who may well have looked as described, taking after his mother's Armenian family. But, if so, he would have resembled most of the Syrians, Armenians, and Turks in the county of Edessa. Racism wasn't a well-defined concept in the twelfth century. People made judgments based on religion and nationality more than color. But anyone reading this unflattering description of Jocelyn may safely assume that any stories of his life coming from William's quill will have the worst possible slant.

In Latakia, Alice lived comfortably in a mixed society. We know from a charter issued by her grandson that there were Greeks who made bricks, shoes, and barrels. Along with them were Armenian blacksmiths, a butcher, a baker, and an archer. The charter also mentioned a Frank and half a dozen Jews. The charter transfers the taxes owed to the principality to the Hospital in Jerusalem.[11] The makeup of the town was much the same in Alice's time.

In 1132 Fulk discovered that Alice had received promises of military support from her cousin Jocelyn II, count Pons of Tripoli, and William of Saone, whose extensive territory surrounded Antioch. Inside Antioch, however, there was a definite contingent that wanted nothing to do with her, particularly the aged Latin Patriarch, Bernard. While she still had her supporters within the city, when Antioch was threatened by a Muslim force, a delegation of community leaders sent to Fulk for help.[12] They may have preferred a steward who might have had plans to incorporate Antioch into his own domain to a woman with only a few armed followers.

There is no hard evidence that Fulk had any designs on Antioch for himself. But it was a strategic city, claimed not only by the Byzantine emperor, who had held it until 1084, but also by Roger, count of Apulia and Sicily. Roger was Bohemond II's closest relative, apart from Constance. He was busy establishing what would become a Norman empire in Italy and Sicily. He had let it be known that he was also interested in Antioch, which he would have a good claim to should Constance die without heirs.[13] Roger was also the son of Adelaide, the third wife of Baldwin I. According to their marriage contract, if Baldwin I died without heirs, Roger would become king of Jerusalem.[14] However, the marriage had ended with Adelaide storming back home. As well, there was some question about the legality of it, since Baldwin's second wife, Arda, was still alive. So Roger's claim to Jerusalem was shaky and might not have stood up in court. Even so, it was a consideration that Fulk had to include in his plans.

However, as Roger grew more powerful, he occasionally reminded people of that agreement. Therefore, Fulk may have been more concerned with Roger's designs on Jerusalem than Antioch. The king may have had a letter from the pope that said Melisende was heir to the throne, but Roger was closer to Rome and more able to put pressure on the next pope. It's possible that Fulk simply wanted to continue the tradition of the king of Jerusalem acting as protector in times of trouble in Antioch. This was William's belief and this has been accepted for centuries, but Alice's possible motives should be examined, too.

Even though Jocelyn had allied with Alice, many of the citizens within the city were unwilling to have him as temporary overlord. So, when the plea came, Fulk may have sighed but set out for Antioch anyway with his troops. His first obstacle was that to get there, he had to go through the county of Tripoli or cross Muslim territory with his army. But Count Pons would not grant him passage. This must have caused some family discussion as Pons was also Fulk's brother-in-law. The count had married Cecelia, the daughter of Fulk's mother, Bertrada, and Phillip of France. The half-siblings had known each other in France, as Fulk seems to have visited his mother several times in his youth.[15] Although Cecelia and Fulk seem to have been fond of each other, either Cecelia had no influence over her husband or she agreed that Fulk had over-reached in his actions in Antioch.

The king was forced to sail around Tripoli up the coast to Antioch. He did this three times in the first three years of his reign in his attempts to keep Alice from taking lordship of the principality. Melisende may have wanted to see her sister, but there is no evidence that she accompanied her husband or that she supported his efforts.

Fulk must have been getting a good idea of why his father-in-law had had no interest in governing a contentious principate with fluid borders several days away from his own lands. He finally appointed Reynald Maseoir, the new constable of Antioch, as his representative. Reynald had fought at the Field of Blood and distinguished himself as a military leader.[16] Fulk apparently trusted Reynald not to change sides and give the keys of Antioch to Alice.

On one of these trips, while waiting to set sail from Sidon for Antioch, Fulk's sister Cecelia came to him with the news that Count Pons was trapped by Zengi in his castle of Montferrand. "Most urgently and persistently, as women will, she begged and besought the king to lay aside everything . . . and to hasten at once to relieve the desperate situation of her husband."[17] Fulk was not only fond of his sister, he also knew that Zengi was a great threat to Pons. He hurried to the count's rescue and the two men were reconciled.

In Jerusalem, Melisende was consolidating her base of support through donations to Latin, Syrian, and Armenian religious institutions. She gave property to the Syrian/Jacobite monastery of St. Mary Magdalene in Jerusalem, where the Syrian patriarchs had been expanding the housing for pilgrims since 1125.[18] She was also working on plans to build the fortress of Bethgibelin, on the borders with Fatamid Ascalon, as well as her pet project of the establishment of a convent at Bethany, which she wanted to build so that Yvette could be abbess when she was older. Melisende "felt that it was unfitting that a king's daughter should be subject to the authority of a mother superior, like an ordinary person."[19]

While this went counter to the concept of monastic humility and obedience, it's like Melisende to insist that her little sister have a position equal to her rank.

There was mistrust of Fulk's intentions in the north, despite his avowed reluctance to take control of Antioch. Yet, when news came that a Muslim force had crossed the Euphrates and was menacing Antioch, Fulk called the armies together and both Pons of Tripoli and Jocelyn II of Edessa responded.

Again we have different versions of the story of this encounter. Al-Qalanisi reports that, while the Franks were engaged in fighting in the north, a part of the Muslim army took advantage of their absence to penetrate the Kingdom of Jerusalem, which had not been seriously attacked in many years. The Muslims raided Tiberias, Nazareth, and Acre, burning, killing, and looting. When the Franks returned and saw the devastation, "they were grieved, dispirited and disheartened; their unity was dissolved."[20]

William says nothing about raids in the Kingdom of Jerusalem but reports that the king's expedition was a great victory, with lots of booty brought to Antioch. He says that Fulk became a hero to the citizens there.[21]

In the light of what happened afterward, al-Qalanisi's report makes more sense, although Fulk may have triumphed in the north and returned to discontent in Jerusalem. The neglect of his duties at home might provide a reason for the subsequent revolt of Hugh of Jaffa and Romanus of Le Puy, against Fulk.

Hugh, count of Jaffa, was another of Melisende's second cousins. His father, Hugh of Le Puiset, was one of ten children of Baldwin II's aunt, Alice, for whom his daughter was named. Hugh had been born in Apulia because his mother, Mabel de Roucy, had decided to immigrate to Jerusalem with her husband while pregnant, and they were in Apulia when it was time for the birth. Because he was a delicate child, Hugh was left at the court of Bohemond II.[22] Hugh was probably raised with Bohemond II, who was close to his age. He may even been among those who gathered to welcome the prince when Bohemond came to marry Alice. So, although he didn't settle in the Levant until he was an adult, Hugh had the right credentials.

His parents died without ever meeting him again, but they left him their lands. When Hugh finally reached the Levant, he took possession of his father's fief of Jaffa, a port city that is now a southern suburb of Tel Aviv.

Although he was a stranger in his new home, Hugh had relatives all over the land, and he was also good-looking, charming, and athletic. William admits that "In him the gifts of nature seem to have met in lavish abundance."[23]

Shortly after his arrival, Hugh had married Emma, the redoubtable widow of the stalwart support of the throne, Eustace Grenier.[24] Emma had twin sons by her first husband: Eustace of Sidon and Walter of Caesarea. She had married Hugh shortly after Eustace's death, in 1124. In 1134, Hugh was about twenty-seven and his step-sons a few years younger. Trying to figure out how much older Emma was is difficult because we don't know how old she was when she married and the twins were born. If she had been only sixteen or seventeen at that time, she would have been in her mid-thirties when she married Hugh and capable of having more children. It was less of a December-May marriage than that of Fulk and Melisende.

Fulk didn't get along with this good-looking young man. William says that there were rumors that Melisende and Hugh were overly friendly. But I think that William is trying to make sense of a story that he doesn't understand. Hugh was Melisende's second cousin and the rules about incest were strict. The marriages of third cousins were sometimes annulled for reasons of consanguinity. Even if the queen and the count were lovers, it wouldn't explain the support Hugh received in the course of his opposition to the king.

Romanus of Le Puy quickly vanishes from William's account. He had been the lord of Transjordan, lands east of the Jordan River. The lordship had been taken from him in the time of Baldwin II; it is not certain why. His participation in Hugh's revolt is also unclear. The particulars of the "revolt" and the other participants are never given. For once, there was no battle. But there was a lot of gossip, which is what William based his account on.

William says that, one day, when the court was full and many nobles were present, Hugh's stepson, Walter, rose and accused Hugh not of adultery but high treason and conspiracy. Adultery with the queen was high treason, but it's also possible that Walter believed that Hugh was part of a resistance to Fulk's authority. William adds that this accusation was "at the instigation of the king." Fulk wanted to rid himself of this gadfly. Hugh denied the charge but said he would "submit to the judgment of the court."[25]

This indicates to me that Hugh was not worried about being hanged for treason and that he knew he had friends among the court, not least of whom was his cousin, the queen. Both Hugh and Romanus had been often at court when Baldwin II was alive. They had witnessed charters, including ones that named Melisende as heir to Jerusalem, so Romanus wasn't an outcast from Baldwin II's court.[26]

After some debate, it was decided by the assembled court that Walter and Hugh would meet in single combat. A day was assigned and Hugh went back to Jaffa, perhaps to train. When the time came, however, he didn't show up for the duel.

It was assumed that this was proof of Hugh's guilt. But mightn't he have gone back to Jaffa and told Emma that she was about to either lose a husband or a son, which did she prefer? Emma may have counseled Hugh to just stay home and see if the whole storm blew over. In his telling of the story, William clearly forgets that Emma and Melisende were very much involved.

When Hugh didn't appear, the court, that is the council of nobles, had no choice but to declare him guilty. Fulk may have put some pressure on the nobles. At this point Melisende's opinion was either not expressed or ignored.

Hugh then seems to have decided to go to the city of Ascalon, still under Fatimid control, to ask for help in fighting the king. It wouldn't have been the first time Christians and Muslims had joined forces but times were changing. The army of Ascalon took advantage of Fulk's problems with his vassal and pillaged the countryside within the Kingdom of Jerusalem. Hugh did not go with them but stayed in Jaffa planning his next move. He may not have actively sought Muslim military help, but instead simply offered the Muslims a truce, promising not to attack them if they invaded Fulk's land. This was equally traitorous in the eyes of William and of Fulk. It also caused a number of Hugh's vassals to abandon him.[27]

While it isn't certain that Hugh actually did go to the Fatimids, he did take refuge, at least for a time, with another of Fulk's enemies—Alice. Her court in Latakia now included her own scribes and officers and she still had the seal of Antioch. In a charter she issued in 1134, Hugh of Jaffa was a witness.[28] It seems that the sisters had maintained their attachment to their cousin. Hugh found safety in Latakia while he considered his options.

Whatever course Hugh might have taken, it was seen by many in Jerusalem as an attempt to undermine the king. This was probably true. Fulk, who came from a long line of warrior Angevins, was incensed at the raids and raced to Jaffa, where he hoped to confront Hugh. By now, Hugh was back in his own territory, furious at his change of fortune and determined to face down the king. However, after trying to convince the count to surrender and failing, most of his friends and vassals deserted him. Several of them later appear among Fulk's entourage, having been given Hugh's property as a reward for their betrayal.

It took the intercession of Patriarch William of Jerusalem and others, including, very likely, Melisende and Emma, to reach a settlement. It was finally decided that Hugh of Jaffa would go into exile for three years. When he came back, all would be as it had been. At least that was the plan. It seems a small price for high treason. Fulk must have known that his accusations were weak.

While he was preparing for his time in exile, Hugh went back to Jerusalem. He doesn't seem to have worried about how he would be received there. He still had many friends. "One day he happened to be playing dice on a table before the shop of a merchant named Alfanus in the street which is called the street of the Furriers," William tells us.[29] The chronicler is not usually this precise, but his informant must have told the story well. While happily throwing the dice, totally ignorant of danger, Hugh was suddenly attacked by a Breton knight, who stabbed him repeatedly.

News spread quickly and people crowded into the streets. The citizens of Jerusalem were horrified at this crime. People began to mutter that Fulk must be behind it. Everyone knew how the king hated the handsome count. And, with mob logic, they therefore assumed that Hugh had been framed because of Fulk's jealousy and was completely innocent of the earlier charges.[30] In an instant, Hugh became a hero and Fulk the worst villain. This sudden shift in attitude among the populace may also have been a reaction to the way the king had allowed the countryside to be pillaged by Muslims while he was fighting invaders in Antioch and, perhaps, a general resentment toward the arrogance of the foreign king. Fulk had angered many of the pullani by appointing his own men, often new arrivals, into key positions in the government and in the church, including William, the new Patriarch of Jerusalem. This had not gone unnoticed by the core of first settlers and their families.[31]

It has been suggested, with good support from charter evidence, that the accusation of treason was a pretext for Walter of Caesarea to advance his own career and get back at both his step-father and his mother. At the death of his twin, Eustace, sometime before 1128, Walter should have become lord of Sidon. But Hugh and Emma seem to have continued administering the town, without allowing him any power.[32] Walter's dramatic denunciation of Hugh gave him the chance to confront him with royal support. Custom declared that Walter should have the satisfaction of a duel with his step-father, which he must have thought he would win. He may not have counted on the strong contingent at court that supported Hugh and, by extension, Melisende. One also wonders if Walter was kept from the lordship of Sidon because his mother was not convinced that he could manage it well. The citizens of Sidon must have agreed with her; if they hadn't, there would have been little she could do about it.

Somehow, Hugh of Jaffa survived his wounds. Fulk made a point of having the Breton knight tried and convicted by law. The man's sentence was to have his "members" cut off. William doesn't say which ones but states that the man's tongue was not removed. Fulk wanted Hugh's assailant to continue telling everyone that the king had nothing to do with the attack.

Once he partially recovered, Hugh still had to go into exile for three years. He went back to his birthplace in Apulia in Italy, where his relative, Count Roger, took him in and gave him an estate to live off of since his lands had been, for the moment, confiscated. But even being in his homeland didn't help Hugh recover completely from his wounds. He died not long after. It's not known if Emma was with him but it's possible that she accompanied her husband, choosing him over Walter, for her dower city of Jericho was later donated by Melisende to help support the convent of Bethany.[33]

Why does this story of jealousy and betrayal matter? Partly because, in a few pages, William gives a panorama of customs, legal procedures, daily activities, and public opinions, as well as a heart-wrenching soap opera. But even more, it matters because of what it did to Melisende.

She had been quiet long enough. Now she came roaring out like a lion. Anyone who had sided with Fulk "came under the displeasure" of the queen. She refused to speak to them or allow them at court. Her anger was so strong that many were afraid for their safety. Fulk finally realized that he had mar-ried a woman with her own mind and an extensive power base. "Even the king found that no place was entirely safe among the kindred and partisans of the queen."[34]

It took time and a lot of mediation, but Fulk and Melisende managed to reconcile, at least on the surface. Fulk seems to have changed completely in his attitude toward his wife. "From that day forward, the king became so uxorious that . . . not even in unimportant cases did he take any measures without her knowledge and assistance."[35] Walter of Caesarea did not get the county of Jaffa. He vanishes from the records for a few years. When he reappears, in February 1138, he is still only lord of Caesarea, and he is far down the list of charter witnesses, indicating that his status was not high.[36]

The tale of Hugh, Fulk, and Melisende does have the ring of backstairs gossip. One might find the entire episode hard to credit if not for two things. First, almost every charter Fulk issued after this was "with the consent and approval of Queen Melisende."[37] The second sign of some accord between them is that the next year Melisende gave birth to another son. And yes, it's fairly certain that Amalric was indeed Fulk's son. One indication of this is that Baldwin IV, Amalric's son, would have both the Angevin red hair and freckles.

However, what none of the chroniclers and few later historians mentioned when discussing this case was that it didn't matter who the father of Melisende's sons was. She was the daughter of the king. It was through her line that the crown descended. Fulk may not have understood this when he agreed to give up Anjou to his son and move to Jerusalem, but it was finally made clear to him. None of Fulk's children in Europe ever tried to claim Jerusalem as part of their inheritance.

If Melisende had not had children; if she had died before Fulk, he might have been able to rule on his own. He might have convinced the nobles to bring his younger son, Elias, from Europe to inherit. There's no way to know what would have happened. But I think that, without heirs through Melisende, another council would have met to choose a king with some connection to the family. With the convoluted intermarriage among the nobility, there were a number of candidates. It's likely that the battles for succession would have started a civil war. The kingdom of Jerusalem might have died in the 1140s instead of lasting another hundred and fifty years.

It seemed that Melisende finally had the upper hand in her marriage and, more importantly, in the kingdom. But Fulk still had one more surprise for her, one he had probably already set in motion by the time of Walter's accusations. Melisende would be angered by this, but the real victim would be Alice, princess of Antioch.

FOURTEEN

PRINCE NOT-SO-CHARMING

ANTIOCH AND JERUSALEM, 1136–1143

THE QUESTION OF HOW TO PROTECT ANTIOCH WAS still paramount to Fulk and to most of the other people of the Latin States. Both the Greek emperor, John Komnenus, and the Seljuk emir, Zengi, coveted the principate and had some grounds for claiming it; Antioch had been Greek for centuries and had had a short span under Muslim control. After the death of her husband, it was said that Alice had tried to arrange a betrothal between the infant Constance and the emperor's youngest son, Manuel.[1] This may have been true. If Alice wanted autonomy from Fulk then being under the protection of the emperor was the logical choice. If Constance married a younger son, it was likely that he would put his energy into Antioch rather than let it be subsumed by the Byzantine Empire. I find it less likely that she sent an offer to Imad al-din Atabeg Zengi.[2]

When Bohemond died in 1131, the atabeg Zengi seemed to be just another of the Muslim lords looking for a territory of his own to rule. He was a Turk but was not from the Seljuk clan, which governed most of Syria. Alice had seen emirs and atabegs come and go with alarming regularity in her life.

There was no political reason for her to do more than offer him the same terms of truce that her predecessors had. She had no way of knowing that he was different from the Ortuqid family who had been dominant in the area for the past thirty years.

Imad al-din Zengi, atabeg of Mosul, was born about 1084. His father, Aq Sunkur, was a mameluk, or military slave of the sultan of Baghdad. In the struggles for power, Aq Sunkur chose to support the loser and, consequently, was executed when his son was about ten. As a young man, Zengi was in the army of Jawali at Mosul at the same time that Baldwin II was a prisoner there. He also fought in the service of al-Bursuqi and Mas'ud of Mosul.[3]

Appointed atabeg of Mosul by the caliph of Bagdad in 1127, he used the position as so many others have done, as a base for expanding his holdings. Aleppo and the area around it were always inviting to conquerors. But Zengi had a force of will, a military ability, and a terrifying streak of cruelty that made him different from the emirs and atabegs who had gone before. He was also deeply devout. He is credited with instigating the first organized *jihad* against the Franks, which led to the conquest of Jerusalem by a member of his family, Saladin, sixty years later.[4] This religiosity was not apparent at the beginning of his career, as he spent the most of the 1130s conquering and terrorizing the Seljuk.

By 1128 he had control of Aleppo as well as Mosul. Then he wrote to the various emirs of Damascus, Hamah, Hims, and other towns, inviting them to form a coalition to drive the Franks from the land. After many oaths, his proposal was accepted. If Zengi's intentions had been pure, the army might have reached Jerusalem then and Melisende never would have been queen.

Instead, Zengi brought the emirs and their armies into his camp and "received them with honor . . . but, after neglecting them for some days he perfidiously plotted against them, arrested . . . a number of officers and plundered their tents, baggage and animals."[5] He took the military leaders and court officials back to Mosul and held them for ransom.[6] This inauspicious beginning foreshadowed Zengi's activities for the next twelve years or so. From Damascus, a city Zengi attacked often but never was able to take,

Ibn al-Qalanisi wrote furious accounts of the atrocities committed by the atabeg. Even Ibn al-Athir, who was a member of the Zengid family, couldn't completely whitewash his ancestor's reputation.

For these reasons, apart from religious qualms, I think it highly unlikely that Alice even considered offering her infant daughter as a wife to the atabeg of Mosul.

We know that at Latakia, Alice had her own court and a scriptorium where official documents were written. She had her own constable, Walter of Sourdeval. In a charter to the Hospitallers in 1134, he gave property in Latakia "with the permission of Alice, Princess of Antioch."[7] She was in touch with the lords of other Latin States and had her supporters, many of whom, like Walter of Saone and his brother, Garenton, had also been born in the Levant. Other witnesses to her charters were William, duke of Jabala, and Theobald, duke of Latakia. These may have been offices she created herself or established titles.[8]

She seems to have been managing her own affairs just as any ruler would. Outside of the conclusions drawn by later, and often hostile, sources, I see no evidence that she intended to usurp the position of her daughter. She might just as possibly have been doing her best to ensure that there was something for Constance to inherit and that the child would not simply be a puppet directed by a husband chosen by Fulk.

But that was precisely what Fulk had in mind. His decision to find a husband for Constance would have repercussions that would influence the future of the Latin States and stretch as far as the kingdom of England. There are echoes of it to the present day.

When Fulk left Antioch in 1135, Alice returned to the city and regained power for a short time. The fact that there was a significant number of people who accepted her indicates that she was respected and that her abilities were recognized. It wouldn't have been possible for her to bribe half the city, as William of Tyre insisted.[9]

Fulk did have reason to be concerned. Antioch was not only threatened by Zengi and Emperor John. There was also the possibility that Roger of Sicily might appear with a fleet to stake his claim. No one, including Alice, believed that Antioch could survive without a strong military leader. Fulk wanted to be certain that this leader was loyal to him and not Alice.

During one of his expeditions to Antioch, sometime before the revolt of Hugh of Jaffa, Fulk consulted with the leaders of the city, particularly its venerable patriarch, Bernard, who had been the spiritual and, sometimes, temporal leader of Antioch since 1100. The plans to bring a husband for Constance from Europe must have been put in motion before the Patriarch's death in 1134.[10]

William of Tyre describes the council in terms that imply that the nobles of Antioch begged Fulk to consider all the young men he knew in Europe who might be willing to come to the Holy Land to marry a child who was, at that moment, five or six years old. "The king listened graciously to their request; he commended them for their loyal solicitude and began to consider the matter with them."[11]

After some debate, the choice fell upon Raymond of Poitiers, the younger son of the formidable William IX, duke of Aquitaine. William had led the relief Crusade of 1101 and so Raymond already had a connection to the land, even if he had never been there. The duke had also held Fulk prisoner for a time, when Fulk was on his way back to his father's land in Anjou after visiting his mother and King Philippe in Paris.[12] However, Fulk seems not to have borne a grudge any more than Baldwin II did toward his captors in Mosul.

Raymond's life before receiving this invitation is something of an enigma. He had no large estates of his own. He is called "of Poitiers," the main town of the county of Poitou, on the Loire River in northern France. His brother, William X, apparently inherited almost everything. This was at a time when most estates were broken up to give each child a share. There seems to have been no mention in the Poitevin records of Raymond. It seems likely to me that he was not a legitimate child. Duke William was known to have had a number of bastards. This normally would have made Raymond ineligible for a marriage with the princess of Antioch. However, I think that Raymond was also the son of the aptly named Dangerosa, the wife of the viscount of Châtellerault, near Poitou. Like Fulk's mother, Bertrada,

Dangerosa had left her husband and moved in with Duke William, probably around 1110. William's wife, Philippa, retired to the convent of Fontevraut but that didn't free the duke to marry his mistress.[13] If Raymond were the son of this liaison, that would be reason enough to exclude him from his father's lands. But the fact that his mother was also part of the aristocracy meant that he couldn't be ignored.

Raymond was probably raised at the court of Henry I of England, a man who had enough bastards of his own to be sympathetic. This is where the envoys found him in 1135. He appears on a few of Henry's charters even though he did not hold any property in England.[14]

If Raymond was the son of Dangerosa then he was at least ten years younger than many historians have assumed, probably a year or two younger than Alice or in his mid-twenties when he arrived in Antioch. This still made him nearly twenty years older than his bride.

Raymond may have been chosen partly because he was from a good family and eager for a holding of his own, but even more because he had proven military skill. A later French chronicler would boast that Raymond speared a hundred Saracens or miscreants with his spear and slew another hundred with his sword.[15] He was illiterate but "did not disdain the company of educated people."[16]

King Henry I died in November 1135 and his nephew, Stephen, was anointed king soon after, leading to years of civil war as Fulk's daughter-in-law, Matilda of England, fought for her right to succeed her father. Having lost his patron, Raymond was at loose ends. In his position, even having to wait for a child to come of age seemed a decent trade for becoming prince of Antioch. He accepted.[17]

In order to get to Antioch, Raymond had to pass through either southern Italy or Constantinople. Since the rulers of both places had good reasons to prevent him from reaching his goal, he traveled through Italy in a variety of disguises. His crossing was further complicated by the fact that the papacy was undergoing another schism. In 1130, Honorius, the pope chosen to reconcile the division between the popes and the Holy Roman Emperor, died. Two groups of cardinals met and each group elected a new pope. Both men were Italian. One, Gregorio Paperaschi, took the name Innocent II. The other, Pietro Pierleoni, chose Anacletus II. Rome liked Anacletus; he was consecrated at St. Peter's. Innocent was consecrated at Santa Maria Nuova, but, shortly afterward, he lost the support of an important Roman family and was forced to flee to France. Much of this was the usual papal politics. However, another dimension was added in this case. The great-grandfather of Anacletus was a Roman Jew.[18] He had converted and many of his children and grandchildren had married Christians. This was the crucial difference between the families of the two popes, both of old Roman stock. Europe was divided. France and England particularly supported Innocent. Rome and Roger of Sicily supported Anacletus.

Fulk and most of the clergy of the Latin States also supported Innocent. Many feared Roger would take over Antioch and bring the partisanship of the schism into an already diverse population. This may have been an argument that helped to sway the new Patriarch of Antioch, Ralph of Domfront, to join with Fulk in his plot to marry little Constance to Raymond.

Ralph had been chosen by the "people of the town," not the bishops, as was usual.[19] In his few years in office, Ralph managed to alienate most of the clergy as well as Raymond of Poitiers, although he had been instrumental in the establishment of Raymond in Antioch. William of Tyre says of Ralph, "He was a military man, very magnificent and generous, a great favorite both with the people and the knightly class."[20] While this may sound complimentary, William does not consider these good traits for a man who was a religious leader, expected to be an arbitrator.

Raymond arrived at Antioch in 1136 or 1137. He had sent some of his servants and retainers on ahead, so, according to William again, Alice got wind of his coming earlier than Fulk had hoped. If she was aware that Raymond was on his way, I think it more than likely that she had spies in Antioch who told her that Raymond had been sent for, but they didn't know why.

William continues, "Meanwhile, Ralph, the crafty patriarch of Antioch, a man well versed in wiles, induced her [Alice] to believe that Raymond . . . had been sent for to be her own husband. . . . Alice's credulous mind readily accepted that false hope."[21]

Since only William mentions this, it's not certain that this is what happened. Such a pairing could make sense. Alice was only about twenty-six at the time. She was politically wise enough to know that Antioch needed a strong fighting man to defend it. Raymond had good connections, but no prospects. It might have occurred to her that there were those, both in Antioch and Jerusalem, who might want the prince of Antioch to be dependent on them and not have any local family to call on for aid, but there was little she could do overtly to prevent this. However, it's likely that Alice would be suspicious of anyone chosen by Fulk.

Whatever the preamble, as soon as Raymond appeared, Constance was brought, without Alice's knowledge, to the church of St. Peter in Antioch and married to him by Patriarch Ralph.[22]

By any standards, including those of twelfth-century European nobility, the marriage of Constance, princess of Antioch, and Raymond of Poitiers was illegal. Children of royalty were betrothed very young, sometimes at birth. Matilda of England had been sent to Germany at the age of eight to

The Church of St. Peter, Antioch. Photograph courtesy of Penelope Adair.

prepare for her eventual marriage to the Holy Roman emperor.[23] But the actual wedding could not take place until the girl had reached puberty. She also had to consent, although some did so unwillingly.[24] Constance was too young on both counts. Added to these impediments, Patriarch Ralph had not been canonically elected. But, once the ceremony had been performed, it seems to have been a *fait accompli*. Alice apparently didn't have the support to get the marriage annulled. In fury, she was forced to return to Latakia. "Ever after, she pursued the prince with relentless hatred."[25]

Wouldn't any mother?

It is very unlikely that Melisende knew about any of Fulk's machinations. She hadn't been in Antioch with Fulk and everyone involved seems to have been sworn to secrecy. The sisters, all four of them, seem to have been very fond of each other. Earlier, Melisende had intervened with Fulk to prevent him from harassing Alice in her rule of Latakia.[26]

Newly married and blissfully ignorant of the political intrigue taking place around him, Raymond went south to help Fulk fight against Zengi, whose power was increasing.[27] He would soon learn that he had made a bargain with the devil in the form of Patriarch Ralph. He would also discover that Emperor John of Constantinople was furious enough about this secret wedding to attack Antioch. First, though, the emperor needed to finish the siege he had undertaken on the town of Anazarbos in Armenian Cilicia.[28]

His siege having succeeded, Emperor John set off for Antioch, capturing various places that had once been Greek but since had become part of the state of Antioch, such as Tarsus. He was angry with Raymond not only because the marriage he had been negotiating between his son and Constance had been thwarted, but because Antioch was considered specifically to be under the jurisdiction of the Greek emperors and no marriage should have been contracted without his permission. This dependence had begun with an oath taken by Bohemond I in 1098 to the effect that if he conquered the city, he would return it to the empire. This wasn't done. Bohemond created his own principality regardless of his promise. Emperor Alexis was unable to enforce the oath and didn't press the matter. John was in a better position to exact revenge and he hadn't forgotten.[29]

Now the emperor decided that it was time to assert his claim. In late August 1137, he and his army appeared at the gates of Antioch.[30] Both the Greek and Latin sources agree that John besieged Antioch for a short time. Soon Raymond decided that his hold on the populace was too tenuous to endure a long siege. He admitted that negotiation was in order and sent ambassadors to John. In the end he promised fealty to the empire and gave the emperor the freedom of the city "in war or in peace."[31] Raymond kept his word—for a while.

Meanwhile, Alice remained unmolested in Latakia. It is not recorded where Constance was. It's possible that she wasn't allowed to see her mother for fear that Alice would flee with her daughter.

It is a mystery to me why there wasn't more of an uproar about this flagrant breach of both canon and civil law. Princess Constance and Raymond eventually had four children. The eldest, Bohemond III, was born when she was sixteen or seventeen, so it is hoped that Raymond honored the prohibition and waited until she was of age to consummate the marriage. Alice seems to have died before 1140, when her supporters, Walter of Surdavalle and Garente of Saone, are among the witnesses to a charter issued by Raymond and Constance giving land to the canons of the Holy Sepulchre.[32] The men may have decided to cut their losses and switch sides but the lack of any other mention of Alice in the records supports the theory that she was no longer living. The cause of her death is a mystery. The coastal cities were particularly prone to malaria, but there are many other illnesses or accidents that could have killed her.

Despite starting life as a pawn, Constance was her mother's daughter. She will be heard from later. And, by the way, her daughter Maria would marry the emperor's son Manuel and become empress of Byzantium.

Also in 1137, Pons of Tripoli died in battle against Zengi. The new count was his son, Raymond. Raymond of Tripoli was Fulk's nephew, being the son of his half-sister Cecelia. Raymond was by then also married to Melisende's sister Hodierna. It's not certain when they were married, but it was before December 1138, when Hodierna witnessed a royal charter issued by Fulk, Melisende, and young Baldwin in the city of Acre.[33]

It is intriguing that Raymond of Tripoli doesn't appear on the charter. He may have been on campaign, although winter was usually not a time for warfare. Hodierna may have decided that she missed her big sister and come to Acre, not far from Tripoli. She may even have needed advice on how to handle her new husband.

Later, Raymond and Hodierna donated heavily in memory of Pons, to the Holy Sepulchre, the Hospitallers, and several churches in and near Jerusalem. In most of Raymond's charters Hodierna is listed as consenting to the gifts.

Raymond was not only saddened but incensed by the death of his father. He took what was left of the army of Tripoli and attacked a village of Syrians in revenge for what he perceived as their betrayal of the count by not sending reinforcements to aid Pons. Raymond invaded the town, brought many of the inhabitants to Tripoli in chains, and had them tortured and killed. William of Tyre calls these acts "proofs of valor," by which Count Raymond "won the affection of all his people and universal approval."[34] It might also be seen as indicating that Raymond had a violent temper and sought disproportionate revenge. Many of the people he punished were not the ones who had made the decision to ignore the summons to battle.

The next few years passed as usual for the various armies. Alliances were made and broken. Battles were fought. Land changed hands. Zengi continued taking over the territory of other Muslims, one town at a time, occasionally fighting the Franks but, for the most part, biding his time as his power grew. His threat was strongest in 1139, when Damascus and Jerusalem mounted a joint expedition to take back the coastal town of Banyas, which Zengi had recently captured. Assisting Fulk at this time was his European son-in-law, Thierry, count of Flanders, who had married Fulk's daughter, Sybille, a few years earlier.[35] Thierry made several trips to Jerusalem, each time bringing much-needed help.

Eventually the arguments among the rulers of the Latin States were submerged in the face of the growing threat of the militant Zengi, but even then they underestimated him

During this period, Melisende and Fulk seem to have worked out their differences. We have already seen that Fulk issued no more charters without Melisende's approval. It was also in this period that the exquisite book of psalms and prayers known as the Melisende Psalter was made at the scriptorium of the church of the Holy Sepulchre. Perhaps a peace offering from Fulk to his wife, it is beautifully decorated with illuminations that are in a blend of Byzantine and Western styles. In this picture of "The Entry into Jerusalem," the Church of the Holy Sepulchre/Dome of the Rock is seen clearly in the background. This is the most spectacular of the manuscripts from Jerusalem that has survived, but it is known that scriptoria existed in the major cities and many monasteries.

This period of relative calm gave Melisende and Fulk the opportunity to direct building projects. One of their great joint accomplishments was the fortress of Bethgibelin twelve miles east of Ascalon, blocking the pass to Jerusalem.[36] Begun in 1134, it was "a strong fortress surrounded by an impregnable wall, with towers, ramparts and a moat."[37] It was reputed to be the site of the biblical Beersheba, where Abraham had "established a well."[38] There seems to have been enough water still there to fill a moat around the fortress. Bethgibelin was given into the care of the Hospitallers in 1136.

By the 1130s, the Hospitallers had expanded from caring for sick and feeble pilgrims. Now, along with the Templars, they also had a military role. It's not certain when they added armed knights to their order, but they would not have been given the care of strategically important fortresses if they didn't have a trained force to man it.[39]

The two military orders were often rivals for donations and glory in battle. Despite this rivalry, even in moderately peaceful times, both were needed to defend the kingdom. All the Frankish settlements were chronically short of men of fighting age.

The Levant had been the scene of countless invasions over the centuries, and when the Crusaders and the Armenians arrived, they found fortifications in most of the towns.[40] Sometimes the walls were so strong that conquest required someone on the inside to help the invaders, as at Antioch

"The Entry into Jerusalem" from the Melisende Psalter. © The British Library Board, Egerton 1139 f5v.

The minaret of Aleppo built before Melisende was born (left). Destroyed 2013 (right). Photographs courtesy of AP Photo/Aleppo Media Center (AMC).

or Edessa. Aleppo and Damascus never fell to the Franks, despite repeated attempts. The eleventh-century minaret of Aleppo lasted until 2013, when it was destroyed in the Syrian civil war.

Many of these castles have survived the centuries, at least the outer shells. One of the best preserved was Krak de Chevaliers, constructed on the site of a smaller fortress called "castle of the Kurds" near the town of Homs in present-day Syria. It protected the route between Tripoli and the valley of the Orontes.[41] In 1142, Raymond of Tripoli also gave it to the Hospitallers to defend. It also survived until 2013, when it was heavily bombed.

In the early 1140s, other fortresses were begun on the frontier. Blanchegarde was close enough to Ascalon that the city could be seen from the towers of the castle.[42] Another of the castles built to protect the kingdom from assault from Ascalon was at the town of Ibelin. The former constable of Jaffa, Barisan the elder, was granted the castle. A relative newcomer, Barisan had supported Fulk in his struggle with Hugh of Jaffa. Ibelin may have been his reward for loyalty. Barisan took the name of the town as his family name. The Ibelin family would play an important role in the future of the Latin States.[43]

Other castles were constructed along the borders with Damascus and Arabia. The lords entrusted with guarding them were granted lands to provide for their support. They also were permitted to collect tolls from all travelers, including Muslim caravans and pilgrims on their way to Mecca.[44]

While the castles are the most impressive of the constructions built by the Latin lords, churches and monasteries were as important. Melisende's interest in the convent of St. Lazarus at Bethany was ongoing. Sadly, there is nothing left today of the buildings or the records. It was only two miles from Jerusalem, on the eastern slope of the Mount of Olives, but it was still in danger of attack. "The queen at great expense caused to be built a strongly fortified tower of hewn and polished stone" for the protection of the convent.[45] The nuns also received the income of Emma's town of Jericho, which had been taken over by the crown.

Yvette was still too young to be the abbess of St. Lazarus so Melisende installed an experienced woman in that position. When the woman, Matilda, died, Yvette did become abbess at the age of twenty-four, "with the sanction of the patriarch and the willing assent of the holy nuns."[46] Melisende endowed the convent with gem-studded chalices and other sacramental objects, silk, vestments, and other items for the comfort of the nuns. She also gave them several books, many probably written at the scriptorium of the Holy Sepulchre. They would have included books of psalms, the writings of

Bethany, site of the monastery. Photograph courtesy of Denys Pringle.

the Church Fathers, such as Augustine and Jerome, and stories of the lives of saints. What else the library contained, if there were books of local history or even accounts of the struggles of the first crusaders, is impossible to know.

Melisende also donated to the monastery of Notre Dame de Josaphat, one of the oldest in the area. In the time of Melisende's father, the abbot, Guilduin, had been yet another of his cousins. Guilduin had benefited from the death of his brother, Galeran, in Muslim captivity when the abbey inherited Galeran's estates.[47] The church associated with this monastery was reputed to be the site of the tomb of the Virgin Mary. It was here, close to the tomb of the Virgin, and to that of Morfia, that Melisende would choose to be buried.[48]

Melisende was also one of the major forces behind the continual rebuilding of the city of Jerusalem. After Fulk's death she had the market streets rebuilt and covered. Many of the shops were given for the support of the convent of Saint Anne, which Melisende also contributed to.[49]

Just outside the walls of Jerusalem was a monastery devoted to caring for lepers, St. Lazarus. While some skin ailments, such as psoriasis, were mistakenly diagnosed as leprosy, the later stages of the disease were unmistakable. Melisende and Fulk donated richly to St. Lazarus. There are accounts of noblemen who contracted the disease and spent their final days there. At some point, long after Melisende's day, the Knights of St. Lazarus would also form a military order. Afflicted men who were already trained for war and still able to hold a sword wanted to fight. They were fierce in battle, preferring a quick death to the horror of a lingering one.[50]

The king and queen spent autumn 1143 in the coastal town of Acre. One fine day, they decided to go riding outside of the city. They brought several members of the court with them and were preceded by servants who were walking along the roads. Since Fulk was particularly fond of hunting, these servants may have been beaters, looking for game in the brush.[51] Suddenly a hare leapt out of a furrow. As it ran off, it was pursued by the courtiers, Fulk among them. Racing across the plain, the king's horse stumbled and fell. As Fulk was thrown, the saddle landed on his head. "His brains gushed forth from both ears and nostrils," William of Tyre relates.[52] Fulk may have died instantly or lingered in a coma for a few days, but the fall was fatal. He died on November 10, 1143.

His body was taken to Jerusalem, where he was buried at Calvary next to his predecessors: Godfrey, Baldwin I, and Baldwin II.

Despite his battles with the native lords and Melisende, Fulk was a good choice as king. He could fight, was an able administrator, and knew when to give in. William says that Melisende flung herself on the ground at the place where Fulk fell, where "she embraced his lifeless body. Tears failed her through continual weeping."[53]

This was the customary way for a grief-stricken widow to behave and William was writing for the couple's son, Amalric. But I suspect that Melisende had grown used to, even fond of, her husband and his sudden death was a shock.

William concludes, "King Fulk left two children who had not yet attained the age of manhood. Baldwin, the elder, then thirteen years old, and Amalric aged seven. The royal power passed to the Lady Melisende, a queen beloved of God, to whom it belonged by hereditary right."[54]

Al-Qalanisi notes Fulk's death and that Melisende and her elder son were "appointed to the kingship; the Franks were satisfied with this."[55]

Melisende now ruled alone.

FIFTEEN

MELISENDE REGINA SOLA

JERUSALEM, 1143–1149

ON CHRISTMAS DAY, 1143, MELISENDE AND HER SON Baldwin III, were crowned queen and king in the church of the Holy Sepulchre in Jerusalem. With great ceremony they were anointed by William, Patriarch of Jerusalem, before all the nobility, bishops, and abbots who could be assembled.[1]

Melisende had not become regent for her son. Nor was she relegated to a role as queen mother.[2] The joint coronation was to remind the kingdom that she was the lawful ruler. The fact that she allowed the under-age Baldwin to be part of her second coronation may have been the result of debates among the court and church officials, rather than her choice. Or, she may have wanted the succession assured. She was actually the first ruler of Latin Jerusalem to receive the crown by inheritance. Her father had been elected king as had Baldwin I. It was not unusual for a minor son to be recognized as king while his father lived. Both the Angevin and Capetian kings followed the custom of having their heirs anointed in their own lifetime.[3] In this, Melisende was also emphasizing her own right to rule.

Even though he wore the crown, it is evident from the records that Baldwin was not making decisions about government policy.

Bernard, the Cistercian abbot of Clairvaux, was already a correspondent of Melisende's. Her letters to him did not survive but he wrote her just after Fulk's death. He expresses his condolences and then advises her that, "the eyes of all will be upon you, and on you alone the whole burden of the kingdom will rest. You must set your hand to great things and, though a woman, you must act as a man . . . so that all may judge you from your actions to be a king rather than a queen."[4] Melisende had no problem with this counsel.

Melisende wasn't exceptional in ruling on her own. From 1100 to 1600 there were twenty reigning queens who were neither wives of kings nor regents for minor sons.[5] Apart from the contemporary European women—Urraca of Castile, Matilda of Tuscany, and Ermengarde of Narbonne—there were a number of women who may not have had the title of queen, but certainly exercised the power just as well.

In the Near East, Melisende was not an anomaly, either. While she was the first woman to inherit Jerusalem, she was not the first to exercise power, despite there being men, especially sons, available.

In her panegyric of her father, Alexis, Anna Komnene takes time to praise her grandmother, Anna Dalessene. Shortly after he became emperor, Alexis officially turned over all administrative power to his mother, while he handled military affairs. Anna reproduces the document proving this in her book.[6] The division of power was apparently a good one. Alexis had no head for administration and his mother did. Anna says, "My grandmother had an exceptional grasp of public affairs, with a genius for organization and government. She was capable, in fact, of managing not only the Roman Empire, but every other empire under the sun, as well."[7] The passage concludes, "not only was she a credit to her own gender, but to men as well: indeed, she contributed to the glory of the whole human race."[8]

Whether Anna's grandmother had all the skills and talents her doting granddaughter attributes to her is not as important as the fact that Anna Dalessene was accepted as the final authority on administration of the Byzantine Empire.

Another example of a powerful ruling woman comes from closer to Melisende's time and place. At about the same time that Hugh of Jaffa was rebelling against Fulk (1134), there was trouble in Damascus. Its young emir, Shams al-Muluk, who was about twenty-two, had proven himself to be an able general, taking Banyas from the Franks and defending Damascus.

However, his governing ability apparently consisted of extortion and torture. Ibn al-Qalanisi excoriates the emir, so it's difficult to know how many of the accusations he makes are true. The list ranges from slander, confiscation of property, physical abuse, and "various abominable forms of threatening and abusive language."[9] Even worse, in the mind of this Damascene gentleman, Shams tyrannized humble people who had no way to fight back.

When he had alienated most of his people, Shams sent secret word to Zengi promising that he could have Damascus if the atabeg would allow him to wreak revenge on all his enemies. If Zengi didn't arrive soon, Shams promised to hand the city to the Franks. He started moving valuables to a castle he owned, named Sarkhad, while continuing to arrest "his officers, secretaries, and officials."[10]

It seemed that everyone in Damascus wanted to be rid of their psychotic emir, but no one had the courage to go against him. So the influential people of the city went to the Khatun, Safwat al-Mulk Zumurrud, the daughter of the emir Jawali, and mother of Shams. She was acutely aware of how her son was ruining the city and agreed to take care of the matter.

Safwat began by giving Shams a good lecture. This produced no change in his behavior. She considered what the next step should be. After long thought, "her benevolence, sound spirit of religion, and well-balanced intelligence moved her further to consider how this evil might be excised and the well-being of Damascus and its inhabitants restored."[11]

There was nothing else to do, she concluded. Catching him without his bodyguard, Safwat ordered her guards to kill her son. His body was displayed to the general rejoicing of the people. Safwat's younger son, Shihab al-Din Mahmud, became emir. The citizens came to the palace and swore to "render obedience to him *and to his mother*" (italics mine).[12]

Writing much later, and using al-Qalanisi's account, among others, ibn Al-Athir adds that Shams had planned to kill his mother, so she killed him first. "God knows best!"[13]

Damascus didn't fall to Zengi at that time, but Safwat's story doesn't end with this. She was a tough, intelligent woman who had learned how to get power and use it. Her contemporaries respected her for this. In the Near East, survival was too important to ignore anyone capable. Like Melisende, rank and ability were more important to her people than gender. In June 1138, Safwat accepted a marriage proposal from Zengi, who, like her, already had grown sons.[14] This alone took courage as Zengi's reputation for cruelty was known throughout the Islamic Near East. Safwat was also aware that it was her grandfather, Tutush, who had killed Zengi's father, the Mamluk, Aq Sunqur.[15] Yet, for the safety of the country, she went into his household.

SHORTLY AFTER HIS FATHER'S DEATH, BALDWIN III learned that a Frankish outpost had been taken by Turks, "at the invitation of certain people dwelling in that vicinity."[16] This seems to have been an area that the Latins had conquered, south of the Dead Sea, north of Petra. This was an area inhabited by Bedouins and Syrian Christians but there were also a number of Muslim farmers and herders. Apart from collecting taxes, there doesn't seem to have been a Latin presence there.

This was the boy's chance to prove he could defend the realm as well as his father. He raised an army and went to the village, which was called Montreal by the Franks. The local people fled to their fortress, now in the hands of the Turks. After a few days of siege, Baldwin or his advisers decided that it would be impossible to take it with the number of men they had. It was then decided to destroy the livelihood of the defenders. The land there was covered with ancient olive groves that had provided for the people. The trade in olive oil was highly profitable. Baldwin's army uprooted and burnt as many of the trees as they could. Seeing this, the local people surrendered on condition that the Turks be allowed to leave in peace. Baldwin agreed. He left a garrison at the fort, perhaps to be sure that taxes were paid as much as the people protected. The locals were left to replant their olives and hope they could survive until they bore fruit.[17]

This story isn't confirmed anywhere other than in William of Tyre. It probably occurred, but doesn't make sense. Historian Hans Eberhard Mayer believes that, at thirteen, Baldwin was already chafing to be free of his mother's control and that she resented it, which is why she didn't let him lead the next expedition.[18] Perhaps, but that would imply that Melisende was going against the wishes of the court, including those who had seen Baldwin in action. It is just as likely that she allowed him to go to strengthen the prestige of the monarchy, but that the boy-king was not in charge by any means and that his conduct did not inspire confidence in those with him. This is my interpretation of the evidence available. I am presenting an alternate view of the event which I believe is as credible as the one put forth that assumes Melisende was greedy for power at the expense of her son.

In the years immediately after Fulk's death, all Melisende's skill and administrative experience were needed. Zengi was slowly devouring the semi-independent emirates to the north and east of Jerusalem. In Constantinople, the new emperor was Manuel, the youngest son who had been considered as a husband for Melisende's niece Constance. A few months before Fulk's death, the emperor John had also been killed in a hunting mishap. He had speared a wild boar and in the struggle with the beast, the emperor had received a scratch from one of his own arrows. The tip may have been poisoned. A few days later, John died of blood poisoning.[19]

Manuel was still in his teens but two of his older brothers had died and the third, Isaac, was bypassed so Manuel was now in charge. The new emperor directed the Byzantine army to follow his father's route through the Armenian territory of Cilicia, which had always been a buffer between Antioch and Constantinople. Their intention was to finally get Antioch to surrender to rule from Constantinople. Once again, the northern states were threatened.

By 1142 or 1143, Constance would have been of age for the marriage to be consummated. With Alice dead, there was no one left to dispute Raymond's rule of Antioch. Roger of Sicily seems to have abandoned his claim.

But Raymond had not counted on the tenacity of the Emperor Manuel, whose army was at the gate to remind the prince of his oath to the empire.

Meanwhile Zengi had spent most of his energy consolidating power in the east, fighting Kurds and other Seljuk emirs. By 1144 he finally felt strong enough to attack Edessa, a prize that had been threatened so many times since Baldwin I had acquired it.[20]

Jocelyn II was count of Edessa at the time. William of Tyre, who, it may be remembered, didn't like him, says that Jocelyn left Edessa unprotected because he preferred to stay at his childhood home of Tel Bashir where "he had time for luxurious pleasures . . . and he felt no responsibility for the noble city."[21]

In December 1144, Zengi, having planned carefully, made his move. When his spies told him that Jocelyn and most of his men had left, Zengi and his army took their position by night. He then blocked all exits from Edessa and proceeded to bombard the stone walls. To bring them down more quickly, he employed one of the most effective of tactics against a heavily fortified castle. He sent sappers to dig tunnels beneath the stone walls. They set wooden beams to support the tunnels. When they reached a likely spot, the sappers set fire to the wood and, if they had calculated accurately, the entire wall collapsed.

This time the sappers were spot on. The walls of Edessa, inadequately guarded, fell, and Zengi's army poured in. The chroniclers all say that the people were slaughtered, except for those who were taken as slaves, and the city was plundered. There was probably carnage as usual, but the sources also state that the Armenian Christians, at least, were left to clean up. Again it appears that those who write of glorious victories don't really count the farmers and craftsmen who managed to avoid their swords. Al-Athir assures his readers that only Franks were killed; Syrians and Armenians were given back their homes after the Turks were through looting them. He adds that all the native people taken as slaves were returned to their homes.[22] Michael the Syrian does not say that only Franks fell, but he does tell the story of Zengi's encounter with the Syrian bishop Basilius bar Soumana.

It seems that Zengi spotted the old man with his tonsure, naked and bound. He asked the bishop who he was. The repartee that followed is probably apocryphal but Zengi was impressed with Basilius's bravery and his command of Arabic. As a result, Zengi spared the Armenians and Greeks, but killed the Franks. So there may well be truth in Al-Athir's praise. Basilius remained as the bishop of Edessa and gave advice to the atabeg until Zengi's murder shortly afterward.[23]

William adds that during the invasion, those who could took refuge in the citadel. However, the crush was so great that many were trampled to death, including the Latin archbishop Hugh. William considers this only right as Hugh had hoarded church funds instead of paying for the defense of Edessa, thus making the defeat his fault.[24]

News of the siege reached Jocelyn, who immediately sent out a call for help. His support of Alice against Raymond had earned the enmity of the prince of Antioch. Raymond also had his hands full with Manuel's assault. In any case, he refused to send his men to fight Zengi.

Melisende responded as soon as she heard about Zengi's attack, She sent her men north under the leadership of her cousin, Manassas of Hierges, who was another recent arrival from the family, the grandson of her namesake aunt, Melisende. The queen had appointed him her constable. Manassas led the army jointly with a second-generation knight called Phillip of Nablus, the son of an early settler named Guy of Milly. Both father and son were intensely loyal to Melisende's family.

Melisende must have been horrified at the fall of her childhood home. She knew the streets, gardens, and people, and the loss would have been heartbreaking. Memories of the scent of fruit blossoms and the cooing of the doves were part of her being.

Baldwin III was not part of the expedition. Had he begged to go with the army and been forbidden by his mother? It's not recorded. Baldwin had probably never been to Edessa. His Armenian grandmother had died before he was born. Sentiment wouldn't have driven him. Perhaps his first military foray the year before had been enough for the present. Perhaps Melisende feared for his life if he came up against Zengi. She must have remembered how her father had been captured twice and what the price of his ransom had been. There are any number of reasons why Baldwin did not lead the Jerusalemites to Edessa.

In any case, it was too late. Edessa fell December 23. It was a bleak Christmas for the Latin States.

It took several months for news of the loss of Edessa to reach Europe, first to the pope, Eugenius III, a Cistercian who was temporarily locked out of Rome. The pope sent word across Christendom. The shock reverberated throughout the West. It was inconceivable that God would allow this ancient Christian city to fall to the infidel. People were accustomed to hearing sermons urging people to take the cross to defend the Holy Land. But coupled with these pleas were a mass of songs and epic poems about the great men who had taken Antioch, Edessa, and Jerusalem. They had become legendary in strength and honor and it was assumed that their successors were equally endowed. I don't think most people understood just how precarious the situation was. They believed that God had guided the Crusaders to free the Holy Land. Once that had been accomplished it was clear that God would take over the protection of the holy places.

Help did eventually come from the West—three years later. In the meantime, Jocelyn tried to retake Edessa and almost succeeded. Raymond of Antioch went to Constantinople and declared himself a vassal of Emperor Manuel, thus ending the threat. Melisende dealt with the twin trials of keeping a fractious kingdom running and living with a teenaged son eager to prove himself a man and a king.

Soon after Edessa fell, the Armenian Catholicos Nerses Snorhali wrote a lament of several hundred lines. The voice of the city is that of a woman, torn between abject grief at her defilement and fury at those who attacked her and those who never appeared to help.

Snorhali agrees with William of Tyre that Antioch abandoned Edessa, leaving the city to her fate.

I quarrel with you, O Antioch,
Dear sister, with words of censure

Why did you not speedily
Come to my aid?
But did you allow that out of envy
I was delivered into the hand of the infidel?[25]

Much of the poem is biblical metaphor, but Snorhali gives a poignant picture of the watch for the rescue forces of Jerusalem, "observing the roads, day and night, always they hoped for arrivals. Still they did not come . . . since they procrastinated and delayed coming to the aid of my Count [Jocelyn]."[26]

Snorhali excoriates Zengi by name, giving an account of the situation that corroborates William's later report, with the atabeg waiting until Jocelyn and the army had gone before beginning his siege. From the context, it's clear that the poem was written soon after the event, before 1146, when Zengi was murdered. The poet also writes of the deadly stampede at the citadel, which he said was locked. Snorhali deviates from the focus of the Latin chroniclers, telling us that the Jacobite bishop, Basil, and the Armenian bishop, John, were among the leaders of the defense of Edessa, along with the Latin archbishop. John managed to survive and he may have given Snorhali the detailed information that he used in his poem, though the grief-stricken emotion comes from the poet's heart.[27]

There were many who would echo the sorrow that Snorhali imagined for his city of Edessa.

So gather your daughters.
Be seated and weep for my sake.
Cry out with a voice full of protest
Stir each soul to lamentation.
For the soothing of a heart on fire
Can only be brought about so.[28]

SIXTEEN

OF KINGS, QUEENS, AND TOURISTS

FRANCE AND THE LATIN STATES, 1144–1148

IN WESTERN EUROPE THERE WAS HORROR AT THE loss of the oldest Christian city, but there wasn't a rush to send armies. Leaders were embroiled in their own problems and quarrels. Pope Eugenius wanted to mount a major military pilgrimage for many of the same reasons Urban II had. Politics in Italy had driven him from Rome, where another anti-pope had been chosen and he needed something to unite the faithful. This wasn't the only reason; Eugenius was also appalled by the fall of Edessa. However, the pope soon realized that his influence was not enough to mount a crusade. Eugenius could imagine only one person with the moral authority to convince the nobility to set out on an expensive and dangerous expedition, his mentor, Bernard.

Bernard, abbot of the monastery of Clairvaux, was an aristocrat from Champagne, brilliant, devout, tireless, and incredibly charismatic. It was said that his preaching in Paris had caused countless students to leave their studies and enter Cistercian monasteries. The Cistercians were a new reform order that rejected the wealthy trappings and property of the Benedictine order, which was long-established and rich. Their current popularity was directly due to the example set by Bernard. The abbot had already given his enthusiastic support to the Templars. His uncle, Andrew of Monbard, was a member of the order and currently in Jerusalem. Andrew was well acquainted with Melisende. Bernard was the natural person to ask for help in promoting a new crusade.

A year after the fall of Edessa, on December 1, 1145, Eugenius issued an official bull exhorting Christians to travel to the Holy Land to wage war. The bull, *Quantum Praedecessores,* was named after the first two words of the document, meaning, "in as much as those who came before us."[1] Eugenius promised the usual remission of sins for those who would undertake to go. The only ruler who showed much interest was the twenty-five-year-old king of France, Louis VII. Louis was the second son of Louis VI and had been intended for the church. But his older brother, Philip, had died as a result of an accident involving a skittish horse and a runaway pig in the streets of Paris.[2] Louis became king in 1137. That same year he married Eleanor, who had become duchess of Aquitaine when her father, William, died while returning from a pilgrimage to Compostela only a few weeks earlier. Eleanor's family had participated in earlier relief parties sent to the Holy Land.

King Louis was open to the idea of crusading partially because he was religious and partly because he had a bad conscience over an incident that had taken place a few years before during his conflict with the count of Champagne, Thibault. While besieging the town of Vitry, Louis had burnt down a church in which the inhabitants had taken refuge.[3] Either the deaths of innocent citizens or the fact that they had died in a place of sanctuary haunted him. The call to arms from the pope impelled him to action. At his Christmas court in Bourges, Louis announced that he was going to free Edessa.

The response was underwhelming. Louis couldn't whip up any enthusiasm for the expedition. Undaunted, he consulted Abbot Bernard, who also wasn't very enthusiastic at first. But after Pope Eugenius issued his bull a second time, and sent a letter of pleading, Bernard took up the cause with a vengeance.[4]

The abbot traveled all over France and sent letters to important lords and clergy preaching the crusade. He went as far as Toulouse in the south and Cologne and Trier in the east. His passionate sermons galvanized listeners. The following Easter, March 31, 1146, at the church of Mary Magdalene at Vézelay, France, a crowd of people assembled to take the cross. Louis stood next to Bernard on a makeshift podium, the cross on his chest prominently displayed. Bernard spoke to the assembly with such power that the two men were engulfed by eager volunteers. Bernard had to cut up his white robe to make more crosses. When, under the crush of people, the podium collapsed, it was considered a miracle, as no one was killed.[5]

This crusade was the first led by a ruling king. After much persuasion and a public challenge at the cathedral of Speyer in Germany, Bernard also convinced Conrad, the aging king of the Germans, to come along with his nephew and successor, Frederick.[6]

Bernard's prime reason for going to Germany had not been to recruit Conrad. The abbot had dropped everything and hurried to the Rhineland upon learning that a "renegade" Cistercian monk named Radulf had been going about preaching that it was necessary to rid Europe of the infidels in their midst before fighting the ones in the East. This sparked a massacre of Jews in the towns. Bernard was horrified that one of his monks was inciting people to murder. He stopped Radulf, sending him back to his monastery, and gave several sermons forbidding anyone to harm the Jews.[7]

By the time Louis and Conrad had assembled their armies, it seemed an impressive and invincible force, but the Second Crusade was not too different from the forces that had come to the Holy Land in 1101 and 1121, despite the presence of royalty. It might have become simply another military action, of interest only to Crusade historians, if not for the participation of one person.

Louis's wife Eleanor was intensely involved in the enterprise. Like her husband, the queen was in her twenties, bright, literate, stylish, and lacking only the one thing that would make her life complete, a son. In seven years of marriage, she had only given birth to a daughter, Marie. She had even gone to Abbot Bernard, who disapproved of her frivolous lifestyle, for advice on why she hadn't conceived again. Eleanor may have felt that the problem was not in her behavior, but her husband's. She had famously complained about Louis's lack of interest in paying the marriage debt. "I have married a monk!" she was heard to wail.[8]

So, one of the first at Vézelay to take the cross after Louis was Eleanor. Much has been made of her decision by contemporaries, later historians, and writers of fiction. I don't find it strange that she would do so. Many women accompanied their husbands on crusade. Eleanor may have been eager for adventure, but she took her religion as seriously as did Louis. If he could expiate his sins by going to the Holy Land, so could she, and at the end of the journey there might be a healthy male child.

If that was her plan, things turned out quite differently than she imagined.

It would be more than a year after Louis took the cross before the combined armies of the French and Germans set out. Life did not stand still in Jerusalem while the Europeans got themselves organized.

Melisende kept up her correspondence with Abbot Bernard. His letters to her aren't dated but they are probably from around this period, after the death of Fulk. We don't have her letters but she seems to have been politely welcoming to friends of the abbot. In one he asks her to look after a young relative of his.[9] The young man was strong of arm and had a gentle disposition. He had gone to Jerusalem to join Bernard's uncle, Andrew, in the Templars. Bernard asks the queen to write to him frequently, to give him news of the family and of Jerusalem.

In Bernard's uncle Andrew, Melisende had found a friend and supporter. During the early years of her widowhood, she was solidifying her ties to the Knights Templar, which had become a powerful presence in the kingdom.

In another missive, Bernard asks Melisende to take care of a group of Premonstratention monks on pilgrimage, "who are equipped with the armor of God and the sword of the spirit."[10]

While other letters to the queen haven't survived, Melisende must have had her hands full with similar requests. Even though Edessa was gone, the main pilgrimage routes were open, and Jerusalem was happy to receive visitors. The goldsmiths of the city were kept busy creating souvenir crosses and reliquaries. Latin and Syrian craftsmen had separate ateliers where they produced works of art like the True Cross of Denkendorf, a silver-plated reliquary studded with amethysts, pearls, and filigree.[11] It was made to hold a sliver of the True Cross. This, along with its worth and workmanship, means that it was probably made as a gift to a special donor or a monastic house back in Europe. Poorer pilgrims would have bought crosses and medallions made from tin or pewter.

Melisende and Baldwin donated funds to the "poor of St. Lazarus" several times. In 1145, she made a joint gift with Raymond and Constance of Antioch to the Hospitallers, of a town near Krak des Chevaliers, not far from Aleppo.[12] This confirms that Alice had died, as Melisende was firmly in her sister's camp regarding Constance's unlawful marriage and would not have made a joint gift with them against her sister's wishes. The fact that this was a joint gift may have been because it was made in Alice's memory. It also suggests that Melisende was trying to make peace with Raymond.

In Edessa, Zengi was busy consolidating his lands. He fought off an Armenian attempt to retake the city. The plot was discovered and the Armenians involved were seized and punished by "slaying, crucifying and scattering throughout the land."[13] However, he also ordered that all captives from Edessa who had been sold into slavery must be returned. This caused consternation among many, including Zengi's friend Zayn al-Din Ali. He had received a beautiful Frankish girl whom he was highly attracted to. He sent her back regretfully because of the "awe and fear" he had for Zengi.[14]

This story has a postscript. Later, Zengi's successor sacked Edessa again and by chance, the same girl fell again into Zayn al-Din Ali's possession. Fearing that he might have to return her once more, he made sure to "enjoy" her immediately.[15]

The horror of the girl at this turn of fortune was not mentioned. The people of Edessa: Armenian, Syrian, and Frank, suffered equally as a result of the wars. While there were many strong women, it was still possible for them to become property in the course of a day's fight. Muslim women shared the same fate, sometimes worse, for the Franks did not keep harems where they would at least be fed and clothed.

Good harvests and bad, the kindness of neighbors and the cruelty of invaders were all unavoidable parts of life in the Near East, then and now.

In 1146, Melisende was in Jaffa, where she and Baldwin donated again to the Hospitallers. That same month, February, they were in Tyre, where they gave to the monastery of Saint Mary of Josaphat.[16] At this point the joint rulership, with Melisende in charge, appeared to be working smoothly.

The queen was also acquiring new advisors. The growing importance of Philip of Nablus is apparent from Melisende's charters. Early in her reign there are two charters, one made at Nablus, the other confirming a donation made by Philip and his brother, a man named Henry the Buffalo, and I wish I knew how he came by that name. Philip didn't have a title. His family must have had some property for they had been included at court from the time of Baldwin I, but they seem to have been something like general utility men, always on call. Philip would become one of Melisende's staunchest allies.

Melisende did not neglect other Christian establishments. In 1148 or 1149 she gave (or perhaps sold) the taxes from the village of Dayr Dakariyya to the Syrian Orthodox convent of St. Mary Magdalene and to the church of Saint Simon the Pharisee, in Jerusalem.

From these few documents, it's clear that the queen was travelling through the kingdom, attending to business.

In their histories, William of Tyre and Ibn al-Qalanisi concentrated on battles almost exclusively. From their joint narratives, it appears the Franks and Zengi had a series of skirmishes in which Baldwin III participated. None of them were successful for the Christians and their young king, although William tries to put a good face on matters. He states several times that Baldwin acted with the advice of unnamed, more experienced, companions.[17] Even with this counsel, each foray ended in embarrassing retreat. This lack of ability may have been part of the reason that, when Baldwin came of age at fifteen, Melisende didn't gracefully retire, nor, at that time, was she requested to.

In the north, Michael the Syrian, while interested in the fate of Edessa, was more focused on ecclesiastical infighting. He notes that in the 1140s the bishop of Laqabin was deposed for fornication, and other bishops were shifted about, some unfairly. These events worried him more than warfare, which had subsided, at least for the moment.

The fate of Edessa greatly worried many of the clerics, however, especially after the fate of the Armenians who tried to revolt against Zengi, only to be defeated and crucified on the city walls.[18] The men were faced with an ancient conundrum: "Why did God allow him [Zengi] to massacre priests and holy monks, rape virgins and so forth?"[19] The scholars tried to answer, often reaching beyond Orthodox teaching. One side insisted that God had not decreed the capture of the city and that if the Franks had arrived in time, Edessa would have been spared.[20] They grappled with the question of God's will, suggesting that the Edessenes must have sinned, although in what way was unknown. These answers didn't sit well with Michael, but he admitted that, even if the Armenians had been oppressed, Zengi actually treated the Syrians with some kindness, allowing them to remain in their homes.

The threat from Zengi was about to end. In on September 14, 1146, the atabeg was busy trying to take the Muslim town of Qal'at Ja'bar. While asleep in his tent, he was murdered by some of his Mameluks. As with the death of Il-Ghazi, several chroniclers say that Zengi put up no fight because he had passed out from drink. Ibn al-Qalanisi doesn't mention this but puts the blame on an attendant of Zengi's "of Frankish origin, who nursed a secret grudge."[21]

Al-Athir relates that his own father was there when the atabeg took his last breath. He told his son that Zengi was a "good-looking man of swarthy complexion and pleasant eyes." At his death the atabeg was past sixty, and his hair had turned gray.[22] Al-Qalanisi adds that the armies of the atabeg scattered, taking whatever money and treasures they could find, burying Zengi where he died without even wrapping him in a shroud.[23]

This was not the first time that Mameluks had assassinated their masters. Mameluks were men who had been bought as boys, raised Muslim, and trained to fight. They were often bodyguards for important men and women. It had been Shawat's Mameluk guards who had killed her son for her. For the most part, they were loyal and were often freed and given land by their masters if they served well. However, later in the century, the Mameluks of Egypt would overthrow the caliphs and rule the country, expanding their range eventually to defeat the Turks of the Levant and place many of the Latin settlements under their authority.

Usually the Mameluks were not Turkish. Most were Armenian, Georgian, Greek, or even Frank. One of the men who killed Zengi may have been of Western extraction. Ibn al-Qalanisi says that after murdering Zengi the man, Yaranqash, went first to Jerusalem, where he stayed for a time. He then went to Damascus, where he expected to be greeted as a hero. Instead he was executed.[24]

Zengi's place in Aleppo was taken by his son, Nur ad-Din Mahmoud. The Christians and Damascenes who had celebrated the death of Zengi soon learned that his successor was just as dangerous. Nur ad-Din also wanted Damascus, and he was not interested in truces with Christians of any sort. A devout Muslim, Nur ad-Din did not inspire rumors of wine indulgence or hunting with Frankish lords.

By the time Conrad, Louis, Eleanor, and their companions of the crusade reached the Holy Land, they would be faced with the first serious *jihad* led against them by a man of genuine faith.

Many of the participants in the Second Crusade had family members who had fought in 1098–1099. Louis's uncle Hugh of Vermandois and Eleanor's grandfather William X had both fought and returned to tell the tale. Either the tales had been embellished with glory or the children hadn't paid attention—if they had truly understood the terrible violence of the First Crusade, Louis and Eleanor would not have attempted a second.

Two chroniclers accompanied the crusaders. Recording the deeds of the French was Odo of Deuil, a monk of St. Denis, the royal abbey north of Paris. His tale, like all the accounts, is quite subjective, colored by his own perceptions of events. However, letters back and forth between King Louis and Suger, the abbot of St. Denis, co-regent of France, add another dimension to the story told by the monk.

On the German side, the crusade was recorded by Otto, bishop of Friesing, half-brother of emperor Conrad. Both Odo and Otto detail the summoning of the armies and the journey. They speak of the arrival of the armies at Constantinople. Then, as the armies enter the Latin States, both men become extremely tight-lipped. There are a few comments about the places they visited, and then they display a fascination with the departure of the crusaders. There are no stories of deeds of valor or great victories.

This was because by any measure, for the Christians, at least, the crusade was a complete disaster.

The French found that the Greek cities, governed by Emperor Manuel, refused to take them in. Odo of Deuil complains that the money changers gouged the pilgrims and that the hostile villages lowered goods for sale down on ropes from the walls rather than meet them face to face. Finally, angry and hungry, the French "procured supplies for themselves by pillage and plunder."[25]

Odo has no good things to say about the Greeks. They lied and cheated. They even aligned with the Turks to harass the French passing through their territory.[26]

The rigors of journey had been more difficult than anyone had expected. Part of the German army had been caught in a flash flood when they camped by a river, with heavy losses. Then, while the French were going through the mountains, the vanguard went farther ahead than it was supposed to, camping at what the leaders thought was a better site. The rest of the army arrived at what they thought would be the end of the day's journey to find the Turks waiting, having slipped between the widely separated division of the army. The result was a rout. "The glorious reputation of the Franks was lost."[27] The king escaped through luck. William of Tyre tells how survivors made their way back to safety, straggling in as village or family groups: "One sought his father, another his master. Here a woman was searching everywhere for her son, another for her husband. The camp resounded with lamentations."[28]

William of Tyre blamed the mix-up on the leader of the vanguard, who came from Aquitaine, and his native guides.[29] But soon European writers of Latin chronicles and popular songs, as well as tavern and wash-line gossip, created the story that Eleanor and her ladies, who called themselves "Amazons," were responsible, because they wanted to find a more comfortable spot for the night.[30]

It was now the beginning of January; the weather was rainy and frigid. There wasn't enough food to feed the soldiers and the pilgrims who had come with them. Louis finally decided to take his wife, her ladies, and many of the noblemen and sail from the coast of Turkey to Antioch. The bulk of the army was left to make their way to Antioch as best they could overland. The king put them in the care of Everard de Barre, commander of the Templars in France, who had accompanied the king from Paris. He and the Templar knights with him had already shown themselves to be the best suited to keep the pilgrims together and safe.[31] Louis had good reason to be thankful that he had brought 139 Templars from Paris as a letter from abbot Suger reminded him.[32]

The king left as much money as he could with his lieutenants before he, Eleanor, and some of their court boarded the ship.[33]

The welcome given the king, queen, and their companions at Antioch must have made the town seem like paradise. Raymond and Constance greeted them with ceremony and comfort. Raymond showered the courtiers with gifts and honors.

The first thing that Louis had to do was write home for money. He sent word to Abbot Suger that he had arrived safely at Antioch, explained that he had given most of his cash to the people in his care so that they could survive the land journey, and told the abbot to send money as soon as possible. He also asked that Suger and the men he had left in charge of the treasury, Samson, archbishop of Reims, and Raoul, count of Peronne, pay back the French Templars for the money he had borrowed from the commander over the course of the journey.[34]

Louis also had Suger pay back a few other loans and oversee the property of Reginald de Bulis, Dreux de Monchy, Albert d'Avolt, and Albert's son

Hugh, who had all died on the journey.[35] It's likely that this would be the first news that the families of these men would have had of their deaths. Many more would never know what happened to the kin who set out for Jerusalem.

Raymond had ulterior motives in giving the king and queen of France such a fulsome welcome. The prince of Antioch hoped to convince Louis to forget about retaking Edessa, which he may have considered a lost cause and whose lord, Jocelyn, he intensely disliked. The nearby Muslim towns of Shaizar and Aleppo would make much better targets and increase the security and wealth of the principality of Antioch. Since Nur ad-Din was established at Aleppo, this might be a chance to defeat the new emir and regain all that his father had conquered in the land around Antioch. Raymond hoped that his niece Queen Eleanor could be won to his cause and could persuade her husband to agree.

The story of what followed, which William of Tyre may have heard while he was still in Europe, has remained the stuff of romantic legend ever since.

William states flatly that when Louis refused to help Raymond attack Aleppo, Raymond was furious. The prince decided to get back at Louis by seducing his niece Eleanor. Eleanor was fed up with her monkish husband and, according to William, "Contrary to her royal dignity, she disregarded her marriage vows and was unfaithful to her husband."[36] Odo of Deuil, who was there, says nothing to either confirm or deny this. His account ends with the king's arrival at Antioch.

Over the centuries, friendships between historians have been shattered over the question: did she or didn't she?

William seems very sure of his facts, but I suspect that he picked up much of his information from Roman gossip: It was clear that something was wrong when Louis and Eleanor came through Rome in 1149 still not speaking to each other.

Someone who was in Rome in 1148 was the English cleric John of Salisbury, who was working at the papal court. John's information is still secondhand but he may well have seen the king and queen on their return trip and had certainly seen them during his years as a student in Paris. John was an astute observer of temperaments. He agrees with William that Louis was upset by Eleanor's obvious enjoyment of her uncle's company, but he doesn't connect the attention to Raymond's military schemes. John says that when Louis wanted to go on to Jerusalem to fulfill his pilgrim vow, Eleanor told him she was going to stay at Antioch awhile. In a fit of jealousy or just plain anger at her attitude, Louis had his wife forcibly brought with him to Jerusalem: "the mutual anger growing greater, the wound remained, hide it though they might."[37]

In her own lifetime this story was embellished until some said that Eleanor had determined to divorce Louis even before they had started their journey to Jerusalem. Not only that, but she was supposed to have arranged her second marriage with Henry II while in bed with his father, Geoffrey.[38] A hundred years later, the stories grew to include a tempestuous affair with Saladin, who, at that time, was actually a boy living in Egypt.[39]

I don't see why I shouldn't add my opinion to everyone else's. I think that Eleanor flirted with her uncle, if for no other reason than to make Louis mad. But I doubt that it was more than that. Raymond did want Louis's help to take Aleppo, and may have been hoping that Louis would reconsider his allegiance. Sleeping with Louis's wife would certainly have burned any bridges, putting a permanent end to any possible alliance.

Another reason why an affair is unlikely is that the amount of privacy in a palace in the middle of winter was negligible. Royalty couldn't just wander out to the barn for a quick roll in the hay. People noticed. As well, Raymond was Eleanor's uncle. By medieval standards sex with him qualified as incest.

There is one final and compelling reason to believe that no affair happened. Constance, Raymond's wife, the princess of Antioch by inheritance, was right there all the time. The one person who is consistently forgotten in this story, she would have been about twenty and had probably had three of her four children: Marie, Philipa, and Bohemond III.[40] She may have been pregnant at that time with their last child, Baldwin. Constance had been married more than half her life, but she had been a princess for all of it. The fact that her first son was named after her father and the second after her grandfather, instead of her husband, underlined the fact that Raymond was only prince through his marriage to her. She was also cousin to Louis, her grandmother and his father being siblings. Constance was no more a pushover than her mother or her Aunt Melisende had been. Fulk had learned who had the right to rule Jerusalem, and Constance must have made this equally clear to Raymond. It would have been politically and personally unwise for him to humiliate her in her own court.

The rumors about Eleanor reflect a modern saying: sex sells.

The story of Eleanor and Raymond calls to mind a tale told by William of Newburgh, who was writing at the same time in England. William recounts the fall of Edessa, but adds a new twist. He writes that Jocelyn II raped the daughter of an Armenian man of Edessa. Because of this rape, the man waited until Christmas Eve and betrayed the city by opening the gates to the Turks. Archbishop Hugh in this account is slaughtered while saying Mass instead of trampled by a mob.[41] To European Christians, it was much more comforting to believe that Edessa was lost through the sin of its count and the betrayal of a non-European citizen than to believe that the Muslim armies were stronger than theirs.

In a similar way, many people in Europe wanted to be convinced that the queen committed adultery; it made later Christian defeats more palatable. Despite his agreement with the gossip, William of Tyre believed that Louis should have helped Raymond. If he had, "one or the other of the cities would have been taken."[42] In hindsight, William is probably right: it might have been better if Louis had attacked Aleppo with Raymond. If they had won, Nur ad-Din might have been stymied.

In spring of 1148, Louis, Eleanor, and their companions finally arrived at Jerusalem in some disarray and ill temper to find Conrad, who had fallen ill and stayed in Constantinople to recover, waiting for them. Baldwin and Melisende tried to make them feel at home, but it can't have been a happy house party. Melisende and Baldwin must have been relieved to see the friendly face of Thierry of Flanders, Fulk's son-in-law, who was making his second trip to fight for the kingdom. Thierry had been among the group Louis left behind with the Templar knights. Together, the count and the Templars had led the remnants of the French through Cilicia and to Jerusalem.[43]

In noting powerful women, it's important to mention Sybille, Thierry's wife. Thierry had left her in charge of Flanders, which she managed well, despite an invasion by a land-hungry neighbor. Her only concession to her sex was to arrange a week-long truce so she could give birth to her son Peter.[44]

Apart from Thierry, Melisende must have found her guests trying. Louis and Eleanor were at the point of separation. Conrad was tired from his illness and was certainly regretting his moment of weakness in letting Bernard shame him into taking the cross. Many of the others were worn out and traumatized by the rigors of the journey. And plans had not been made to retake Edessa, as all of the Latin States expected.

By June 1148, there had still been no assault on the Turks. The court had gone to Acre to meet reinforcements who had come by sea. There a council was finally held to decide the best place to attack. Raymond of Antioch refused to participate, preferring to defend his territory against Nur ad-Din, who was menacing Antioch from his base in Aleppo.[45] There might have been a tang of sour grapes in his decision as well, since his advice had been ignored.

The new arrivals included Lombards and other Italians as well as a group of English and Norman knights who were fresh from a successful crusade in Portugal, where they had taken the city of Lisbon from the Muslims.

William of Tyre lists the clerics and nobles who were at Acre. As was often the case, many of the crusaders had family members with them. Louis's younger brother Robert was there and, even though there was still much animosity between France and Champagne, Henry, the son and heir of Count Thibault, was also in the king's party. Baldwin's brother-in-law, Thierry of Flanders, had brought his brother Henry, bishop of Toul.[46]

There should also have been an army from Provence led by Count Alphonse-Jordan, the son of Raymond I of Tripoli. Alphonse had been born in the Holy Land and baptized in the Jordan river, hence his name. This contingent had arrived in the Holy Land, but almost immediately Alphonse-Jordan died, so the Provençals were not able to attend the council. It was said that Alphonse-Jordan had been poisoned and rumors circulated that the poisoning had been ordered by Raymond, count of Tripoli, who feared that Alphonse-Jordan had come to lay claim to his land.[47] Raymond did not attend the council, either, and most of the crusaders from Provence returned home without taking part in a battle.

The list William gives of the Jerusalemites includes most of the bishops, the commanders of the Templars and Hospitallers, Baldwin III, and Melisende.[48] The other men from the kingdom of Jerusalem include Melisende's cousin and constable, Manasses of Hierges, the ever-loyal Philip of Nablus, and the counts of Tiberias, Sidon, Transjordan, Beirut, and Toron. Surprisingly, Walter of Caesarea was also in attendance, although it's not certain if he is the same Walter who had accused Hugh of Jaffa of treason fourteen years before. The name was beginning to appear again as witness to the king's charters and it could be that Walter was preparing to return to the court at Jerusalem when Baldwin III ruled without his mother

Balian the Old, lord of Ibelin, attended the council along with his household. He may also have already been preparing to take the side of Baldwin III, should the king decide to break free of his mother's suzerainty.

Once the council attendants were in place, they set about choosing a plan of attack. Most realized that Edessa was a lost cause, too far and too heavily guarded to be regained. There were really only two vulnerable cities: Sunni Damascus or Shi'ite Ascalon. Otto of Friesing says that the decision had already been reached by Baldwin III, Louis, and Conrad, while in Jerusalem, to attack Damascus.[49] Others say that the matter was still open. Whatever the case, eventually the lot fell upon Damascus. The debate about why continues to this day.

While there had been a truce with Damascus since 1139 and a combined Frankish-Damascene force had routed Nur ad-Din only a short time before, it's not surprising that the city was the target of the crusaders. There had been several attempts by both Baldwins to take it before. In between hostilities there had been trade between the two lands, resulting in mutual accommodation, treaties regarding pasture rights for the Bedouin, and protection for pilgrims on their way to Mecca. However, caught between Nur ad-Din and the Franks, the current emir of Damascus, Anar, had made an alliance with Aleppo and even sent his daughter to be married to Nur ad-Din to seal the bargain.[50] By doing so, he hoped to avoid a complete take-over of Damascus by the ambitious son of Zengi.

So, it may have seemed that the emir of Damascus had already broken the truce. It may have been enough of an excuse for the Latins. Even if Anar had honored his promise, I think that the lure of reward was too great to dissuade them. The French and German armies, unfamiliar with the customs of the Near East, were in favor of taking such a rich prize. Damascus was the jewel of the Syrian plains. The Spanish traveler Ibn Jubayr described it when he visited on his way to Mecca later in the century.

> Damascus is the paradise of the Orient and dawning place of her gracious and resplendent beauty. She is on a hill having meadows and springs, with deep shade and delicious water. . . . The gardens encircle it like the halo round the moon and contain it as if it were the calyx of a flower. To the east, as far as the eye can see, and wherever you look on its four sides its ripe fruits hold the gaze.[51]

In the generally arid Near East, the fruit orchards and grain fields of Damascus were looked at longingly by both Turks and Franks. Another Spanish traveler, the Jewish Benjamin of Tudela, also visited Damascus in the early 1160s. He comments on the wealth of the city, especially the abundance of water. "The Amana flows through the city and, by means of aqueducts the water is conveyed into the houses of the great people, and into the streets and market places."[52]

Benjamin is also awed by the glass, one of the fine crafts made in the city. He is amazed to see a "chamber built of gold and glass and if people walk round the wall they are able to see one another, even if the wall is between them."[53]

Damascus also had a thriving ceramics industry and was known for its goldsmiths and weavers, who made a cloth that we still call "damask." The greatest prize for the European knights was to capture a sword made of Damascene steel. Hundreds of these were brought back to the West and they changed the style and technique by which swords were made there.[54]

There was a Syrian Christian quarter in the city and a Jewish quarter large enough to have an academy.[55] All four branches of Muslim jurisprudence were represented by *madrasas*. And, for the wealthy, there was a racecourse and polo ground just outside the walls.[56]

Even after years of renovation, Jerusalem couldn't hold a candle to Damascus.

The council decided that their combined armies would attack at once. They arrived at the outskirts of the city of Damascus in mid-July 1148.

As to what happened next, there is very little information from the European chroniclers. Odo of Deuil was apparently too traumatized by the journey and the rift between Eleanor and Louis at Antioch to write. Otto of Freising refuses to say anything more than that the expedition to Damascus "must be related elsewhere, and possibly by others."[57] William of Newburgh intersperses the whole tale of the Damascus crusade among other local events that he finds much more interesting. His only comment is to sniff, "They then returned ingloriously, having accomplished nothing of note."[58]

The assembled armies brought the piece of the True Cross that was in the care of the canons of the Holy Sepulchre and was guarded by the Templars. This was supposed to have guaranteed victory. But the Latins hadn't counted on the citizens of Damascus having their own holy objects to call upon for protection. Damascus had many religious connotations and traditions. It was believed that Cain and Abel had lived there.[59] In the Qur'an there is a passage that is interpreted to mean that the infant Jesus and Mary were given shelter in Damascus on their flight into Egypt.[60] Members of the family of the Prophet were buried in Damascus. In the eyes of the citizens, they also lived in a city of God.

As the Franks were approaching, the frightened Muslims of Damascus put their faith in a sacred relic, a copy of the Qur'an that had belonged to the first caliph, Uthman, and was stained with his blood. Now it was brought out into the courtyard of the Great Mosque. The people gathered around it, wailing and praying for a miracle to save them.[61]

The siege itself has been described and discussed by many authors. It was a muddle of bad decisions, exacerbated, according to one Arab writer, by the Franks, who had camped in the orchards, eating so much of the ripe fruit that many of them came down with dysentery.[62] Ibn al-Qalanisi was inside the city and as afraid as anyone by this unified force. After the first day of fighting, "all the people [were] discouraged and straitened in spirit through fear because of the horror they had just witnessed."[63]

Messages had been sent by carrier pigeon, begging Nur ad-Din and others to come and drive off the attackers. In the meantime, the townsmen formed their own militia, sneaking out and harassing small parties of the enemy.[64]

Eventually, word came that a coalition of Muslims under Nur ad-Din was on its way. In the face of a unified foe, the Europeans decided that it was time to go home. Emperor Conrad died shortly after his return to Germany. Most of the others slunk back to Europe as quietly as possible.

Louis wasn't as eager as his companions to return. He lingered in the Holy Land through the autumn, sightseeing. Eleanor hadn't thawed in her feelings toward him, apparently, and he was equally unhappy with her.

It's a shame that there is no record of encounters between Eleanor and Melisende. But Eleanor must have noticed that both Melisende and

The Great Mosque of Damascus. Photograph courtesy of Denys Pringle.

Constance were careful to remind people that they were rulers by inheritance. Eleanor was queen of France by marriage, but, as duchess of Aquitaine, her territory stretched across western France and brought in much more income than the small area controlled by Louis.[65] It is intriguing to note that, when Eleanor's second husband, Henry, became king of England, she was crowned alongside him, contrary to custom.[66] Might she have been told of Melisende's two coronations, which emphasized her as joint ruler?

Louis's letters home to Abbot Suger were mostly to ask for money. Now the abbot, who had been a childhood friend of Louis's father and had known the king all his life, wrote back sounding very much like a parent at the end of his patience. With much flowery phrasing and deference, the message still comes down to, "Come home. You've sulked long enough. Ralph and I have paid your debts. Please leave the Holy Land by Easter."[67] Louis must also have written Suger about his problems with Eleanor, for the abbot closed his letter with, "Whatever the anger in your soul for your wife, keep it to yourself until you return home."[68]

Suger managed to patch the marriage together for a short time, with some help from Pope Eugenius. When the couple stayed at the papal court, Eugenius made them sleep in the same bed and told them he expected some marital activity.[69] The next year Eleanor had a second daughter, Alice. But ultimately even the pope couldn't keep the marriage together, and after Suger died, in 1151, the king and queen divorced. Eleanor immediately married Henry Plantagenet, Fulk's grandson, making Baldwin III the uncle of the next king of England. This may have been commented on in Jerusalem, but for the most part inhabitants of the Holy Land had more important matters to concern them.

SEVENTEEN

MELISENDE'S FINAL CONFLICT

JERUSALEM, ASCALON, ACRE, AND BETHANY, 1150–1161

THE FAILURE OF THE SECOND CRUSADE WAS DEMOR-
alizing for everyone involved. In its wake the Europeans searched for someone on whom to fix the blame. Some said that a traitor had been bribed to
encourage the armies to attack at the wrong place. Others said that Raymond
of Antioch, angry that Louis hadn't agreed to his plans, had used his influence to cause the disaster.[1] Bernard of Clairvaux was castigated for preaching
the crusade; his reputation never recovered completely.[2] As the news of the
disaster spread west, the rumors grew. Many believed that it was the sinful behavior of the participants that caused their downfall. Conrad blamed
the Jerusalemites. Gerhoh of Reichersberg was certain that all had been led
astray by the Devil.[3] None of these allegations were backed up with facts.

It didn't help that a much less prestigious Christian army had invaded
the Spanish peninsula and taken the city of Lisbon from the Moors. Their
feat was celebrated in the West as the Reconquista of Spain continued. This
made the contrast to the failure in the East all the more striking.

Before everyone left the Holy Land for Europe, Baldwin III made an attempt to convince the Crusaders to try again. This time they would attack Ascalon he insisted. He knew it would work. But no one was willing to make the attempt. The young king did not have the military prestige of his father and grandfather.

Although Melisende was at the council at Acre, we don't know if she agreed with the decision to attack Damascus. Her father had tried more than once to take it and settled for tribute and truce. Of all the unconquered Muslim cities, it was the one that had always been most willing to compromise and arrange treaties with the Latins. But it was also a tempting prize. Whether she was for or against the attack, she was never accused of being part of any plot to thwart the crusaders.

The Muslims were cheered by the fact that the rulers of Europe were unable to defeat them, but this didn't change the political dynamics of the region as much as some may have thought. The main result of the Second Crusade was that Nur ad-Din gained more influence in the region and, eventually, he was able to absorb Damascus into his lands.

The real disaster was the reaction of the faithful in Europe. The story of the failures and infighting among the leaders of the crusade disgusted many who might have donated to the cause or come to fight. Writing thirty years later, William of Tyre notes that fewer pilgrims of any sort came to Jerusalem even in his time, and "those who do come fear lest they be caught in the same toils [as the armies of Louis and Conrad] and hence make as short a stay as possible."[4]

In terms of manpower and funds for arms, the Latin States had always been dependent on frequent infusions from the West. Despite this uncertain support, the Franks continued to attempt to expand their power. But the attack on Damascus had triggered something that had been growing by fits and starts among the Muslims for several years. The opposing Sunni and Shi'ite sects and feuding families began to form serious non-aggression pacts and, even more, promises of mutual aid. So when, in June 1149, Raymond of Antioch set out to lay siege to the Aleppan fortress of Neva, Nur ad-Din wrote Damascus for help. The emir, Anar, was busy arranging for grain from the area to be brought for storage in Damascus, but he sent a battle-hardened lieutenant and army at once.[5] It seems to have been enough to keep the emir of Aleppo content.

Raymond of Antioch may have made too many enemies among his own people, or, as William suggests, "he was a man of undaunted and impetuous courage who allowed himself to be ruled by the advice of no one in matters of this kind."[6] He didn't bring enough soldiers to accomplish his mission and didn't bother asking any of the other lords for help. Raymond and his outnumbered army met Nur ad-Din and the armies of Aleppo and Damascus on June 29, 1149. The Antiochenes were routed. Raymond was killed and his head and right arm sent to Baghdad as trophies.[7] Antioch was once more left with a young woman and minor child in authority.

Raymond may have had character flaws, but his military reputation was impressive. Far away in England, William of Newburgh had heard of his valor and had a fond memory of hearing tales of his exploits from a monk who had once been in Raymond's service.[8]

Unlike her mother, Constance was the reigning princess. She was barely into her twenties and had already produced four children, two girls and two boys. After Raymond's defeat, Nur ad-Din advanced to Antioch, camping outside the gates in the hope of starving them out. Constance had few defenders of the city since most of the forces of Antioch had gone with Raymond. It's not certain how many soldiers returned, but not enough. She sent messengers to her aunt and cousin in Jerusalem asking for help. In the meantime, she organized the people to keep the enemy from breaking into the city.

Meanwhile Nur ad-Din scoured the area around Antioch and went as far as the sea, which he had never seen before.[9] He raided monasteries and fortresses, gathering booty to pay his army and provisions to keep them during a siege of Antioch.

Constance and the Latin Patriarch Aimery, as well as most of the townspeople, prepared to defend the city, although they also sent offers of treasure to bribe Nur ad-Din to retreat to Aleppo and leave them in peace.[10] Constance knew well what measures to take to save her city.

When he received word of Raymond's death, King Baldwin III was called upon to go up to Antioch as his father and grandfather had done, to sort things out. But the young king wasn't made of the same stuff. He did what he could, gathering what men he had available, and headed up to Antioch. In an effort to encourage the people of the city to take heart, Baldwin laid siege to the nearby Muslim fortress of Harim, hoping to draw Nur ad-Din from Antioch. But, "after spending several days there without success, he gave up and returned to Antioch."[11] Nur ad-Din eventually lifted the siege once he felt that he had depleted their supplies and will power, satisfied that he had crippled his nearest enemy. Antioch would not pose a threat to Aleppo for years.

It's not clear if Baldwin assumed any formal authority in Antioch. William says that he "remained at Antioch until affairs were reduced to order as far as time and place permitted."[12] Constance, with the help of the citizens of Antioch, then took over governing the principality, but they were still very short of manpower.

Another casualty of Raymond's death was Jocelyn II, former count of Edessa. The prince of Antioch would have been pleased that his old nemesis suffered as a result of his downfall. Upon learning of Raymond's defeat, the sultan of Iconium, north of Edessa, decided to take advantage of the confusion and attack Jocelyn's home of Tel Bashir, which he still held. In response to Jocelyn's call for help, Baldwin, busy at Antioch, sent his constable, Humphrey of Toron, to assess the military needs there.

This action shows the first major crack in the joint rule of Melisende and her son. Manasses of Hierges was still Melisende's constable in Jerusalem, but it appears that Baldwin was spending more time in Acre, setting up a rival court, which he took with him to Antioch. Now nearly twenty, the young king was tired of ruling only with his mother's consent. But the defeat at Damascus and the young king's failure in subsequent endeavors had not allowed him to gain the support he needed to take over on his own.

Since not enough help was forthcoming, Jocelyn managed to pay off the sultan with suits of armor and the return of prisoners taken in one raid or another. Afterward, the count went to Antioch to thank Baldwin personally for sending Humphrey and perhaps to see if his experience was needed in protecting the principality. Baldwin and Constance turned down his offer.

On his way home, Jocelyn was captured by Nur ad-Din's men. Ibn al-Athir says that he was out hunting and a local Turkomen took him prisoner, knowing that Nur ad-Din would pay a high price for him.[13] Michael the Syrian says that God caused a tree to grow where there had never been one before so that Jocelyn fell over the roots and was captured for his many sins.[14] William, who disliked Jocelyn more than either of the others did, tells us that he was taken when he "turned aside to relieve the needs of nature."[15]

Taken to Aleppo in chains, Jocelyn eventually died in prison. His wife, Beatrice, was left to hold Tel Bashir as best she could, "far beyond the strength of a woman, she busied herself in strengthening the fortresses of the land and supplying them with arms, men and food."[16] Eventually, she would be forced to sell her estates to the Greeks in return for a pension to support herself and her children.

William laments the fact that the two remaining Latin States in the north were now under the control of women, "in punishment for our sins."[17]

Edessa was lost but in Antioch the archbishop, Aimery, took charge of the military, using his own money to pay mercenaries and to feed the regular guards until Nur ad-Din decamped. Constance assumed the civil power and governed with no known complaint from the Antiochenes.

Once things were less chaotic, the threat from Nur ad-Din over and daily life back to normal, the next important task was to find a new husband for Constance. Baldwin III and his counselors felt that it was essential to select someone who could defend the territory as well as remain loyal to the king, unlike too many of the other men who had controlled the principality. The emperor Manuel also felt he had a stake in whom the next prince would be. Since Raymond had been forced to submit to Manuel's suzerainty to avoid invasion, Antioch was technically a vassal state of the Byzantine Empire.

They forgot that Constance was no longer a child and had ideas of her own.

The Assisses of Jerusalem, laws compiled in the thirteenth century but based on early customs, have a section that is unique. There is no parallel in Western Europe, Byzantium, or the Muslim world. I believe that it grew from the abundance of women in the Latin States who were in charge by default. It also may have had something to do with the number of them who refused to be treated as marriage pawns. This law states that an heiress must be offered three choices of a husband by the king. If none appeal to her, then the king must find three more men. If she refuses them all, she is allowed to choose her own husband.[18]

That is just what Constance did. The king chose three men that he knew would be loyal to him: Ives de Nesle, Walter of Falkenberg, and Ralph de Merle.[19] She turned them all down. The Emperor Manuel sent a certain John Roger to Antioch to marry Constance. She took one look at him and announced that he was too old. Poor John Roger returned to Constantinople and entered a monastery.[20]

"The princess dreaded the yoke of marriage and preferred a free and in-dependent life,"[21] William of Tyre said with scorn. He believed that she was shirking her responsibilities, but I certainly don't blame her. She had already been cast upon the altar of duty once. Like her mother and aunt, Constance may have been confident in her own ability to make decisions. No outside lord could understand her principality as well as she. Her first charter, made at Latakia, undid a gift her mother had unjustly made to Guarner of Burgo of land that belonged to Ralph Boer. Unfortunately, Guarner's children had already sold the land to the Hospitallers. Constance, "who had the jurisdic-tion of this land," decided how the case should be settled and "confirmed it with the seal of the principate."[22]

That doesn't sound as if Constance was living a "free and independent life." It sounds as if she was attending to her responsibilities as princess of Antioch.

Nevertheless, her cousin Baldwin and many others felt that she needed a man. The king called a council that met in Tripoli in 1150. Melisende at-tended, although by then there was an open break between her and her elder son. They had set up separate chanceries and were each issuing their own charters.

Aimery, Patriarch of Antioch, came to the council along with many other church officials. How he felt about Constance remaining single isn't known, but a new prince would reduce the current power that the Patriarch was wielding. The assembly had many pressing matters to discuss, including Baldwin's desire to invade the territory of the Fatimids and capture Ascalon. But the main goal of the meeting was to force Constance to come to a marriage decision. Jerusalem couldn't concentrate on southern expansion if the northern border state of Antioch had no able military leader.

Constance held firm. "Neither the king, nor the . . . queen nor the countess of Tripoli, her two aunts, was able to induce her to yield and thus provide for herself and her land."[23] Brava Constance!

It's possible that neither Melisende nor Hodierna tried very hard to make their niece marry against her will. Neither of them had found much joy in marriage, Hodierna was at that time at the point of leaving her husband, Raymond of Tripoli.

The council broke up, chagrined at the young princess and at a loss as to what to do next. Constance went back to Antioch. If she remarried, the choice would be hers. In 1153, she married a charming newcomer who had fought with Baldwin III. His name was Reynaud de Chatillon. He seems to have been disliked by most of the men he knew but women adored him.

After the council, Hodierna refused to stay any longer in Tripoli with her husband. No one seems to know what had happened between the couple. I've found no account that says what Raymond might have done. Hodierna would have known from the women around her that a husband's adultery was not cause for a wife to leave. My guess is that it might have something to do with the ferocity that Raymond showed after his father, Pons, died. He may have had a temper that was let loose on his wife and children as well as Syrian villagers. But that's only a guess. Melisende seems to have reconciled the pair somewhat, but it was decided that Hodierna would benefit from an extended time away from her husband. Raymond apparently made no effort to keep his wife in Tripoli.

Melisende offered to let Hodierna come live with her in Jerusalem. The count either rode with them for a while and turned back home or was out on another task. The two women were still on the road when a messenger raced after them with the news that Count Raymond of Tripoli had been murdered by a party of Assassins at the Tripoli city gates as he was returning with two friends, who died with him. This unexpected tragedy brought about a torrent of xenophobia in Tripoli, in which mobs of Franks "without discrimination put to the sword all those who were found to differ in language or dress from the Latins."[24]

Someone may have paid the Assassins to kill Raymond, although they had never been known to target Christians. Or he may have done something to antagonize them. It's also possible that he was assassinated by people dressed as Batini or using their methods. They could have been supporters of Bernard, the illegitimate son of the count of Toulouse, Alphonse-Jordan, who also claimed the lordship of Tripoli. Bernard had recently died under suspicious circumstances and it has been hinted that Raymond had something to do with his demise.[25]

No one seems to have suggested that Hodierna sent men to murder her husband.[26] She does not seem to have had the force of will of her older sisters, but it is interesting that the attack came just at the point when she had decided on a separation.

On receiving the news, Hodierna immediately returned to Tripoli with her children, Raymond and Melisende. Raymond was about twelve, close to the age Baldwin III had been when Fulk died. King Baldwin ordered that all the nobles of the land swear allegiance to Hodierna and her children. She assumed the regency of Tripoli. Since she wasn't the heiress, no one seems to have demanded that she remarry for the defense of the county. Perhaps Guillaume Duc, viscount of Tripoli, assumed that responsibility.[27]

It was also possible that Raymond had been involved in a dispute with another faction in Tripoli. The composition of the county was much different from Jerusalem or Antioch. The "Franks" were mainly Provençals, and spoke a form of French very different from that of the northerners. There was a large Italian contingent, many from Genoa, including the lords of the town of Gibelet, who gave military assistance when required but were mainly engaged in trade.[28] The main Jewish community of the county was also in Gibelet.

Tripoli produced a number of luxury goods. It was famous for the silk made there along with a dye made from rose madder, grown in the region. Sugar cane was grown and processed and soap and oil made from olives. The wines from the grapes of the surrounding countryside were considered excellent. Citizens also wove cotton and carpets (something not common in the West) and made high-end glass and ceramics.[29] In this manufacture, Jews, Syrian Christians, and even a few Muslims became rich. Tripoli was probably the most cosmopolitan of the Latin States.

In the mountains of the county lived the Muslim Druze and some Ismali'ites, who may have been part of the Assassins. The largest Christian group was the Maronites, whose dogma had formed in the seventh and eighth centuries. They followed the Eastern rite of the church but, as early as 1182, reunited with Rome and acknowledged the pope as head of their faith.[30] Most of the Christians of Lebanon today still follow Maronite practices.

Hodierna's regency was intended to preserve the count's share of the wealth for her children. Her understanding of the diverse population helped her to govern. It was likely through her influence that Raymond III and Melisende became fluent in Arabic.

Baldwin was now titular regent of Antioch and Tripoli, as well as king of Jerusalem. At the moment, Jerusalem, Antioch, Tripoli, and what was left of Edessa were being governed by women. Baldwin must have felt outnumbered by his female relatives.

Now a grown man, Baldwin had been chafing for a while at the reins his mother kept him under. But Melisende wasn't interested in abdicating in his favor. If she had been regent, instead of queen by inheritance, there would have been no question of her stepping down. Baldwin would have ruled alone from the age of about fifteen. The fact that it took another two years for him to attempt to take sole power may say something about his abilities and Melisende's. His military career had been a series of failures. He had not yet married. But at the time that he and Melisende were at the council in Tripoli, he was already planning a palace coup.

Melisende had fought many battles in her life. She had successfully resisted the attempts of her husband to shut her out of the government. She had supervised the reconstruction of Jerusalem and several fortresses between the city and Muslim territory. For five years past her son's coming of age, she had ruled the kingdom. By all contemporary accounts, she was a competent ruler.

What she had no way to fight was the blackening of her reputation by later historians. In the twentieth century alone, she has been called a "power-hungry Queen Dowager"[31] and "an authoritarian, even vindictive, woman."[32] Eminent Crusade historian Hans Eberhard Mayer, in the only serious monograph written on Melisende's rule, persists in calling her the "Queen Mother." While he admits that Baldwin's military career had been a series of defeats, he still sees Melisende as woman who plotted to keep her son from power.[33]

I have read the same charters and chronicles as other historians and come to a different conclusion. I believe that Melisende and a large part of the nobility of the kingdom did not think that Baldwin was ready to be the sole ruler. As she reminded those who wanted her to abdicate, Melisende was not regent for her son. The fact that she had been crowned jointly with him showed that. She was not a dowager, nor a queen mother. Those titles, had they been in existence then, were for queens who were the widows of reigning lords. Alice and Hodierna were regents; Melisende and Constance were heirs. In Steven Runciman's interpretation of the events, he points out that, "legal opinion seems to have been that right, if not expediency, was on her side."[34]

In other words, as Baldwin's opposition to his mother grew, most of the nobility moved to his side because he was male, but it was acknowledged that Melisende did have the right to rule with him or on her own.

Aware of the growing dissension, Baldwin arranged for a second double coronation to be held on Easter Sunday, 1150, at the Church of the Holy Sepulchre. However, unbeknownst to Melisende, he "deferred the time for the ceremony in order that his mother should not be crowned with him. Then, unexpectedly, on the following day, without summoning his mother, he appeared in public, crowned with the laurel."[35]

The secrecy of this act indicates to me either that he didn't want Melisende to make a scene, which would accord with the negative opinions of her, or that he knew that her supporters would protest and perhaps stop the coronation altogether.

After much negotiating, Baldwin and Melisende agreed to split the kingdom. He would have Tyre and Acre and she Jerusalem and Nablus, a town that, I believe, had been Morfia's dower land. Melisende retired for the time being to Nablus.

This division didn't last for long. Considering the pressure being exerted upon the Latins by Nur ad-Din, it wasn't feasible to have two competing governments.

Melisende had many supporters. Not least among them was her younger son, Amalric. At the moment he was the count of Jaffa, the old county of Hugh of Le Puiset. There is little mention of Amalric up to this point. He is mentioned in a few of his mother's charters but I have none that he issued alone.

William, who was writing for Amalric, puts the blame for Baldwin's actions on friends of his who had conceived a hatred not of Melisende, but of her constable, Manasses. He insists that they were responsible for what happened next. It wasn't enough, he says, to make her divide the kingdom, "Not even in this was the persecution against the queen stilled. On the contrary, the still-smoldering fire was rekindled on trivial pretexts and blazed forth into a conflagration far more dangerous than before."[36] At the instigation of his friends, Baldwin demanded that Melisende give up all her land to him.

Baldwin and his followers, many from the area around Tyre, such as the Ibelin family, set out to besiege Melisende in Jerusalem. She and her supporters, including Aimery, Philip of Nablus, and the Templar Andrew of Montbard, took refuge in the Tower of David. Baldwin fired at her with catapults but didn't make a dent in the fortifications. This bombardment lasted a few days when the Patriarch of Jerusalem, along with other neutral parties, intervened.

They managed to convince Melisende to surrender Jerusalem to her son and retire to Nablus. Baldwin swore that he would not bother her there in any way. Baldwin III at last was sole ruler of Jerusalem.

From France, Abbot Bernard wrote Melisende that he had heard rumors of her troubles. There must have been negative gossip about her determination to keep power. In the light of the recent civil war in England over the right of Henry I's daughter, Matilda, to the throne, people may have had a jaundiced view of female rule. Bernard tells her that he might have believed the stories if not for a letter from his uncle, Andrew of Montbard, explaining the situation and praising her behavior. The abbot gives her what encouragement he can.[37]

Melisende did not issue any more charters without the assent of Baldwin, much as Fulk had done after his abortive attempt to assert his power. But the mother and son seem to have had some sort of reconciliation. She was his mother, after all. Amalric and Phillip of Nablus also re-entered Baldwin's circle. After the death of his wife, Phillip joined the Templars and eventually became grand master. Always loyal to the family, Phillip eventually retired from the Templars at Amalric's request and died on a mission to Constantinople in the king's service.

Historians have seen Melisende's actions through a lens of centuries of primogeniture. If she had been male, then Baldwin would have been seen as an upstart and a traitor. As it was, it is clear that there were many who were satisfied with her governance and not comfortable with allowing Baldwin complete control. None of the chroniclers living at that time in the Near East have said that she was power hungry. In a time and place where nearly every ruler spent most of his time trying to expand his territory, she was fairly consistent. If her son's forays into enemy territory had been successful, she might have decided on graceful retirement. Or she might have arranged, like Emperor Alexis and his mother, that he handle military matters and she run the home front.

But one thing still makes me wonder: why wasn't Baldwin married as a teenager? Even if he had been homosexual, he could have done his duty and produced heirs, as other homosexual kings had done. I haven't found any reference to ambassadors making the rounds looking for acceptable brides. Was Melisende so determined to hold onto her son that she didn't want to compete with a wife? I doubt it. Baldwin didn't marry until 1158, long after Melisende had lost control over his actions. It took the urging of the Haut Court, made up of the nobility of the realm, before he agreed to take a wife.

His bride was Theodora, a cousin of Emperor Manuel. She was about thirteen at the time of the marriage and very probably did not speak French or Arabic. The couple had no children in the five years of their marriage. William of Tyre doesn't even mention that Baldwin III had a wife. What made Baldwin wait so long to marry? Was something wrong with him that no one would talk about? Unless new sources are uncovered, I'm doomed to ignorance.

There is no indication that Melisende was relegated to a backwater, nor that her followers were punished. By 1152, both Philip of Nablus and Amalric are witnessing Baldwin's charters.[38] That same year Melisende adjudicated between citizens and canons of Nablus, "with the consent of her sons, King Baldwin and Amalric, Count of Jaffa."[39] By 1154, she even appears again in Baldwin's charters, giving her consent to one of his donations.[40]

In 1153, Baldwin finally succeeded in capturing that long-desired prize of Ascalon. He must have been elated to have achieved a goal that all the previous kings of Jerusalem had attempted and failed. This made the threat of attack from Egypt negligible and sealed Baldwin's status. Nur ad-Din did not come to the aid of Ascalon as his father had; he was busy taking control of Damascus. While Baldwin was away, Melisende returned to Jerusalem as regent, or perhaps she saw it as taking up her rightful duties once more. But she went back to Nablus after Baldwin's triumphal return.

Melisende continued to keep an eye on the kingdom from Nablus. She remained a patron of artists and religious institutions. Her last charter is from 1160, in which she gives property to the monastery at Josaphat. But sometime later that year, she had a stroke that left her helpless. Yvette, now abbess, brought her to the convent of Bethany that Melisende had founded for her. By that time, Fulk's daughter, Sybille, had come to Jerusalem and also entered the convent. They, along with Hodierna, "watched over her with unremitting care," until her death in 1161.[41] She was buried at the abbey of Josephat, near the tomb of her mother.

Her elder son Baldwin survived her by only a year. Her second son, Amalric, became king.

Melisende has been considered as someone who put her own ambition above the good of her kingdom and her son. I disagree. Baldwin III was a capable king, eventually, but he needed to grow into the role. If he had been competent at the beginning, then she might have been willing to step aside for him. But why should she have done so? Melisende was queen of Jerusalem and she was good at her job. She, her sister Alice, and too many other women who governed have been slandered and ignored, not by the people of their own time, but by later historians, up to the present day.

William's epitaph sums up the opinion of her contemporaries. "For thirty years and more, during the lifetime of her husband, as well as afterwards, in the reign of her son, Melisende had governed the kingdom with strength surpassing that of most women. Her rule had been wise and judicious."[42]

William was mistaken only in that Melisende's strength was not uncommon. Her mother and sisters demonstrate such strength, as did many others, including the woman who walked alone into an enemy camp to retrieve her stolen child. Melisende's legacy was in setting an example for another generation. She only had three grandchildren, two girls and a boy. Her grandson was the tragic leper king, Baldwin IV. Amalric's two daughters, Sybille and Isabella, each became queen. Alice's daughter, Constance, ruled Antioch until well after her son Bohemond had come of age. Eventually he had to prove he could rule before she would retire to Latakia.

The damage done by the failed Second Crusade led to the rise of the emir Saladin and the fall of the city of Jerusalem to him twenty years after Melisende's death. But the coastal cities remained in the hands of the Franks. The last foothold, Acre, survived until 1291.

Melisende's tomb at the Abbey of Josephat near Jerusalem. Photograph courtesy of Denys Pringle.

The histories of the Latin States have too often ignored the contribution made by women, and also the effects of the constant warfare on the diverse population of the region. A new look at the variety of peoples and the interactions among them, male and female, will not only revise our image of the Crusades but bring about a better understanding of conflicts in the Near East today.

NOTES

INTRODUCTION

1. Hans Eberhard Mayer, "Studies in the History of Queen Melisende of Jerusalem." *Dumbarton Oaks Papers* 26 (1972): 93, 95–182.

ONE: ARRANGING THE CHESSBOARD

1. Her date of birth isn't certain. Most people didn't record birth years, especially for girls.
2. Anna Komnene, *The Alexiad,* trans. E. R. A. Sewter (1969; reprint, London: Penguin Classics, 2002), 275.
3. Christopher Tyerman, *Fighting for Christendom: Holy War and the Crusades* (Oxford: Oxford University Press, 2004), 186.
4. There are many forms of Shi'ite Islam, but the fundamental battle between them and the Sunni continues today.
5. Nílgün Dalkesen, *Gender Roles and Women's Status in Central Asia and Anatolia Between the Thirteenth and Sixteen Centuries,* Unpublished dissertation (Middle East Technical University, 2007), 113.
6. Claude Cahen, "The Turkish Invasion," *A history of the Crusades,* Vol. I., ed. John Baldwin (University of Wisconsin, 1969), 140.
7. Pierre Aubé, *Les Empires Normands d'Orient* (Paris: Perin, 1991), 45–87.
8. Komnene, *The Alexiad,* 31.
9. Ibid., 41.
10. Ralph Bailey Yewdale, *Bohemond I, Prince of Antioch* (Amsterdam: Hakkert, 1970), 5, quoting Orderic Vitalis, book IV.
11. Komnene, *The Alexiad,* 295.
12. One suspects that Anna was more fascinated than she would admit with Viking men who looked like the hunks on the covers of romance novels.
13. Jean-Luc Déjean, *Les Comtes de Toulouse 1050–1250* (Paris: Fayard, 1979), 29–30.
14. Ibid., 78.

TWO: CHILD OF THE FIRST CHRISTIAN CITY

1. Gilo of Paris, *Historia Vie Hierosolimitane,* ed. and trans. C. W. Grocock and J. E. Siberry (Oxford: Oxford University Press, 1997), 132–133. I have revised the translation a bit.
2. Steven Runciman, "Some Remarks on the Image of Edessa," *Cambridge Historical Journal* 3, no. 3 (1931): 240.
3. L. W. Barnard, "The Origins and Emergence of the Church in Edessa during the First Two Centuries A.D.," *Vigiliae Christianae* 22, no. 3 (September 1968): 162.
4. Ibn al-Athir, *The Chronicle of Ibn al-Athir for the Crusading Period, Part 1,* trans. D. S. Richards (Aldershot, UK: Ashgate, 2006), 47.

5. Anna Komnene, *The Alexiad,* trans. E. R. A. Sewter (reprint; London: Penguin, 2009), 169–170.

6. Matthew of Edessa, *Armenia and the Crusades, Tenth to the Twelfth Centuries: The Chronicle of Matthew of Edessa,* trans. A. Dotourian (Latham, MS: University Press of America, 1993), 193.

7. Benjamin Z. Kedar, "Multidirectional Conversion in the Frankish Levant," in *Varieties of Religious Conversion in the Middle Ages,* ed. J. Muldoon (Gainsville, FL: University of Florida Press, 1997), 190–199.

8. Michael the Syrian, *Chronique de Michel le Syrien, Patriarche Jacobite d'Antioche (1166–1199),* vol. 3, ed. and trans. J.-B Chabot (Paris: 1905), 186. This sounds like a slander made by an enemy, but you never know.

9. Michael the Syrian, *Chronique de Michel le Syrien,* 189.

10. Ibid., 187.

11. Some say that Toro's wife did the same, but I suspect that's scholarly prurience. I don't find it in any primary source.

12. Matthew of Edessa, *Armenia and the Crusades,* 169.

13. Christopher MacEvitt, *The Crusades and the Christian Worlds of the East: Rough Tolerance* (Philadelphia: University of Pennsylvania Press, 2008), 68.

14. William of Tyre, *A History of Deeds Done Beyond the Seas,* trans. Babcock and Krey (New York: Octagon Books, 1976), 1:416.

15. Matthew of Edessa, *Armenia and the Crusades,* 177; William of Tyre, *A History of Deeds Done Beyond the Seas,* 411.

16. Ralph Bailey Yewdale, *Bohemond I, Prince of Antioch* (Amsterdam, Hakkert, 1970), 170; Claude Cahen, *Pre-Ottoman Turkey,* trans. J. Jones-Williams (New York: Taplinger Publishing 1968), 86.

17. Yewdale, 109, quoting Orderic Vitalis.

18. Ibid., 132.

19. Michael the Syrian, *Chronique de Michel le Syrien,* 188.

20. William of Tyre, *A History of Deeds Done Beyond the Seas,* 1:482.

21. Ibid.

22. The only Qatya I've been able to find is in the Sinai, miles away from northern Syria.

23. Michael the Syrian, *Chronique de Michel le Syrien,* 189.

24. Matthew of Edessa, *Armenia and the Crusades,* 192.

25. Ibid.

26. William of Tyre, *A History of Deeds Done Beyond the Seas;* Matthew of Edessa, *Armenia and the Crusades,* 93. The amount given for the ransom varies from thirty to seventy thousand bezants, depending on the source, but it was more than Baldwin had on hand.

27. Richard of Salerno was a Norman of Italy who had been imprisoned with Bohemond earlier. E. G. Rey, *Les Familles d'outre-mer Première Série* (Paris: 1869), 181.

28. Albert of Aachen, *Historia Ierosolimtana,* ed. and trans. S. B. Edgington (Oxford: Oxford University Press, 2007), 9: 47, 720–3.

29. Matthew of Edessa, *Armenia and the Crusades,* 197.

30. Ibid.

31. Ibid., 19. Matthew was convinced that he was living in the End Times so he saw everything as an omen of doom. However, Michael the Syrian also commented on the comet. Michael the Syrian, *Chronique de Michel le Syrien,* 193.

32. Ibid. This is also reported by Ibn al-Qalanisi, *The Damascus Chronicle of the Crusades,* ed. and trans. H. A. R. Gibb (Mineola, NY: Dover, 2002), 69.

33. Albert of Achen, *Historia Ierosolimtana,* 9:46.

34. Ibn al-Qalanisi, *The Damascus Chronicle of the Crusades,* 55.

35. Jonathan Riley-Smith, *The First Crusaders* (Cambridge: Cambridge University Press, 1997), 169–188.

THREE: WORLDS COLLIDING

1. Matthew of Edessa, *Armenia and the Crusades,* trans. A. Dosturian (Latham, Maryland: University Press of America, 1993), 162.

2. Ibn al-Qalanisi, *The Damascus Chronicle of the Crusades,* trans. and ed. by H. A. R. Gibb (reprint, Mineola, New York: Dover, 2002), 50–51.

3. Ibn al-Athir, *The Chronicle of Ibn al-Athir for the Crusading Period, Parts 1 & 2,* trans. by D. S. Richards (Aldershot: Ashgate, 2005), 80.

4. Ibid.

5. Ibid., 112.

6. Ibn al-Qalanisi, *The Damascus Chronicle of the Crusades,* 79.

7. Ibn al-Athir, *The Chronicle of Ibn al-Athir,* 136.

8. Ibid. One difference between the Turks and the Arabs was the amount of power and autonomy the Turkish women had. This will be discussed later.

9. Ibn al-Athir, *The Chronicle of Ibn al-Athir,* 137. He says it was the plasterers, specifically. Perhaps Jawali's wife had been redecorating and not paid them.

10. Ibid., 138.

11. Fulcher of Chartres, *A History of the Expedition to Jerusalem, 1095–1127,* trans. by Frances Rila Ryan (New York: Norton, 1969), 410.

12. Ibid.

13. Matthew of Edessa, *Armenia and the Crusades,* 175. Matthew seems to imply here that no Armenian would do such a thing.

14. Anonymous, *Gesta Francorum: The Deeds of the Franks and the Other Pilgrims to Jerusalem,* ed. and trans. Rosalind Hill (Oxford: Clarendon Press, 1962), 33.

15. Ibn al-Athir, *The Chronicle of Ibn al-Athir,* 139.

16. Matthew of Edessa, *Armenia and the Crusades,* 201.

17. Ibn al-Athir, *The Chronicle of Ibn al-Athir,* 141.

18. Matthew of Edessa, *Armenia and the Crusades,* 201; Albert of Achen, *Historia Ierosolimtana,* 10:38; Fulcher of Chartres, *A History of the Expedition to Jerusalem,* 197; Ibn al-Athir, *The Chronicle of Ibn al-Athir,* 141.

19. Michael the Syrian, *Chronique de Michel le Syrien,* 197.

20. Ibid.

21. Ibn al-Athir, *The Chronicle of Ibn al-Athir,* 142.

22. Matthew of Edessa, *Armenia and the Crusades,* 201–202.

23. Ibid.

24. Ibid.

25. D. S. Rice, "Medieval Harran," *Anatolian Studies* 2 (1952): 37.

26. Ibid.

27. Quoted in D. S. Rice, "Medieval Harran," 39.

28. Matthew of Edessa, *Armenia and the Crusades,* 201.

29. I figured this out by assuming that Baldwin had endured enforced celibacy during his imprisonment and that seeing his wife would be high on the list of "things to do when I'm free." And, like all men of his time, he needed a son so producing one immediately was important.

30. Ibn al-Qalanisi, *The Damascus Chronicle of the Crusades,* 100–101.

31. Robert Lawrence Nicholson, *Jocelyn I, Prince of Edessa* (Urbana: University of Illinois Press, 1954), 48.

32. Ibn al-Qalanisi, *The Damascus Chronicle of the Crusades,* 103.

33. Ibid.

34. Ibn al-Athir, *The Chronicle of Ibn al-Athir,* 274.

35. Ibn al-Qalanisi, *The Damascus Chronicle of the Crusades,* 102; Matthew of Edessa, *Armenia and the Crusades,* 204.

36. Matthew of Edessa, *Armenia and the Crusades,* 204.

37. Ibn al-Qalanisi, *The Damascus Chronicle of the Crusades.*

38. Nicholson, *Jocelyn I, Prince of Edessa,* 29.

39. Ibn al-Qalanisi, *The Damascus Chronicle of the Crusades,* 104. Ibn al-Qalanisi is the only one who mentions this, but it would certainly make sense that the starving people of Edessa would seek refuge elsewhere.

40. Matthew of Edessa, *Armenia and the Crusades,* 205.

41. Ibn al-Qalanisi, *The Damascus Chronicle of the Crusades,* 105; Matthew of Edessa, *Armenia and the Crusades,* 206; Fulcher of Chartres, 198.

42. Gilo of Paris, *Historia Vie Hierosolimitane,* 168–169 (Book VII).

43. Baha al-Din Ibn Shaddad, *The Rare and Excellent History of Saladin,* trans. D. S. Richards (Aldershot: Ashgate, 2002), 147–148.

44. Ibn al-Qalanisi, *The Damascus Chronicle of the Crusades,* 107; Fulcher of Chartres, *A History of the Expedition to Jerusalem, 1095–1127,* 199–200.

45. Fulcher of Chartres, *A History of the Expedition to Jerusalem, 1095–1127,* 200.

FOUR: THE FRONTIER COUNTY

1. Ibn al-Athir, *The Chronicle of Ibn al-Athir,* 145.

2. Ibid.

3. Ibid. I don't know if he was making a social comment when he juxtaposed these two events. The reader must draw her own conclusions.

4. Matthew of Edessa, *Armenia and the Crusades,* 210.

5. Ibid.

6. Matthew of Edessa, *Armenia and the Crusades,* 211.

7. Robert Lawrence Nicholson, *Jocelyn I, Prince of Edessa* (Urbana: University of Illinois Press, 1954), 48.

8. It's not certain when Hodierna was born, only that it was before 1118.

9. William of Tyre, *A History of Deeds Done Beyond the Seas,* chapter 22, quoted in Nicholson, *Jocelyn I, Prince of Edessa,* 46.

10. Ibn al-Qalanisi, *The Damascus Chronicle of the Crusades,* 133; Matthew of Edessa, *Armenia and the Crusade.*

11. *Die Urkunden der Lateinschen Könige von Jerusalem,* vol. 1, ed. and trans. Hans Eberhard Mayer (Hannover: Hahnsche, 2010); no. 3, 98195, charter number 64, 176. Jocelyn appears frequently as a witness after this time.

12. Baldwin was in Tel Bashir from 1113; Matthew of Edessa, *Armenia and the Crusades,* 212. I'm assuming his family was with him.

13. Ibid.

14. Ibid., 213.

15. Ibid.

16. Ibid.

17. Ibid.

18. Ibn al-Qalanisi, *The Damascus Chronicle of the Crusades,* 140.

19. Fulcher of Chartres, *A History of the Expedition to Jerusalem, 1095–1127,* 209.

20. Ibid.

21. Ibn al-Athir, *The Chronicle of Ibn al-Athir,* 163.

22. Ibid. Ibn al-Athir also reports the rumor.

23. Ibid., 163. He is the only one who mentions this so it may be something imagined, but it is interesting that al-Athir might think it to be true.

24. Ibid., 141.

25. Ibid., 142. A Christian chronicler would make the same claim of pre-battle repentance, for Roger of Antioch.

26. Ibid., 166.

27. Kemal ad-Din, "La Chronique d'Alep," *Recueil des Historiens des Croisades Orientalis, III* (Paris: 1884), 602.

28. Matthew of Edessa, *Armenia and the Crusades,* 216.

29. Ibid.

30. Walter the Chancellor, *The Antiochene Wars,* trans. Thomas S. Ashbridge and Susan B. Edgington (Aldershot: Ashgate, 1999), 81.

31. Walter the Chancellor, *The Antiochene Wars,* 81.

32. Matthew of Edessa, *Armenia and the Crusades,* 217.

33. Ibn al-Qalanisi, *The Damascus Chronicle of the Crusades,* 149.

34. Kemal ad-Din, "La Chronique d'Alep," 607; Ibn al-Athir, *The Chronicle of Ibn al-Athir,* 171.

35. D. S. Rice, "Medieval Harran: Studies on its Topography and Monuments," *Anatolian Studies* 2 (1952).

36. Michael the Syrian, *Chronique de Michel le Syrien,* 200; also noted in: Fulcher of Chartres, *A History of the Expedition to Jerusalem, 1095–1127,* 210; Matthew of Edessa, *Armenia and the Crusades,* 217.

37. Walter the Chancellor, *The Antiochene Wars,* 83. The aftershocks went on for five months. Having gone through the 1996 Northridge, CA, earthquake, I can say this is about right. They can really get on one's nerves.

38. Ibid.

39. Matthew of Edessa, *Armenia and the Crusades,* 217.

FIVE: OH, JERUSALEM!

1. Fulcher of Chartres, *A History of the Expedition to Jerusalem, 1095–1127,* trans. by Frances Rila Ryan (New York: Norton, 1969), 26.116.

2. Hugh of Poitiers, *The Vézelay Chronicle,* trans. John Scott and John O. Ward (Binghampton, NY: Center for Medieval and Early Renaissance Studies, 1992), 140.

3. Jonathan Sumption, *Pilgrimage: An Image of Mediaeval Religion* (New Jersey: Rowman and Littlefield, 1975), 199.

4. William of Tyre, *A History of Deeds Done Beyond the Seas,* 1:374.

5. Anonymous, *Gesta Francorum,* 91.

6. Gilo of Paris, *Historia Vie Hierosolimitane,* 246–247.

7. Anonymous, *Gesta Francorum,* 92.

8. Fulcher of Chartres, 26:122.

9. Ibid., 132.

10. Ibn Al-Athir, *The Chronicle of Ibn al-Athir,* 23; Al-Qalanisi says that the Franks went back on their word, Al-Qalanisi, *The Damascus Chronicle of the Crusades,* 47.

11. Shalom Goiten, "Tyre-Tripoli-'Acre: Geniza Documents from the Beginning of the Crusader Period," *The Jewish Quarterly Review* 66, no. 2 (October 1975): 76.

12. Fulcher of Chartres, 123; Gilo of Paris, *Historia Vie Hierosolimitane,* 249.

13. Fulcher of Chartres, 124. It sounds to me like the articles luring people to the California Gold Rush.

14. Ibid., 150. Fulcher states that there were no more than 300 knights in the whole kingdom and wonders why the Muslims didn't take advantage of this.

15. Adrian Boas, *Jerusalem in the Time of the Crusades* (Abingdon, England: Routledge 2001), 110.

16. S. D. Goiten, *A Mediterranean Society: The Jewish Communities of the World as Portrayed in the Cairo Geniza,* vol. 1 (Berkeley: University of California Press, 1967).

17. William of Tyre, *A History of Deeds Done Beyond the Seas,* 1:518.

18. Fulcher of Chartres, 221–222.

19. Ibid.

20. He brought his first wife on crusade with him but she died in Marash. His second wife, Arda, was Armenian. He repudiated her and forced her to enter the convent of St. Anne so that he could marry Adelaide of Sicily, who brought ships and money. The marriage failed spectacularly and Adelaide returned to Sicily, taking what was left of her dowry.

21. Usamah ibn-Munqidh, *An Arab-Syrian Warrior in the Period of the Crusades: Memoirs of Usamah ibn-Minqidh,* trans. Philip K. Hitti (New York: Columbia University Press, 1929), 93–94.

22. William of Tyre, *A History of Deeds Done Beyond the Seas,* 1:520.

23. Matthew of Edessa, *Armenia and the Crusades,* 221.

24. Ibid.

25. William of Tyre, *A History of Deeds Done Beyond the Seas,* 1:521.

26. Malcolm Barber, *The Crusader States* (New Haven: Yale University Press, 2012), 119, discusses this.

27. William of Tyre, *A History of Deeds Done Beyond the Seas,* 1:521–522.

28. Matthew of Edessa, *Armenia and the Crusades,* 221–222.

29. William of Tyre, *A History of Deeds Done Beyond the Seas,* 1:522. As I have pointed out, birth dates weren't generally recorded for men or women at this time. Many people didn't know exactly how old they were.

30. Ibid., 1:461. After the fact, it was said that Arda had been briefly captured by Muslims and her virtue was suspect. Even at the time, this sounded thin. Baldwin wanted a richer bride.

31. Ibid., 1:409.

32. Ibid., 1:507.

33. Eusebius, *The Church History,* chapter 43 (Grand Rapids: Kregel Academic & Professional, 2007), 334.

34. Ibid.

35. William of Tyre, *A History of Deeds Done Beyond the Seas,* 1:385.

36. *Anonymous Pilgrims I-VII (11th and 12th Centuries),* trans. Aubrey Stewart (London: Palestine Pilgrims' Text Society, 1894), 6:8–9. The Templars later obtained this bathtub and carried it in processions. They did not have the cup from the Last Supper, no matter what you made have read or seen in films.

37. Boas, *Jerusalem at the Time of the Crusaders,* 103.

38. Ibid.

39. *Anonymous Pilgrims I-VII,* 6:70.

40. This is the source of the image of the skull at the foot of the cross in many representations of the crucifixion.

41. Boas, *Jerusalem at the Time of the Crusaders,* 109. Built in 691 c.e. by the Caliph "Abd" al-Malik.

42. Fulcher of Chartres, 26:118.

43. Ibid.

44. Boas, *Jerusalem at the Time of the Crusaders,* 115.

45. Jonathan Sumption, *Pilgrimage: An Image of Mediaeval Religion* (New Jersey: Rowman and Littlefield, 1975), 199.

46. Helen Nicholson, *The Knights Hospitaller* (Woodbridge: Boydell Press, 2001), 3–4.

47. *Die Urkunden der Lateinschen Könige von Jerusalem,* vol. 1, ed. and trans. Hans Eberhard Mayer (Hanover: Hahnsche, 2010), no. 3, 98.

48. *The Rule, Statutes and Customs of the Hospitallers 1099–1310,* trans. E. J. King (London: Methuen, 1934), 1. King believes that Gerard came from Provence but gives no evidence for this.

49. Victor Azarya, *The Armenian Quarter of Jerusalem* (Berkeley: University of California, 1984), 58.

50. Ibid.

51. Boas, *Jerusalem at the Time of the Crusaders,* 126. Of course, the church of St. James of Compostela in Spain said they had the head, but it was well known that some relics—the Image of Edessa, for example—could replicate themselves.

52. *Anonymous Pilgrims I-VII,* 5:28.

53. Ibid., 29.

SIX: THE FIELD OF BLOOD

1. William of Tyre, *A History of Deeds Done Beyond the Seas,* 1:525.

2. Al-Athir, *The Chronicle of Ibn al-Athir,* 196.

3. Stefan Heidemann, "Financing the Tribute to the Kingdom of Jerusalem: An Urban Tax in Damascus," *Bulletin of the School of Oriental and African Studies,* University of London, Vol 70, No. 1 (2007) 117–142.

4. Al-Athir, *The Chronicle of Ibn al-Athir,* 196.

5. William of Tyre, *A History of Deeds Done Beyond the Seas,* 1:524.

6. Fulcher of Chartres, *A History of the Expedition to Jerusalem, 1095–1127.* Translated by Frances Rila Ryan. New York: Norton, 1969, 226. If this were the real reason, it seems very strange that they hadn't tried it before.

7. C. E. Bosworth and Sir Gerard Clausen, "Al- Xwarazmi on the Peoples of Central Asia," *The Turks in the Early Islamic World,* ed. by C. E. Bosworth (Aldershot: Ashgate, 2007), 168.

8. Usamah, *An Arab-Syrian Warrior in the Period of the Crusades: Memoirs of Usamah ibn-Minqidh,* trans. Philip K Hitti (New York: Columbia University Press, 1929), 93–94.

9. Carole Hillenbrand, *The Crusades, Islamic Perspectives* (reprint, Edinburgh: Edinburgh University Press, 2010), 80.

10. Matthew of Edessa, *Armenia and the Crusades,* 223.
11. *Qu'ran Sura (The Koran),* trans. J. M. Rodwell (London: Phoenix, 1969), 2:213–214.
12. Hillenbrand, *Islamic Perspectives,* 100.
13. Hillenbrand, "Jihad Poetry in the Age of Crusade," *Crusades—Medieval Worlds in Conflict,* ed. Thomas Madden et al. (Farnham, Surrey: Ashgate, 2010), 12.
14. Thomas Asbridge, *The Creation of the Principality of Antioch 1098–1130* (Woodbridge: Boydell, 2000), 41.
15. Kemal ad-din, "La Chronique d'Alep," 612.
16. Ibid., 613.
17. Ibn Al-Athir, *The Chronicle of Ibn al-Athir,* 21.
18. Ibid., 21.
19. Ibn Al-Athir, *The Chronicle of Ibn al-Athir,* 55–56; Sadakat Kadri, *Heaven on Earth: A Journey Through Shari'a Law from the Deserts of Ancient Arabia to the Streets of the Modern Muslim World* (New York: Farrar Strauss Giroux, 2012), 69.
20. Ibn al-Qalanisi, *The Damascus Chronicle of the Crusades,* 149.
21. Ibid., 150.
22. Asbridge, *The Creation of the Principality of Antioch 1098–1130,* 79.
23. Walter the Chancellor, *The Antiochene Wars,* 168.
24. Ibn al-Qalansi, *The Damascus Chronicle of the Crusades,* 158.
25. Fulcher of Chartres, 228. William of Tyre states that Jocelyn was at Edessa, but he is relying on both the memory of others and Fulcher's account, which doesn't mention Jocelyn.
26. Ibn al-Qalansi, *The Damascus Chronicle of the Crusades,* 158.
27. Asbridge, *The Creation of the Principality of Antioch 1098–1130,* 76, quoting Walter the Chancellor, *The Antiochene Wars.*
28. R. C. Smail, *Crusading Warfare 1097–1193* (Cambridge: Cambridge University Press, 1956), 179. This is still the best overall description of the battle itself.
29. Ibn al-Qalanisi, *The Damascus Chronicle of the Crusades,* 160.
30. Ibid.
31. Kemal ad-Din, "La Chronique d'Alep," 618.
32. William of Tyre, *A History of Deeds Done Beyond the Seas,* 1:530. I would have thought that, if both sides were affected, it might occur to them that God wanted them to stop fighting.
33. Fulcher of Chartres, 227.
34. Kemal ad-Din, "La Chronique d'Alep," 619.
35. Ibn Al'Athir, *The Chronicle of Ibn al-Athir,* 204–205.
36. Fulcher of Chartres, 229.
37. Usamah ibn-Munqidh, *An Arab-Syrian Warrior in the Period of the Crusades: Memoirs of Usamah ibn-Minqidh,* trans. Philip K. Hitti (New York: Columbia University Press, 1929), 68.
38. Kemal ad-Din, "La Chronique d'Alep," 614.
39. Ibid., 615.
40. Jonathan Riley-Smith, "The Venetian Crusade of 1122–1124," *I Communi Italiani nel regno crociato di Gerusalemme,* ed. G. Airaldi and B. Z. Kedar (Genoa: University of Genoa, 1986), 339. I am grateful to Andrew Buck for sending me this article.
41. "Cartes de l'Abbaye de Notre-Dame de Josaphat," *Revue de L'Orient Latin,* vol. 7 (Paris: 1899), 123, charter no. 207.
42. Fulcher of Chartres, 231; Fulcher shows himself at other times to be a romantic so I think he just assumes the "pious affection" part.
43. Ibid., 301–302.
44. Walter the Chancellor, *The Antiochene Wars,* 97.
45. Asbridge, *The Creation of the Principality of Antioch 1098–1130,* 196–202.
46. Ibid. Obviously God had to have a hand in the peaceful transition of power. Looking at the current world, readers may draw their own conclusions about the accuracy of his statement.

SEVEN: KEEPING THE HOME FIRES BURNING

1. E. G. Rey, *Les familles d'outremer,* (Paris: Imprimerie Impérial, 1869), 718–719.
2. Quoted in Benjamin Z. Kedar, "On the Origins of the Earliest Laws of Frankish Jerusalem: The Canons of the Council of Nablus," *Speculum* 74, no. 2 (April 1999): 323.

3. Ibn al-Qalanisi, *The Damascus Chronicle of the Crusades,* 161.

4. Charles Kohler, "Un Nouveau Récit de L'Invention des Patriarches Abraham, Isaac et Jacob à Hébron," *Revue de l'Orient Latin* vol. 2, 478–502.

5. *Jewish Travellers in the Middle Ages,* ed. Elkan Nathan Adler (New York: Dover, 1987), 98.

6. Genesis 25:10.

7. Benjamin of Tudela, *The Itinerary of Benjamin of Tudela: Travels in the Middle Ages,* trans. A. Asher (1840; reprint Malibu, CA: Pangloss, 1987), 86.

8. Ibid., 86–87. No one mentions t-shirts but it's possible that pilgrims could also buy metal pins as souvenirs, like those available to those going to Compostela in Spain.

9. Joshua Prawer, *The History of the Jews in the Latin Kingdom of Jerusalem* (Oxford: Oxford University Press, 1988), 141–142.

10. Comte de Riant, "Invention des patriarches à Hebron," *Archives de L'Orient Latin Tome II* (Paris: 1884), 412–413.

11. Ibid., 411.

12. Kohler, "Un Nouveau Récit," 500

13. Maria Georgopoulou, "The Artistic World of the Crusaders and Oriental Christians in the Twelfth and Thirteenth Centuries," *Gesta* 43, no. 2 (2004): 115.

14. William of Tyre, *A History of Deeds Done Beyond the Seas,* 378, recounts the first proclamation of this festival.

15. Boas, *Jerusalem at the Time of the Crusaders,* 30–31.

16. Ibid., 33.

17. Steven Runciman, *A History of the Crusades: Vol. I: A History of Jerusalem and the Frankish East* (Cambridge: Cambridge University Press, 1968), 316–317.

18. Nicola A. Ziadeh, *Damascus under the Mamluks* (Norman, Oklahoma: University of Oklahoma Press, 1964), 44.

19. Malcolm Barber, *The New Knighthood: A History of the Order of the Temple* (Cambridge: Cambridge University Press, 1994), 31–59.

20. Fulcher of Chartres, *A History of the Expedition to Jerusalem, 1095–1127,* 232. William of Tyre, *A History of Deeds Done Beyond the Seas,* 1:535. Neither man bothers to give Morfia's name.

EIGHT: FORGING A KINGDOM

1. William of Tyre, *A History of Deeds Done Beyond the Seas,* 1:535.

2. *Letters from the East,* trans. Malcolm Barber and Keith Bate (Farnham, Surrey: Ashgate, 2013), 43. The original is in the records of Santiago.

3. Steven Runciman, *A History of the Crusades: Vol. I: A History of Jerusalem and the Frankish East* (Cambridge: Cambridge University Press, 1968), 253.

4. Kedar, "On the Origins of the Earliest Laws of Frankish Jerusalem," 331. Kedar gives the Latin text of the canons of the council. I relate the gist of them.

5. Ibid., 332.

6. Ibid., *"culpam faciens cum ipsis veniam peto."*

7. Ibid., *"caritative cum eis recipio."*

8. Ibid., 333. *"Quicumque cum alteriusuxore concubuisse proatus fuerit, accepta iudicii sentencia eviretur, et ab haec terra eicitatur. Mecha vero enasetur, nisis vir eius misericordiam facere voluerit. Quod si fecerit, ambo mare transgrediantur."* I have puzzled over this but can only suggest that the lack of Christian women in the kingdom gave them more lenient treatment under the law.

9. Of course, if one were important enough, this could be fudged a bit. In 1148, the wife of Raoul de Vermandois agreed to a divorce because he had already married Petronilla, the sister of Eleanor of Aquitaine.

10. Hans Eberhard Mayer, *The Crusades,* 2d ed. (Oxford: Oxford University Press, 1988), 75. I know Baldwin I was married three times, but the second two were clearly for money and he dismissed both of his wives once he had received their dowries.

11. William of Tyre, *A History of Deeds Done Beyond the Seas,* 1:416.

12. Ibid.

13. Usamah, *An Arab-Syrian Warrior in the Period of the Crusades,* 94.

14. Ibid.

15. Fulcher of Chartres, 158.

16. Fulcher of Chartres, 235.

17. William of Tyre, *A History of Deeds Done Beyond the Seas*, 1:536. How I wish more of those archives had survived!

18. Ibid., 1:538. One might note that he doesn't mention Jews.

19. *Cartulaire de l'Église de Saint Sépulchre de Jérusalem*, no. 45, col. 1154–1155. The text and analysis are also in *Die Urkunden der Lateinschen Könige von Jerusalem*, no. 86, 230–231.

20. Ibn al-Athir, *The Chronicle of Ibn al-Athir*, 197.

21. Sadakat Kadri, *Heaven on Earth: A Journey Through Shari'a Law from the Deserts of Ancient Arabia to the Streets of the Modern Muslim World* (New York: Farrar Strauss, Giroux, 2012), 88.

22. Ibn al-Qalanisi, *The Damascus Chronicle of the Crusades*, 162.

23. The site of this still exists in Jerusalem. The one in Harran was destroyed by the Mongols in 1250. The one in Aleppo was destroyed in the civil war in 2012.

24. Malcolm Barber, *The New Knighthood: A History of the Order of the Temple* (Cambridge: Cambridge University Press, 1994), 78.

25. William of Tyre, *A History of Deeds Done Beyond the Seas*, 1:525.

26. Sharan Newman, *The Real History of the Templars* (New York: Berkley, 2008), 23–27.

27. Ibid., 70.

28. Jean Richard, "Hospitals and Hospital Congregations in the Latin Kingdom in the Early Days of the Frankish Conquest," *Outremer—Studies in the History of the Crusading Kingdom of Jerusalem*, ed. Joshua Prawer (Israel: Yad Izhak Ben-Zvi, 1982), 91. Jocelyn gave the hospital to the Hospitallers in 1134.

29. Boas, *Jerusalem at the Time of the Crusaders*, 80.

30. Suger, Abbot of St. Denis, *The Deeds of Louis the Fat*, trans. Richard C. Custimono and John Moorhead (Washington, DC: Catholic University of America Press, 1992), 131–133. Suger's favorite adjective for Fulk is "warlike."

31. Ibid., 135.

NINE: QUEEN IN TRAINING

1. William of Malmsbury, *A History of the Norman Kings 1066–1125*, trans. by Joseph Stephenson (reprint, Wales: Llanerch Enterprises, 1989), 151.

2. Matilda would later marry Fulk's son, Geoffrey, and become the mother of Henry II of England. Melisende would then become Matilda's mother-in-law. Fulk's daughter, Sybille, would become her step-daughter. It's just as well that Matilda and Melisende never met. They would either have hated each other on sight or joined forces to conquer the known world. I thank Professor Karen Nicholas, SUNY Oswego, for information on dates for Sybille.

3. Quoted in, D. E. P Jackson, "Muslims in the Crusader States," *East and West in the Crusader States*, 23.

4. Hillenbrand, *The Crusades, Islamic Perspectives* (Leuven: Uitgerwerlij Peeters, 1996), 364.

5. Ibid., 88 (#48).

6. Ronnie Ellenblum, *Frankish Rural Settlement in the Latin Kingdom of Jerusalem* (Cambridge: Cambridge University Press, 1998), 69.

7. Ibid., 69–70.

8. Ibid., 154.

9. Denys Pringle, "Magna Mahumeria al-Bira: The Archaeology of a Frankish New Town in Palestine," *Crusade and Settlement*, ed. by Peter W. Edbury (Wales: University College Cardiff Press, 1985), 147–168.

10. *Anonymous Pilgrims I-VII*, 27–28.

11. Ibid.

12. Ibid., 29.

13. Ibid. One gets the feeling that pilgrim V was fed up with trying to read road signs in five alphabets.

14. *Anonymous Pilgrims I-VII*, 36.

15. Shlomo Dov. Goiten, *A Mediterranean Society: The Jewish Communities of the World as Portrayed in the Documents of the Cairo Geniza,* Vol. 1 (Berkeley: California University Press, 1999), 65.

16. Clinton Bailey, "Dating the Arrival of the Bedouin Tribes in the Negev and Sinai," *Journal of the Economic and Social History of the Orient* 28, no. 1 (1985): 21.

17. Ibn Al-Athir, *The Chronicle of Ibn al-Athir,* 2:35.

18. Albert of Aachen, *Historia Ierosolimitana,* 2:206.

19. Ibid., 207.

20. Fulcher of Chartres, *A History of the Expedition to Jerusalem,* 237.

21. Ibid.

22. Ibn Al-Athir, *The Chronicle of Ibn al-Athir,* 232, for the relationship. The Artuq clan paralleled the Montlhery, for the number of cousins and nephews.

23. John L. La Monte, "The Lords of Le Puiset on Crusade," *Speculum* 17, no. 1 (1942): 106–108. La Monte found no trace of the nephew and suspects he didn't exist.

24. Fulcher of Chartres, *A History of the Expedition to Jerusalem,* 238.

25. Nicholas Morton, *The Teutonic Knights in the Holy Land 1190–1291* (Woodbridge, England: Boydell Press, 2007), 5.

26. Mayer in *Die Urkunden der Lateinschen Könige von Jerusalem,* no. 89, 236, reproduces and discusses the agreement.

27. William of Tyre, *A History of Deeds Done Beyond the Seas,* 2:9.

28. Mohamed Ouerfelli, *Le Sucre: Production, commercialisation et usages dans la Méditerranée médiévale* (Leiden: Brill, 2008), 33.

29. Ibid., 39.

30. William of Tyre, *A History of Deeds Done Beyond the Seas,* 2:9.

31. Ibn al-Qalanisi, *The Damascus Chronicle of the Crusades,* 131–132.

32. Kemal ad-Din, "La Chronique d'Alep," 634.

33. Ibid. Ibn al-Qalansi says it was the 8th of November (*The Damascus Chronicle of the Crusades,* 121).

34. Walter the Chancellor, *The Antiochene Wars,* 171.

35. Matthew of Edessa, *Armenia and the Crusades,* 229, gives the fullest account of the capture but Fulcher of Charter and Ibn al-Qalanisi confirm the essentials.

36. Fulcher of Chartres, *A History of the Expedition to Jerusalem,* 240.

37. La Monte, "The Lords of Le Puiset on Crusade," 7.

38. *Lignages d'Outremer,* 2:718.

39. Barber, *The Crusader States,* 143–144.

40. Matthew of Edessa, *Armenia and the Crusades,* 230. William of Tyre says that there were fifty men from Edessa dressed as monks but the essence of the story is the same. I think that Matthew's story is more likely; monks would have gone to the local bishop for a judgment. It was normal for local disputes to be brought to the lord for judgment.

41. Ibid., 92.

42. Ibid., 93.

43. William of Tyre, *A History of Deeds Done Beyond the Seas,* 2:542.

44. Ibid., 2:544.

45. Fulcher of Chartres, *A History of the Expedition to Jerusalem,* 250.

46. Ibid., 251.

47. Helen Nicholson, *The Knights Hospitaller,* 62, This wife was Marie, sister of Roger of Antioch; Jocelyn's Armenian wife had died around 1118. We only know about Stephanie because she became an abbess and left charter records. There may have been other children. One hopes that Jocelyn eventually learned how to hold his children.

48. Ibid., 92.

49. Matthew of Edessa, *Armenia and the Crusades,* 231. Just after this account Matthew notes that at the same time, around Melitine, storks, cranes, and buzzards battled each other. The cranes vanquished the storks and exterminated them. I don't know what to make of this, unless it's an analogy. Information from ornithologists is welcome.

50. William of Tyre, *A History of Deeds done Beyond the Sea,* 2:16

51. Matthew of Edessa, *Armenia and the Crusades*, 232, also listed the sum in dinar and micheles, but always one hundred thousand.

52. Anonymous, "The First and Second Crusades from an Anonymous Syriac Source," 92.

53. Ibid. I haven't found a conversion rate for the dahekan, but it was a lot.

54. For an excellent look at this see Ronald C. Finucane, *Rescue of the Innocents: Endangered Children in Medieval Miracles* (New York: Palgrave Macmillan, 2000).

55. Peter Heather, *The Restoration of Rome: Barbarian Popes and Imperial Pretenders* (London: Macmillan, 2013), 14–17.

56. Anon, *Histoire de Guillaume Le Marechal*, ed. Paul Meyer (Paris: Librairie Reouard, 1891), 20.

57. Ralph Bailey Yewdale, *Bohemond I, Prince of Antioch* (Amsterdam: Adolf M. Hakkert, 1970), 109.

58. The king's nephew, whose name was unrecorded by the Latin chroniclers but is given the name by Michael the Syrian; Matthew of Edessa, *Armenia and the Crusades*, 233.

59. Michael the Syrian, *Chronique de Michel le Syrien*, 225.

60. La Monte, "The Lords of Le Puiset on Crusade," 108.

61. Ibn Al-Athir, *The Chronicle of Ibn al-Athir*, 251.

62. Fulcher of Chartres, 282.

63. William of Tyre, *A History of Deeds Done Beyond the Seas*, 2:25.

64. Hans Eberhard Mayer, "The Succession to Baldwin II of Jerusalem: English Impact on the East," *Dumbarton Oaks Papers* 39 (1985): 140.

65. William of Tyre, *A History of Deeds Done Beyond the Seas*, 2:27.

66. Jonathan Riley-Smith, "The Venetian Crusade of 1122–1124," 305.

67. William of Tyre, *A History of Deeds Done Beyond the Seas*, 2:18.

68. Fulcher of Chartres, *A History of the Expedition to Jerusalem*, 266.

69. Shlomo Dov Goiten, *A Mediterranean Society: The Jewish Communities of the World as Portrayed in the Documents of the Cairo Geniza*, Vol. 3 (Berkeley: California University Press, 1999), 217.

70. William of Tyre, *A History of Deeds Done Beyond the Seas*, 2:19.

71. Ibn al-Athir, *The Chronicle of Ibn al-Athir*, 253.

72. Fulcher of Chartres, *A History of the Expedition to Jerusalem*, 266.

73. Joshua Prawer, *The History of the Jews in the Latin Kingdom of Jerusalem* (Oxford: Oxford University Press, 1988), 51–53. Prawer makes a good case for the continuation of the Jewish community between the Christian takeover in 1124 and the next mention by Benjamin of Tudela in 1170.

74. Shlomo Dov Goiten, *A Mediterranean Society*, 110.

75. Prawer, *The History of the Jews in the Latin Kingdom of Jerusalem*, 54–55.

76. Ibn Al-Athir, *The Chronicle of Ibn al-Athir*, 253.

77. Walter the Chancellor, *The Antiochene Wars*, 144–145.

78. Pierre Aubé. *Roger II de Sicile* (Paris: Payot, 2001), 138–140.

79. Asbridge, *The Creation of the Principality of Antioch 1098–1130*, 146; Fulcher of Chartres also mentions this pact, *A History of the Expedition to Jerusalem*, 297.

80. Fulcher of Chartres, *A History of the Expedition to Jerusalem*, 298.

81. Matthew of Edessa, *Armenia and the Crusades*, 237. Matthew may have been visiting Antioch at the time and actually seen Bohemond.

82. Fulcher of Chartres, *A History of the Expedition to Jerusalem*, 303.

83. Except for servants, priests, counselors, and other hangers-on, but at least no parents.

84. See *Die Urkunden der Lateinschen Könige von Jerusalem*, no. 109, 269, for the place of Morfia's burial and the gifts for her memory.

TEN: FINDING A KING

1. Matthew of Edessa, *Armenia and the Crusades*, 219.

2. William of Tyre, *A History of Deeds Done Beyond the Seas*, 2:42.

3. Bernard S. Bachrach, "The Idea of the Angevin Empire," *Albion* 10, no. 4 (winter 1978): 293–299.

4. William of Malmesbury, *A History of the Norman Kings 1066–1125*, trans. by Joseph Stevenson (reprint, Dyfed, Wales: Llanarch, 1989), 139–140.

5. Du Cange, *Familles d'Outremer*, (Paris: E.G. Rey, 1869), 481. Du Cange adds that on his deathbed, Tancred willed Cecile to Pons.

6. Suger, Abbot of St. Denis, *The Deeds of Louis the Fat*, trans. Richard C. Custimono and John Moorhead (Washington, DC: Catholic University of America Press, 1992), 76.

7. This was almost the only excuse for divorce in the twelfth century. Since, even in the Crusader States, the royal families were related often several times over, this was a handy thing to suddenly "discover" when a marriage proved inconvenient. See Eleanor of Aquitaine, below.

8. I am grateful to Prof. Karen Nicholas for working out dates concerning Sybille.

9. William of Tyre, *A History of Deeds Done Beyond the Seas*, 2:38.

10. Bernard S. Bachrach, "The Idea of the Angevin Empire," *Albion* 10, no. 4 (winter 1978): 293–299.

11. H. Pirie-Gordon, "The Reigning Princes of Galilee," *English Historical Review* 27, no. 107 (July 1912): 451.

12. Reinhold Röhricht, *Geschicte des Königreichs Jerusalem 1100–1291* (Innsbruck: Wagnerschen Universitäts Buchhandlung, 1898), 212.

13. For a complete history of the Templars see Malcolm Barber, *The New Knighthood: A History of the Order of the Temple* (Cambridge: Cambridge University Press, 1994).

14. *Die Urkunden der Lateinschen Könige von Jerusalem*, 144.

15. Reinhold Röhricht, ed., *Regsta Regni Heirosolymitani* (Wagneriana: Libraria Academica, 1893), no. 121, 30.

16. Ibid., no. 122.

17. William of Tyre, *A History of Deeds Done Beyond the Seas*, 2:38.

18. Hans Eberhard Mayer, "Studies in the History of Queen Melisende of Jerusalem," *Dumbarton Oaks Papers* 26 (1972): 111–113.

ELEVEN: PREPARING TO PASS THE TORCH

1. William of Tyre, *A History of Deeds Done Beyond the Seas*, 2:34.

2. Michael the Syrian, *Chronique de Michel le Syrien*, 224.

3. Ibid.

4. Fulcher of Chartres, 292.

5. Ibid., 271.

6. Ibid.

7. Ronnie Ellenblum, *Frankish Rural Settlement in the Latin Kingdom of Jerusalem* (Cambridge: Cambridge University Press, 1998).

8. Especially Joshua Prawer, *The Crusaders' Kingdom* (London: Phoenix Press, 1972), 107.

9. Peter Edbury and John Gordon Rowe, *William of Tyre: Historian of the Latin East* (Cambridge: Cambridge University Press, 1988), 15.

10. Ibid., 23.

11. William of Tyre, *A History of Deeds Done Beyond the Sea*, 2:40

12. "Melissenda filia regis hoc laudat et consentit," *Die Urkunden der Lateinschen Könige von Jerusalem*, no. 105, 263.

13. Barbara Rosenwein, *To Be the Neighbor of St. Peter* (Ithaca, New York: Cornell University Press, 1989), gives an excellent explanation of this.

14. Al-Athir, *The Chronicle of Ibn al-Athir*, 274.

15. Bernard Lewis, *The Assassins: A Radical Sect in Islam*, 2nd ed. (London: Weidenfeld and Nicholson, 2001), 28–30.

16. Marchall G. S. Hodson, *The Secret Order of Assassins: The Struggle of the Early Nizârî Ismâ'ilîs Against the Islamic World* (reprint, Philadelphia: University of Pennsylvania Press, 2005), 112–115.

17. Al-Qalanisi, *The Damascus Chronicle of the Crusades*, 179. The Damascene aristocrat despised the Batini.

18. Ibid., 187–188.

19. Ibid., 192.
20. Ibid., 193.
21. Barber, *The New Knighthood*, 18.
22. Chrysogonus Waddell, *The Paraclete Statutes* (Trappist, Kentucky: Gethsemani Abbey, 1987), 21.
23. Boas, *Jerusalem at the Time of the Crusaders*, 145.
24. William of Tyre, *A History of Deeds Done Beyond the Seas*, 2:39.
25. *Assises de Jerusalem* (Paris: Imprimerie Royale, 1843).
26. Theodore Evergates, *Aristocracy in the County of Champagne* (Philadelphia: University of Pennsylvania Press, 2007), describes how the countesses of Champagne had juridical rights, especially in their dower towns.
27. William of Tyre, *A History of Deeds Done Beyond the Seas*, 2:41.
28. Ibid., 42.
29. Ibn Al-Qalansi, *The Damascus Chronicle of the Crusades*, 198–199.

TWELVE: TRAINING A KING

1. Al- Qalanisi, *The Damascus Chronicle of the Crusades*, 199.
2. William of Tyre, *A History of Deeds Done Beyond the Seas*, 2:77.
3. Hodgson, *The Secret Order of Assassins*, 107.
4. Michael the Syrian, *Chronique de Michel le Syrien*, 228.
5. William of Tyre, *A History of Deeds Done Beyond the Seas*, 2:38.
6. Ibid., 47.
7. Michael the Syrian, *Chronique de Michel le Syrien*, 228.
8. Ibid.
9. William of Tyre, *A History of Deeds Done Beyond the Seas*, 2:51.
10. Usamah, *An Arab-Syrian Warrior in the Period of the Crusades*, 151–152.
11. William of Tyre, *A History of Deeds Done Beyond the Seas*, 2:44.
12. Kemal ad-Din, "La Chronique d'Alep," 661.
13. William of Tyre, *A History of Deeds Done Beyond the Seas*, 2:44.
14. *Die Urkunden der Lateinschen Könige von Jerusalem*, 252, charter no. 97.
15. Michael the Syrian, *Chronique de Michel le Syrien*, 230.
16. Kemal ad-Din, "La Chronique d'Alep," 661.
17. William of Tyre, *A History of Deeds Done Beyond the Seas*, 2:46.
18. Ibid.
19. Al-Qalanisi, *The Damascus Chronicle of the Crusades*, 208.

THIRTEEN: TAMING A KING

1. *Die Urkunden der Lateinschen Könige von Jerusalem*, 298–299, charter no. 129.
2. Ibid.
3. Ibid. If this is the same man, Elias was later rewarded for his loyalty with the bishopric of Tiberias.
4. Ibid., commentary.
5. *Die Urkunden der Lateinschen Könige von Jerusalem*, 300.
6. Al-Qalanisi, *The Damascus Chronicle of the Crusades*, 211–219.
7. Michael the Syrian, *Chronique de Michel le Syrien*, 232.
8. William of Tyre, *A History of Deeds Done Beyond the Seas*, 2:52.
9. Michael the Syrian, *Chronique de Michel le Syrien*, 232.
10. William of Tyre, *A History of Deeds Done Beyond the Seas*, 2:53.
11. Christopher MacEvitt, *The Crusades and the Christian World of the East: Rough Tolerance*, (Philadelphia: University of Pennsylvania Press, 2008), 147–148.
12. William of Tyre, *A History of Deeds Done Beyond the Seas*, 2:53.
13. Pierre Aubé, *Roger II de Sicile* (Paris: Payot, 2001), 380–381.
14. William of Tyre, *A History of Deeds Done Beyond the Seas*, 1:496.

15. Jonathan Phillips, *Defenders of the Holy Land* (Oxford: Clarendon Press, 1996), 56.

16. Thomas Asbridge, *The Creation of the Principality of Antioch 1098–1130,* 175, for his appointment; William of Tyre, *A History of Deeds Done Beyond the Seas,* 2:55.

17. William of Tyre, *A History of Deeds Done Beyond the Seas,* 2:56.

18. Nurith Kenaan, "Local Christian Art in Twelfth Century Jerusalem," *Israel Exploration Journal* 23, no. 3 (1973): 175.

19. William of Tyre, *A History of Deeds Done Beyond the Seas,* 2:133.

20. Al Qalanisi, *The Damascus Chronicle of the Crusades,* 227.

21. William of Tyre, *A History of Deeds Done Beyond the Seas,* 2:58.

22. Melisende and her sisters were lucky. They were almost the only ones in the family not seriously inbred.

23. William of Tyre, *A History of Deeds Done Beyond the Seas,* 2:72.

24. Way to go, Emma! As with several other women of the Latin kingdoms, she chose her second husband on her own.

25. William of Tyre, *A History of Deeds Done Beyond the Seas,* 2:72.

26. *Cartulaire de l'Église de Saint Sèpulchre de Jérusalem,* ed. Eugène de Rozière (Paris: 1849), 83–85.

27. Hans Eberhard Mayer, "Studies in the History of Queen Melisende of Jerusalem," *Dumbarton Oaks Papers* 26 (1972):113.

28. Mayer dates this charter to before Hugh's revolt. But Hugh's visit to Alice shows a certain familial support on both sides and I'm inclined to think he went to her during his time of trial.

29. *Cartulaire de l'Église de Saint Sèpulchre de Jérusalem,* 74.

30. Ibid.

31. Hans Eberhard Mayer, "Angvins *versus* Normans: The New Men of King Fulk of Jerusalem," *American Philosophical Society* 133, no. 1 (1989): 3. Mayer quotes the Norman chronicler Orderic Vitalis as to Fulk's replacing long-time advisors and men who had been among the first Western settlers.

32. Hans Eberhard Mayer, "The Wheel of Fortune: Vicissitudes under Kings Fulk and Baldwin III of Jerusalem," *Speculum* 65, no 4 (October 1990): 860–877. Mayer also corrects a number of long-held assumptions concerning the family of the counts of Jaffa in this article.

33. William of Tyre, *A History of Deeds Done Beyond the Seas.* 2:65.

34. *Cartulaire de l'Église de Saint Sèpulchre de Jérusalem,* 76.

35. Ibid.

36. *Die Urkunden der Lateinschen Könige von Jerusalem,* vol. I, no. 137, 337–321.

37. Starting in April 1136. Röhricht, *Regsta Regni Heirosolymitani,* 40, charter 163.

FOURTEEN: PRINCE NOT-SO-CHARMING

1. John Kinnamos, *Deeds of John and Manuel Comnenus,* trans. Charles M. Brand (New York: Columbia University Press, 1976), 22.

2. Imad al-Din is a common name meaning "pillar of the faith." Atabeg is his title, and Zengi is his family name.

3. Carole Hillenbrand, "'Abominable Acts': The Career of Zengi," in *The Second Crusade,* ed. Jonathan Phillips and Martin Hoch (Manchester: Manchester University Press, 2001), 113.

4. Hillenbrand, "Abominable Acts," 112.

5. Ibn al-Qalanisi, *The Damascus Chronicle of the Crusades,* 202; also noted in Kemal ad-Din, "La Chronique d'Alep," 660, and Ibn al-Athir, *The Chronicle of Ibn al-Athir,* 279.

6. Ibid., 203.

7. E. G. Rey, *Les Familles d'Outre-Mer Première Série* (Paris:, 1869), 2:649.

8. Thomas Asbridge, *The Creation of the Principality of Antioch 1098–1130,* 190.

9. William of Tyre, *A History of Deeds Done Beyond the Sea,* 2:58.

10. Asbridge, *The Creation of the Principality of Antioch 1098–1130,* 202.

11. William of Tyre, *A History of Deeds Done Beyond the Seas,* 2:59.

12. Abbot Suger of Saint Denis, *Oeuvres Complètes de Suger,* ed. by A. Lecoy de la Marche (Paris: 1867), 130.

13. Alfred Richard, *Histoire des Comtes de Poitou, Tome IV* (Pau, France: Princi Negue, 2004), 113.

14. Jonathan P. Phillips, "A Note on the Origins of Raymond of Poitiers," *English Historical Review* 106, no. 418 (January 1991): 67.

15. *Archives Historique de Poitou,* 8:109. *Lettres de Besley,* ed. A. Briquet (Paris: 1880).

16. Richard, *Histoire des Comtes de Poitou,* 210.

17. His birth in 1110 or 1111 would make the comments of William of Tyre about his youth more believable, although William implies that Raymond was still in his teens. That isn't likely. William of Tyre, *A History of Deeds Done Beyond the Seas,* 2:80.

18. The street between the Tiber River and the Jewish ghetto in Rome is still called Pierleoni.

19. William of Tyre, *A History of Deeds Done Beyond the Seas,* 2:60.

20. Ibid.

21. Ibid., 2:78.

22. Ibid., 79.

23. John of Salisbury, *Historia Pontificalis,* ed. and trans. Marjorie Chibnall (Edinburgh: Thomas Nelson and Sons, 1956), 52.

24. James A. Brundage, *Law, Sex and Society in Medieval Europe* (Chicago, University of Chicago Press, 1990) discusses these laws thoroughly.

25. William of Tyre, *A History of Deeds Done Beyond the Seas,* 2:79.

26. Ibid., 2:78.

27. Ibid.

28. Kinnamos, *Deeds of John and Manuel Comnenus,* 23.

29. Asbridge, *The Creation of the Principality of Antioch 1098–1130,* 99–100. William of Tyre also admits this, *A History of Deeds Done Beyond the Seas,* 2:81.

30. William of Tyre, *A History of Deeds Done Beyond the Seas,* 2:85, n. 60.

31. Ibid., 2:93.

32. Röhricht, *Regsta Regni Heirosolymitani,* 37, charters. 148 and 150, for Alice's witnesses; 48, charter 195, for Raymond and Constance's witnesses.

33. *Die Urkunden der Lateinschen Könige von Jerusalem,* no. 141, 324–236.

34. William of Tyre, *A History of Deeds Done Beyond the Seas,* 2:83.

35. Ibid.

36. Also called Bait Jibrim.

37. William of Tyre, *A History of Deeds Done Beyond the Seas,* 2:81.

38. Ibid.

39. Alan Forey, *The Military Orders* (New York: MacMillan, 1992), 18–19.

40. Robin Fedden and John Thomson, *Crusader Castles* (Beirut: Khayat's, 1957), 21–22.

41. Ibid., 84. The current state of Krak de Chevaliers is uncertain. It sustained severe damage in 2012–2013 as the result of bombing during the Syrian civil war.

42. Malcolm Barber, *The Crusader States* (New Haven: Yale University Press, 2012), 162.

43. Ibid.

44. Fedden and Thomson, *Crusader Castles,* 26.

45. William of Tyre, *A History of Deeds Done Beyond the Seas,* 2:132. William doesn't mention who was stationed in the fortress to fight off enemies. Perhaps the nuns trained in siege defense between their hours of prayer.

46. Ibid. This might be taken with a grain of salt since everyone knew that the convent had been built for Yvette. But canon law prohibited lay interference in the election of religious officials. This had been the root of the acrimonious battle between the popes and the Holy Roman emperors, only settled a few years before.

47. *Cartulaire de Josephat,* 43:45.

48. Boas, *Jerusalem at the Time of the Crusaders,* 119.

49. Ibid.

50. Alan Forey, *The Military Orders From the Twelfth to the Early Fourteenth Century.* Macmillan, London, 1992, 22

51. Usamah, *An Arab-Syrian Warrior in the Period of the Crusades,* 226, mentions going hunting with the king and the gift of a falcon from him during one of the many truces.

52. William of Tyre, *A History of Deeds Done Beyond the Seas,* 2:134.

53. Ibid.
54. William of Tyre, *A History of Deeds Done Beyond the Seas*, 2:135.
55. Ibn al-Qalanisi, *The Damascus Chronicle of the Crusades*, 265.

FIFTEEN: MELISENDE REGINA SOLA

1. William of Tyre, *A History of Deeds Done Beyond the Seas*, 2:139.
2. Both terms have been used for her by historians.
3. Note Henry II of England, who anointed his son Henry "the Young King," and Philippe VI of France, who also had his son Philippe crowned at Reims as a young man. Neither son lived to rule on his own.
4. Bernard of Clairvaux, *Opera Omnia*, vol. 1 (Paris: Mabillon, 1839).
5. Armin Wolf, "Reigning Queens in Medieval Europe: Where, When, Why," *Medieval Queenship*, ed. John Carmi Parsons (New York: St. Martin's Press, 1993), 169.
6. Anna Komnene, *The Alexiad*, trans. E. R. A. Sewter (reprint, London: Penguin, 2009), book 3, 92–94.
7. Ibid., 94.
8. Ibid., 96.
9. Ibn al-Qalanisi, *The Damascus Chronicle of the Crusades*, 229.
10. Ibid., 230.
11. Ibid., 231.
12. Ibid., 232.
13. Ibn al-Athir, *The Chronicle of Ibn al-Athir*, part 1, 313 This is his usual response when he doesn't understand a report that he is repeating.
14. Al-Qalanisi, *The Damascus Chronicle of the Crusades*, 252.
15. Carole Hillenbrand, "'Abominable Acts': The Career of Zengi," in *The Second Crusade*, ed. Jonathan Phillips and Martin Hoch (Manchester: Manchester University Press, 2001), 113.
16. William of Tyre, *A History of Deeds Done Beyond the Seas*, 2:144.
17. William of Tyre, *A History of Deeds Done Beyond the Seas*, 2:144–145.
18. Hans Eberhard Mayer, "Studies in the History of Queen Melisende of Jerusalem," *Dumbarton Oaks Papers* 26 (1972): 117.
19. John Kinnamos, *Deeds of John and Manuel Comnenus*, trans. Charles M. Brand (New York: Columbia University Press, 1976), 27-31.
20. Ibn al-Athir, *The Chronicle of Ibn al-Athir*, 90–91, for Kurdish conquests.
21. William of Tyre, *A History of Deeds Done Beyond the Seas*, 141
22. Al-Athir, *The Chronicle of Ibn al-Athir*, part 1, 373. One might remember that Al-Athir was working for Zengi's family, as William was being paid by Melisende's.
23. Michael the Syrian, *Chronique de Michel le Syrien*, 262–263.
24. William of Tyre, *A History of Deeds Done Beyond the Seas*, 2:143. William seems to have forgotten that it was all Jocelyn's fault.
25. Nerses Snorhali, *Lament on Edessa*, trans. Theo Marten van Lint, in "Seeking Meaning in Catastrophe," 53. ll. 67–74.
26. Ibid., 70–71 ll. 89–92.
27. Snorhali, *Lament on Edessa*, 37.
28. Ibid., 58–59 ll. 171–173 (slightly edited by me—I liked "protest" better than "complaint").

SIXTEEN: OF KINGS, QUEENS, AND TOURISTS

1. Eugenius III, *Select Historical Documents of the Middle Ages*, trans. Ernest F. Henderson (London: George Bell and Sons, 1910), 333–336.
2. Yves Sassier, *Louis VII* (Paris: Fayard, 1991), 16. It is said that, after this, all pigs in Paris had to wear bells.
3. Ibid., 127.
4. Bernard of Clairvaux, "ad Dominum Papam Eugenium," *Epistola* CCLVI, 538–539. In which Bernard agrees to take up the cause.

5. Odo of Deuil, *De Profectione Ludovici VII in Orientum,* ed. and trans. Virginia Gingerick Berry (New York: Norton, 1948), 8–11.

6. Otto of Freising, *The Deeds of Frederick Barbarossa,* trans. Charles Christopher Merow (New York: Norton, 1966), 74–75.

7. Ephraim of Bonn, "Sefer Zekhira," *Jews and Crusaders: The Hebrew Chronicles of the First and Second Crusades,* trans. Shlomo Eidelberg (Madison, WI: University of Wisconsin, 1977), 122. Ephraim was thirteen at the time. He and his family survived by barricading themselves in the fortress of Wolkenberg.

8. Yves Sassier, *Louis VII* (Paris: Fayard, 1991), 91.

9. Bernard of Clairvaux, "juvenis consanguinus meus," *Epistola,* CCVI, 434–435.

10. Bernard of Clairvaux, "juvenis consanguinus meus," CCLV, 435.

11. Adrian J. Boas, *Jerusalem in the Time of the Crusades* (Abington: Routledge, 2001), 197–198.

12. *Die Urkunden der Lateinschen Könige von Jerusalem,* no. 170, 349.

13. Ibn al-Qalanisi, *The Damascus Chronicle of the Crusades,* 270.

14. Ibn al-Athir, *The Chronicle of Ibn al-Athir. 2:*8.

15. Ibid., 8.

16. *Die Urkunden der Lateinschen Könige von Jerusalem,* nos. 171–172, 350.

17. William of Tyre, *A History of Deeds Done Beyond the Seas,* 2: 87.

18. Kemal ad-Din, "La Chronique d'Alep."

19. Michael the Syrian, *Chronique de Michel le Syrien,* 266.

20. Ibid., 267.

21. Ibn al-Qalanisi, *The Damascus Chronicle of the Crusades,* trans. and ed. by H. A. R. Gibb (Mineola, NY: Dover, 2002, 1932 reprint), 270.

22. Ibn al-Athir, *The Chronicle of Ibn al-Athir,* 382.

23. Ibn al-Qalanisi, *The Damascus Chronicle of the Crusades,* 271–272.

24. Ibid., 273–274.

25. Odo of Deuil, *De Profectione Ludovici VII in Orientum,* 40–41.

26. Ibid., n. 126–127.

27. William of Tyre, *A History of Deeds Done Beyond the Seas,* 2:177.

28. Ibid., 2:178.

29. Ibid., 2:175–177.

30. Abbot Suger of Saint Denis, *Oeuvres Complètes de Suger,* ed. by A. Lecoy de la Marche (Paris: 1867), letter 50, 229.

31. Odo of Deuil, *De Profectione Ludovici VII in Orientum,* 272–273.

32. Suger, *Ouevres Complétes,* 230.

33. William of Tyre, *A History of Deeds Done Beyond the Seas,* 2:178.

34. Suger, *Ouevres Complétes,* 294.

35. Ibid., 296.

36. Ibid., 180–181.

37. John of Salisbury, *Historia Pontificalis,* ed. and trans. Marjorie Chibnall (Edinburgh: Thomas Nelson and Sons, 1956), 52. I confess to being very fond of John. His personality comes through so clearly in his work.

38. Richard Barber, "Eleanor of Aquitaine and the Media," *The World of Eleanor of Acquitaine,* ed. Marcus Bull and Catherine Léglu (Woodbridge: Boydell, 2005), 25. This is an excellent essay for anyone who has been dizzied by the number of Eleanor legends.

39. Ibn Shaddad, Baha al-Din, *The Rare and Excellent History of Saladin,* ed. and trans. D. S. Richards. (Aldershot: Ashgate, 2002), 35.

40. Jonathan Phillips, *Defenders of the Holy Land: Relations Between the Latin East and the West, 1119–1187* (Oxford: Oxford University Press, 1996), 285.

41. William of Newburgh, *The History of English Affairs, Book I,* ed. and trans. P. G. Walsh and M. J. Kennedy (Wiltshire, England: Aris & Phillips, 1988), 87.

42. William of Tyre, *A History of Deeds Done Beyond the Seas,* 2:181.

43. Phillips, *Defenders of the Holy Land,* 90.

44. Karen Nicholas, private correspondence, Jan. 2013.

45. Ibn al-Athir, *The Chronicle of Ibn Al-Athir for the Crusading Period,* vol. 2, 2:15.

46. William of Tyre, *A History of Deeds Done Beyond the Seas*, 2:184.
47. The Provençal records only say that Alphonse-Jordan was poisoned, but not by whom. He may have just had some bad shellfish. It's one of those maddening mysteries of the Levant.
48. William of Tyre, *A History of Deeds Done Beyond the Seas*, 2:185.
49. Otto of Freising, *The Deeds of Frederick Barbarossa*, 103.
50. Martin Hoch, "The Choice of Damascus as the Objective of the Second Crusade: A Re-evaluation," *Autour de la Première Croisade. Actes du Colloque de la Society for the Study of the Crusades and the Latin East (Clermont-Ferrand, 22–25 juin 1995)*, ed. Michel Balard, vol. 14 (Paris: Publications de la Sorbonne, 1996), 363. For diplomatic purposes, Christians were at a disadvantage in only being allowed one wife at a time.
51. Quoted in Nicola A. Ziadeh, *Damascus under the Mamluks* (Norman, Oklahoma: University of Oklahoma Press, 1964), 24.
52. Benjamin of Tudela, *Travels in the Middle Ages*, trans. A. Asher, ed. Michael Signer (1840; reprint, Malibu, California: Pangloss Press, 1987), 90.
53. Ibid., 91.
54. Afif Banassi, "Fabrication des épées de Damas," *Syria* T. 23, Fascicle 3/4 (1976): 286.
55. Benjamin of Tudela, *Travels in the Middle Ages*, 91.
56. Ziadeh, *Damascus Under the Mamluks*, 26.
57. Otto of Freising, *The Deeds of Frederick Barbarossa*, 103.
58. William of Newburgh, *The History of English Affairs, Book I*, 95.
59. Nicola Ziadeh, *Damascus Under the Mamluks*, 12.
60. Yehosua Frenkel, "The Qur'an versus the Cross in the Wake of the Crusade: The Social Function of Dreams and Symbols in Encounter and Conflict (Damascus, July 1146)," *Quaderni di Studi Arabi*, 20/21 (2002–2003): 109.
61. Ibid., 114.
62. Ibid., 111.
63. Ibn al-Qalanisi, *The Damascus Chronicle of the Crusades*, 284.
64. Ibid., 285.
65. Sassier, *Louis VII*, 59–60.
66. Barber, "Eleanor of Aquitaine and the Media," 17.
67. Suger, *Oeuvres Complètes*, XI, 258.
68. Ibid., 260. Both the above are loose translations, but that is the essence of them.
69. John of Salisbury, *Historia Pontificalis*, 45.

SEVENTEEN: MELISENDE'S FINAL CONFLICT

1. William of Tyre, *A History of Deeds Done Beyond the Seas*, 2:179–180.
2. Giles Constable, "The Second Crusade as Seen by Contemporaries," *Traditio* 9 (1953): 266.
3. Ibid., 268.
4. William of Tyre, *A History of Deeds Done Beyond the Seas*, 2:193.
5. Ibn al-Qalanisi, *The Damascus Chronicle of the Crusades*, 291.
6. William of Tyre, *A History of Deeds Done Beyond the Seas*, 2:197.
7. Ibn al-Qalanisi, *The Damascus Chronicle of the Crusades;* William of Tyre, *A History of Deeds Done Beyond the Seas*, 2:198.
8. William of Newburgh, *The History of English Affairs, Book I*, 96–97.
9. Ibid., 199. No one else mentions this and the image does resemble the scene where Alexander the Great stands on the shore and weeps because he has nothing more to conquer. But it's possible.
10. Ibn al-Qalanisi, *The Damascus Chronicle of the Crusades*, 293. He particularly states that the townspeople played an important part in the protection of Antioch.
11. William of Tyre, *A History of Deeds Done Beyond the Seas*, 2:200.
12. Ibid., 201.
13. Ibn al-Athir, *The Chronicle of Ibn al-Athir*, 2:39.
14. Michael the Syrian, *Chronique de Michel le Syrien*, 295.
15. William of Tyre, *A History of Deeds Done Beyond the Seas*, 2:201.
16. Ibid., 202.

17. Ibid.
18. John of Ibelin, *Le Livre des Assises,* ed. by Peter W. Edbury (Leiden: Brill, 2003), 85.
19. William of Tyre, *A History of Deeds Done Beyond the Seas,* 2:213.
20. John Kinnamos, *Deeds of John and Manuel Comnenus,* trans. Charles M. Brand (New York: Columbia University Press, 1976), 97–98. To be fair, John Roger may have decided to renounce the secular life because he had been frightened by a serious illness, not because Constance rejected him.
21. William of Tyre, *A History of Deeds Done Beyond the Seas,* 2:213.
22. Reinhold Röhricht, ed., *Regsta Regni Heirosolymitani,* no 263 (Wagneriana: Libraria Academica, 1893), 67.
23. Ibid.
24. Ibid., 214.
25. Jean Richard, *Le Comté de Tripoli sous la Dynastie Toulousaine 1102–1187,* (Paris: Geuthner, 1999, 1945 reprint), 7.
26. No one at the time, that is. The French historian, Grousset, states, "It is not allowed to suppose that the countess Hodierna was complicit in the assassination of Raymond III." René Grosset, *Histoire des Croisades et du Royaume Franc de Jérusalem,* vol. 2 (Paris: Librairie Plon, 1955). Grosset believes that all the sisters were "unnatural" in their thirst for power.
27. Richard, *Le Comté de Tripoli,* 83.
28. Ibid., 81.
29. Richard, *Le Comté de Tripoli,* 83.
30. William of Tyre, *A History of Deeds Done Beyond the Seas,* 2:258–259.
31. Joshua Prawer, *The Crusaders' Kingdom* (London: Phoenix Press, 1972), 107.
32. Grosset, *Histoire des Croisades et du Royaume Franc de Jérusalem,* 2:314. Grosset insists that Melisende's "regency" was a dismal failure and that she did nothing to help Edessa. He somehow blames her also for the deaths of Raymond of Antioch and Raymond of Tripoli, apparently through inactivity.
33. Mayer, "Studies in the History of Queen Melisende of Jerusalem," 125 ff.
34. Runciman, *A History of the Crusades,* 2:335.
35. William of Tyre, *A History of Deeds Done Beyond the Seas,* 2:205.
36. Ibid., 2:206.
37. Bernard of Clairvaux, *Epistola,* CCLXXXIX, 1:274. His previous letter is to Andrew, telling his uncle that he has written the queen.
38. Röhricht, *Regsta Regni Heirosolymitani,* 70, charter 276.
39. Ibid., charter 278.
40. Ibid., 74–75, charter 292.
41. William of Tyre, *A History of Deeds Done Beyond the Seas,* 2:283.
42. Ibid.

BIBLIOGRAPHY

PRIMARY SOURCES

Albert of Achen. *History of the Journey to Jerusalem.* Vol. 1: Books 1–6. Translated by Susan B. Edgington. Ashgate: Aldershot, 2013.

Anna Komnene. *The Alexiad.* Translated by E. R. A. Sewter. London: Penguin Classics, 2003.

"Annales de Terre Saint." In *Archives de L'Orient Latin.* Vol. 2. Paris: Société de L'Orient Latin, 1881.

Anonymous Pilgrims, *Palestine Pilgrims Text Society.* Vol. 6. Translated by Aubrey Stewart. London: 1894.

Anonymous. "The First and Second Crusades from an Anonymous Syriac Source." Translated by A. S. Tritton and H. A. R. Gibb. *Journal of the Royal Asiatic Society of Great Britain and Ireland* no. 1 (January 1933): 69–101.

Archives de L'Orient Latin. Vols. 1–2. Paris: Société de L'Orient Latin, 1881.

Assises d'Antioche. Sempad the Constable. Venice: Imprimerie Arménienne Médaillé, 1876.

Assises de Jerusalem, Paris, Imprimerie Royale, 1843

Benjamin of Tudela. *Travels in the Middle Ages Sefer ha-Massaot.* Malibu, CA: Pangloss Press, 1983.

Bernard of Clairvaux. *Sancti Bernardi Opera Omnia.* Vols. 1–4. Edited by Jean Mabillon. Paris: 1839.

Cartulaire du Chapitre du Saint-Sépulchre de Jerusalem. Edited by G. Bresc-Bautier. Paris: Documents relatifs à l'histoire des croisades publiés par l'Academie des inscriptions et Belles-Lettres, 1984.

Cartulaire de l'Eglise du Saint Sépulchre de Jerusalem. Edited by J. P. Migne. In *Patrilogiae Latinae CLV.* Petit-Montrouge: 1854.

Chartes de Terre Sainte provenant de l'abbaye de Notre-Dame de Josaphat. Edited by F. Delaborde. Paris: 1800.

Eugenius III. *Epistolae et Privilegia.* Edited by Migne, Petit-Montrouge: 1855. In *Patrologia Latina No. 180.*

"Fragment d'un cartulaire de l'ordre de Saint Lazare, en Terre-Sainte." In *Archives de L'Orient Latin.* Paris: Société de L'Orient Latin, 1884.

Fulcher of Chartres. *A History of the Expedition to Jerusalem, 1095–1127.* Translated by Frances Rila Ryan. New York: Norton, 1969.

Fulcheri Cartonensis Historia Hierosolimitana. Edited by H. Hagenmayer. Heidelberg: 1913.

Gesta Francorum: The Deeds of the Franks and the Other Pilgrims to Jerusalem. Edited by Rosalind Hill. Oxford: Oxford University Press, 1962.

Gilo of Paris. *Historia Vie Hierosolimitane.* Edited and translated by C. W. Grocock and J. E. Siberry. Oxford: Oxford University Press, 1997.

Godefridi Bullonii, Lotharigia Ducis, postmodem Hierosolytymorum Regis Primis Epistolae et Diplomata. Edited by J. P. Migne. *Patrilogiae Latinae CLV* Petit-Montrouge: 1854.

Hugh of Poitiers. *The Vézelay Chronicle.* Translated by John Scott and John O. Ward. Binghamton, NY: Pegasus, 1992.

Ibn al-Athir. *The Chronicle of Ibn al-Athir for the Crusading Period, Parts 1 & 2.* Translated by D. S. Richards. Aldershot: Ashgate, 2005.

Ibn al-Qalanisi. *The Damascus Chronicle of the Crusades.* Translated and edited by H. A. R. Gibb. 1932. Reprint, Mineola, NY: Dover, 2002.

Ibn-Munqidh, Usama. *An Arab-Syrian Gentleman and Warrior in the Period of the Crusades.* Translated by Philip K. Hitti. New York: Columbia University Press, 1929.

Ibn Shaddad, Baha al-Din. *The Rare and Excellent History of Saladin.* edited and translated D. S. Richards. Aldershot: Ashgate, 2002.

Jewish Travellers [sic] *in the Middle Ages.* Edited and translated by Elkan Nathan Adler, 1930. Reprint, Mineola, NY: Dover, 1987.

John of Ibelin. *Le Livre des Assises.* Edited by Peter W. Edbury. Leiden: Brill, 2003.

Kemal ad-Din. "Estraits de la chronique d'Alep." *Recueil des historiens des croisades: historiens orientaux,* Vol. 3. Académie des inscriptions et belles-lettres, Paris (1905) .

John Kinnamos. *Deeds of John and Manuel Comnenus.* Translated by Charles M. Brand. New York: Columbia University Press, 1976.

Letters of Medieval Jewish Traders. Translated by S. D. Goitein. Princeton: Princeton University Press, 1973.

Marie-Adélaide Neilen. *Lignages d'Outremer.* Paris: L'Académie des Inscriptions et Belle-Lettres, 2003.

Matthew of Edessa. *Armenia and the Crusades.* Translated by A. Dosturian. Latham MD, University Press of America, 1993.

Papsturkunden für Kirchen in Heiligen Lande. Edited by Ruldoph Heistand. Göttingen: Vandenhoeck and Rurpecht, 1985.

Ralph of Caens. *Gesta Tancredi.* Edited by J. P. Migne. In *Patra Logia Latina,* 155. Petit-Montrouge: 1854.

Raymond of St. Gilles. *Historia Francorum qui ceperunt Jerusalem.* Edited by J. P. Migne. Petit-Montrouge: 1854.

Recueil des Historiens des Croisades. Vols. 1–14. Edited by Académie des Inscriptions des Belles Lettres. Paris: 1837–1904.

Odo of Deuil. *De Profectione Ludovici VII in Orienteum.* Translated by Virginia G. Berry. New York: Columbia University Press, 1948.

Otto of Freising. *The Deeds of Frederick Barbarossa.* Translated by Charles C. Mierow. New York: Columbia University Press, 1953.

Regesta Regni Hiersolymitani. Edited by Reinhold Röhricht. Libraria Academica Wagneriana, 1893.

Snorhali. *Lament on Edessa.* Edited and translated by Theo M. van Lint. In *East and West in the Crusader States: Vol. II, Context, Contacts, Confrontation.* Edited by Krijnie Ciggaar and Herman Teule. Leuven, 1999.

Abbot Suger of Saint Denis. *Oeuvres Complètes de Suger.* Edited by A. Lecoy de la Marche. Paris: 1867.

Walter the Chancellor. *The Antiochene Wars: A Translation and Commentary.* Edited and translated by Thomas S. Asbridge and Susan B. Edgington. Aldershot: Ashgate, 1999.

William of Malmesbury. *A History of the Norman Kings 1066–1125.* Translated by Joseph Stevenson.

William of Newburgh. *The History of English Affairs Book I.* Edited and translated by P. G. Walsh and M. J. Kennedy. Warminster, Wiltshire: Aris & Phillips, 1988.

William of Tyre. *A History of Deeds Done Beyond the Sea.* Vols. 1 and 2. Translated by Emily Atwater Babcock and A. C. Krey. New York: Octagon Books, 1976.

SECONDARY SOURCES

Abulafia, David. "Trade and Crusade 1050–1250." In *Cross Cultural Convergences in the Crusader Period: Essays Presented to Aryeh Grabois on His Sixty-fifth Birthday,* edited by Michael Goodrich, Sophia Menache, and Sylvia Schein, 1–20. New York: Peter Lang, 1995.

Alonzi, Luigi. "Terra e Rendite nei Secoli XII-XIII: Normana, Inghilterra, Terrrasanta." *Mediterraneam Ricerche storiche,* Anno VII (Aprile 2010): 13–30.

Asbridge, Thomas. "The 'Crusader' Community at Antioch: The Impact of Interaction with Byzantium and Islam." *Transactions of the Royal Historical Society,* sixth series, 9 (1999): 305–325.

———. *The Creation of the Principality of Antioch 1098–1130.* Woodbridge: Boydell, 2000.

———. "Alice of Antioch: A Case Study of Female Power in the Twelfth Century." In *The Experience of Crusading,* Vol. 2, edited by Peter Edbury and Jonathan Phillips, 29–47. Cambridge: Cambridge University Press, 2003.

Aubé, Pierre. *Les empires normands d'Orient.* Paris: Periin, 1991.

Bachrach, Bernard S. "The Idea of the Angevin Empire." *Albion* 10, no. 4 (winter 1978).

Balard, Michel. *Croisades et Orient latin XIe –XIV siècles.* Paris: Armand Colin, 2001.

Balard, Michel, Bejamin Z. Kedar, and Jonathan Riley-Smith. *Dei Gesta per Francos: Etudes sur les croisades dédiées à Jean Richard/ Crusade Studies in Honour of Jean Richard.* Burlington, VT: Ashgate, 2001.

Baldwin, Marshall. *Raymond III of Tripolis and the Fall of Jerusalem 1140–1187.* Amsterdam: Adolf M. Hakkert, 1969.

———. "Ecclesiastical Developments in the Twelfth Century Crusaders' State of Tripolis." *The Catholic Historical Review* 22, no. 2 (July 1936): 149–171.

Baloup, Daniel and Philippe Josserand, eds. *Regards Croisés sur la Guerre Sainte: Guerre, Idéologie et Religion dans L'Espace Méditerranéen Latin XIe-XIIIe Siècle.* Toulouse: CNRS Université de Toulouse-Le Mirail, 2006.

Bahnasi, Afif. "Fabrication des épées de Damas." *Syria* T. 53, Fasc. 3/4 (1976): 281–294.

Baker, Derek, ed. *Relations between East and West in the Middle Ages.* Edinburgh: Edinburgh University Press, 1973.

Barber, Malcolm. *Crusader States.* New Haven: Yale University Press, 2012.

———. "Philip of Nablus in the Kingdom of Jerusalem." *The Experience of Crusading.* Vol. 2. Edited by Peter Edbury and Jonathan Phillips, 60–75. Cambridge: Cambridge University Press, 2003.

Baron, Salo Wittmayer. *A Social and Religious History of the Jews. Vol. IV: Meeting of East and West.* New York: Columbia University Press, 1957.

Ben-Ami, Aharon. *Social Change in a Hostile Environment: The Crusaders Kingdome of Jerusalem.* Princeton: Princeton University Press, 1969.

Beyer, Gustav. "Neapolis/näblus und sein Gebiet in der Kreuzfahrerzeit. Eine topographische und historisch-geographische Studie." *Zeitschrift des Deutschen Palästina-Vereins* 1878–1945 Bd. 63, H 3/4 (1940): 155–209.

Boas, Adrian J. *Jerusalem in the Time of the Crusades.* Abington: Routledge, 2001.

Bosworth, C. Edmund, ed. *The Turks in the Early Islamic World.* Aldershot: Ashgate, 2007.

Bournoutian, George A. *A History of the Armenian People. Vol. I Pre-history to 1500 A.D.* Costa Mesa, CA: Mazda Publishers, 1995.

Bradbury, Jim. *The Medieval Siege.* Woodbridge: Boydell Press, 1992.

Brundage, James S. "Marriage Law in the Latin Kingdom of Jerusalem." In *Outremer: Studies in the History of the Crusading Kingdom of Jerusalem, presented to Joshua Prawer.* Edited by Benjamin Z. Kedar, H. E. Mayer, and R. C. Smail, 258–272. Jerusalem: Yad Izhak Ben-Zvi Institute, 1982.

———. "Immortalizing the Crusades: Law and Institutions." In *Montjoie: Studies in Crusade History in Honour of Hans Eberhard Mayer.* Edited by Bejamin Z. Kedar, Jonathan Riley-Smith, and Rudolf Heistand, 251–260. Variorum Press, 1997.

Bull, Marcus and Norman Housley, eds. *The Experience of Crusading: Western Approaches.* Cambridge: Cambridge University Press, 2003.

Cahen, Claude. *Pre-Ottoman Turkey.* New York: Tapplinger Publishing, 1968.

———. "Some New Editions of Oriental Sources about Syria in the Time of the Crusades." In *Outremer: Studies in the History of the Crusading Kingdom of Jerusalem, presented to Joshua Prawer.* Edited by Benjamin Z. Kedar, H. E. Mayer, and R. C. Smail, 223–239. Jerusalem: Yad Izhak Ben-Zvi Institute, Jerusalem, 1982.

———. *Orient et Occident au temps des Croisades.* Alençon: Aubier Montaigne, 1983.

Cameron, Avril. "The History of the Image of Edessa: The Telling of a Story." *Harvard Ukranian Studies* 7 (1981): 80–91.

244 ~ DEFENDING THE CITY OF GOD

Caspi-Reisfeld, Keren. "Women Warriors during the Crusades." In *Gendering the Crusades*. Edited by Susan B. Edgington and Sarah Lambert, 94–107. Cardiff: University of Wales, 2001.

Charanis, Peter. "Aims of the Medieval Crusades and How They Were Viewed by Byzantium." *Church History* 21, no. 2 (June 1952): 123–134.

Ciggaar, K., A. Davids, and H. Teule, eds. *Orientalia Lovaniensia Analecta: East and West in the Crusader States*. Leuven: Uitgeveru Peeters, 1996.

Constable, Giles. "The Second Crusade as Seen by Contemporaries." *Traditio* 9 (1953): 213–279.

———. "The Financing of the Crusades in the Twelfth Century." In *Outremer: Studies in the History of the Crusading Kingdom of Jerusalem, presented to Joshua Prawer*. Edited by Benjamin Z. Kedar, H. E. Mayer, and R. C. Smail, 64–89. Jerusalem: Yad Izhak Ben-Zvi Institute, 1982.

———. "The Crusading Project of 1150." In *Montjoie: Studies in Crusade History in Honour of Hans Eberhard Mayer*. Edited by Benjamin Z. Kedar, Jonathan Riley-Smith, and Rudolf Heistand, 67–75. Variorum Press, 1997.

———. "Medieval Charters as a Source for the History of the Crusades." In *The Crusades: The Essential Readings*. Edited by Thomas Madden, 130–153. Oxford: Blackwell, 2002.

Crawford, Robert W. "William of Tyre and the Maronites." *Speculum* 30, no. 2 (April 1955): 222–228.

Daftary, Farbad. "The Isma'ilis and the Crusaders: History and Myth." In *The Crusades and the Military Orders: Expanding the Frontiers of Medieval Latin Christianity*. Edited by Zsolkt Hunyadi, and József Laszlovszky, 21–41. Budapest: Central European University, 2001.

Dédéyan, Gérard. "Regard sur les Communautés Chrétiennes Orientales." *Arabica* 43 (1996): 98–115.

———. "Un émir arménien du Hawran entre la principauté turque de Damas et le royaume latin de Jérusalem 1147." In *Dei Gesta per Francos: Etudes sur les croisades dédiées à Jean Richard/ Crusade Studies in Honour of Jean Richard*. Edited by Michel Balard, Benjamin Z. Kedar, and Jonathan Riley-Smith, 179–185. Burlington, VT: Ashgate, 2001.

Déjean, Jean-Luc. *Les comtes de Toulouse 1050–1250*. Paris: Fayard, 1979.

Dick, Ignatios. *Melkites: Greek Orthodox and Greek Catholics of the Patriarchates of Antioch, Alexandria and Jerusalem*. Roslindale, MA: Sophia Press, 2004.

Du Cange, *Familles d'Outremer*. E. G. Rey, Paris 1869

Edbury, Peter W., ed. *Crusade and Settlement*. Wales: University College Cardiff Press, 1985.

Edbury, Peter and Jonathan Phillips, eds. *The Experience of Crusading. Vol 2: Defining the Crusader Kingdom*. Cambridge: Cambridge University Press, 2003.

Edbury, Peter and John Gordon Rowe, *William of Tyre: Historian of the Latin East*. Cambridge University Press, Cambridge. 1988

Eddé, Anne-Marie. "Francs et musulmans de Syrie au début du XIIe siècle d'après Ibn Abi Tayyi." In *Dei Gesta per Francos: Etudes sur les croisades dédiées à Jean Richard/ Crusade Studies in Honour of Jean Richard*. Edited by Michel Barlard, Bejamin Z. Kedar, and Jonathan Riley-Smith, 159–169. Burlington, Vermont: Ashgate, 2001.

Edgerton, Susan B. and Sarah Lambert. *Gendering the Crusades*. Cardiff: University of Wales, 2001.

Elisséeff, Nikita. "Corporations de Damas sous Nur al-Din: matériaux pour une topographie économique de Damas au XII siècle." *Arabica* T. 3 Fasc. 1 (January 1956): 61–79.

———. "Un document contemporain de Nûr ad-Dîn: Sa notice biographic par ibn 'Asakir." *Bulletin d'étude orientales* T. 25 (1972): 125–140.

———. "The Reaction of the Syrian Muslims after the Foundation of the First Latin Kingdom of Jerusalem." In *The Crusades: The Essential Readings*. Edited by Thomas F. Madden, 221–232. Oxford: Blackwell, 2002.

Ellenblum, Ronnie. *Frankish Rural Settlement in the Latin Kingdom of Jerusalem*. Cambridge: Cambridge University Press, 1998.

———. "Construction Methods in Frankish Rural Settlements." In *The Horns of Hattin*. Edited by Benjamin Z. Kedar, 168–189. Jerusalem: Yad Izhak Ben-Zvi, 1992.

———. "Frankish and Muslim Siege Warfare and the Construction of Frankish Concentric Castles." In *Dei Gesta per Francos: Etudes sur les croisades dédiées à Jean Richard/ Crusade Studies in Honour of Jean Richard*. Edited by Michel Balard, Benjamin Z. Kedar, and Jonathan Riley-Smith, 187–198. Burlington, VT: Ashgate, 2001.

Folda, Jaroslav. "Images of Queen Melisende in Manuscripts of William of Tyre's History of Outremer: 1250–1300." *Gesta* 32, no. 2 (1993): 97–112.

———. "The Church of Saint Anne." *The Biblical Archeologist* 54, no. 2 (June 1991): 88–96.

Frazee, Charles A. "The Christian Church in Cilician Armenia: Its Relations with Rome and Constantinople to 1198." *Church History* 45, no. 2 (June 1976): 166–184.

Frenkel, Yehosua. "The Qur'an versus the Cross in the Wake of the Crusade: The Social Function of Dreams and Symbols in Encounter and Conflict Damascus, July 1148." *Quaderni di Studi Arabici* 20/21 (2002–2003): 105–132.

Friedman, Yvonne. *Encounter between Enemies.* Leiden: Brill, 2002.

———. "Women in Captivity and their Ransom During the Crusader Period." In *Dei Gesta per Francos: Etudes sur les croisades dédiées à Jean Richard/ Crusade Studies in Honour of Jean Richard.* Edited by Michel Balard, Bejamin Z. Kedar, and Jonathan Riley-Smith, 75–87. Burlington, VT: Ashgate, 2001.

———. "Captivity and Ransom, the Experience of Women." In *Gendering the Crusades.* Edited by Susan B. Edginton and Sarah Lambert, 121–139. Cardiff: University of Wales, 2001.

Gaudette, Helen A. "The Spending Power of a Crusader Queen: Melisende of Jerusalem." In *Women and Wealth in Late Medieval Europe.* Edited by Theresa Ehrenfight, 135–148. New York: Palgrave MacMillan, 2010.

Genty, Roger. *Les Comtes de Toulouse: histoire et traditions.* Ferrriéres, France: Poliphile, 1987.

Gerish, Deborah. "Holy War, Royal Wives and Equivocation in Twelfth-Century Jerusalem." In *Advances in the Crusades.* Edited by Helen J. Nicholson. New York: Palgrave, 2005.

Given, Raymond. "New Perspectives on the Crusaders' Armenia: Cilicia from 1071–1148." *Journal of the Georgia Association of Historians.* Vol. XVI, 1995.

Goiten, Shlomo Dov. *A Mediterranean Society: The Jewish Communities of the World as Portrayed in the Documents of the Cairo Geniza.* Volumes 1–5, Berkeley: California University Press, 1999

———. "A Letter From Selucia Cilicia: Dated 21 July 1137." *Speculum* 39, no. 2 (April 1964): 298–303.

———. "Tyre-Tripoli-'Acre: Geniza Documents from the Beginning of the Crusader Period." *The Jewish Quarterly Review* 66, no. 2 (October 1975): 69–88.

———. "'Meeting in Jerusalem': Messianic Expectations in the Letters of the Cairo Geniza." *AJS Review* 4 (1979): 43–57.

———. "Geniza Sources for the Crusader Period: A Survey." In *Outremer: Studies in the History of the Crusading Kingdom of Jerusalem, presented to Joshua Prawer.* Edited by Benjamin Z. Kedar, H. E. Mayer, and R. C. Smail, 306–322. Jerusalem: Yad Izhak Ben-Zvi Institute, 1982.

Goodrich, Michael, Sophia Menache, and Sylvia Schein. *Cross Cultural Convergences in the Crusader Period: Essays Presented to Aryeh Grabois on his Sixty-fifth Birthday.* New York: Peter Lang, 1995.

Gourdin, Philippe, et al. *Pays d'Islam et monde latin, 950–1250.* Paris: Atlande, 2001.

Hamilton, Bernard. "Women in the crusader states: the queens of Jerusalem 1100–90." In *Medieval Women.* Edited by Derek Baker, 143–174. Oxford: Blackwell, 1978.

Harris, Jonathan. *Byzantium and the Crusades.* London: Hambledon, 2003.

Hazard, Harry W. "Caesarea and the Crusades." *Bulletin of the American Schools of Oriental Research, Supplementary Studies* 19 (1975): 79–114.

Heather, Peter. *The Restoration of Rome: Barbarian Popes and Imperial Pretenders,* MacMillan. London, 2013.

Heidemann, Stefan. "Financing the Tribute to the Kingdom of Jerusalem: An Urban Tax in Damascus." *Bulletin of the School of Oriental and African Studies,* University of London. Vol. 70 No. 1 (2007) 117–142.

Heistand, Rudolph. "Gaufridus Abbas Templi Domini: An underestimated figure in the early history of the kingdom of Jerusalem." In *The Experience of Crusading.* Vol. 2. Edited by Peter Edbury and Jonathan Phillips, 48–59. Cambridge: Cambridge University Press, 2003.

———. "Die Herren von Sidon und die Thronfolgekrise des Jahres 1163 im Köingriech in Jerusalem." In *Montjoie: Studies in Crusade History in Honour of Hans Eberhard Mayer.* Edited by Benjamin Z. Kedar, Jonathan Riley-Smith, and Rudolf Heistand, 77–90. Variorum Press, 1997.

————. "Some Reflections of the Impact of the Papacy on the Crusader States and the Military Orders in the Twelfth and Thirteenth Centuries." In *The Crusades and the Military Orders: Expanding the Frontiers of Medieval Latin Christianity.* Edited by Zsolkt Hunyadi, and József Laszlovszky, 3–20. Budapest: Central European University, 2001.

————. "L'archevêque Hughes d'Edesse et son destin posthume." In *Dei Gesta per Francos: Etudes sur les croisades dédiées à Jean Richard/ Crusade Studies in Honour of Jean Richard.* Edited by Michel Balard, Benjamin Z. Kedar, and Jonathan Riley-Smith, 171–177. Burlington, VT: Ashgate, 2001.

Hill, John and Laurita Hill. *Raymond IV, Count of Toulouse.* Syracuse: Syracuse University Press, 1962.

Hillenbrand, Carole. "The Establishment of Artuqid Power in Dayr Bakr in the Twelfth Century." *Studia Islamica* 54 (1981): 129–153.

————. "*Jihad* Poetry in the Age of the Crusades." In *Crusades—Medieval Worlds in Conflict.* Edited by Thomas Madden, James L. Naus, and Vincent Ryan, 9–24. Farham, Surrey: Ashgate, 2010.

————. *The Crusades, Islamic Perspectives.* Reprint, Edinburgh: Edinburgh University Press, 2010.

Hoch, Martin."The Choice of Damascus as the Objective of the Second Crusade: A Re-Evaluation." In *Byzantina Sorbonensia,* Vol. 14. Edited by Michel Balard, 359–369. Paris: Publications de la Sorbonne, 1996.

Hodgson, Marshall G. S. *The Secret Order of Assassins: The Struggle of the Early Nizârî Ismâ'îlîs Against the Islamic World.* 1955. Reprint, Philadelphia: University of Pennsylvania Press, 2005.

————. "Al-Darazi and Hamza in the Origin of the Druze Religion." *Journal of the American Oriental Society* 82. no. 1 (January-March 1962): 5–20.

Hunyadi, Zsolkt and József Laszlovszky. *The Crusades and the Military Orders: Expanding the Frontiers of Medieval Latin Christianity.* Budapest: Central European University, 2001.

Jacoby, David. "The Venetian Privileges in the Latin Kingdom of Jerusalem: Twelfth and Thirteenth-Century Interpretations and Implementation." In *Montjoie: Studies in Crusade History in Honour of Hans Eberhard Mayer.* Edited by Benjamin Z. Kedar, Jonathan Riley-Smith, and Rudolf Heistand, 155–175. Variorum Press, 1997.

Jehel, Georges and Philippe Racinet. *Les Relations des Pays d'Islam avec le Monde Latin.* Paris: Editions du Temps, 2000.

Jotischky, Andrew. *The Perfection of Solitude: Hermits and Monks in the Crusader States.* Harrisburg, PA: Penn State Press, 1995.

Kadri, Sadakat. *Heaven on Earth: A Journey Through Shari'a Law from the Deserts of Ancient Arabia to the Streets of the Modern Muslim World.* Farrar Strauss, Giroux, New York, 2012

Katzir, Yael. "The Patriarch of Jerusalem, Primate of the Latin Kingdom." In *Crusade and Settlement.* Edited by Peter W. Edbury, 169–180. Wales: University College Cardiff Press, 1985.

Kedar, Benjamin Z., trans. "Gerard of Nazareth, a Neglected Twelfth-Century Writer in the Latin East: A Contribution to the Intellectual and Monastic History of the Crusader States." *Dumbarton Oaks Papers* 37 (1983): 55–77.

————. *The Horns of Hattin.* Yad Izhak Ben-Zvi. Jerusalem: 1992.

————. "The Subjected Muslims of the Frankish Levant." In *The Crusades: The Essential Readings.* Edited by Thomas Madden, 233–264. Oxford: Blackwell, 2002.

————. "A Second Incarnation in Frankish Jerusalem." *The Experience of Crusading.* Vol. 2. Edited by Peter Edbury and Jonathan Phillips, 79–92. Cambridge: Cambridge University Press, 2003.

Kedar, Benjamin Z., Jonathan Riley-Smith, and Rudolf Heistand. Eds. *Montjoie: Studies in Crusade History in Honour of Hans Eberhard Mayer.* Variorum Press, 1997.

Kedar, Benjamin Z. H. E. Mayer, and R. C. Smail, eds. *Outremer: Studies in the History of the Crusading Kingdom of Jerusalem, presented to Joshua Prawer.* Jerusalem: Yad Izhak Ben-Zvi Institute, 1982.

Konymjian, Dickran K. "Problems of Medieval Armenian and Muslim Historiography: The Mxit'ar Ani Fragment." *International Journal of Middle East Studies* 4 (October 1973): 465–475.

Lange, Christian and Songül Mecit. *The Seljuks: Politics, Society and Culture.* Edinburgh: Edinburgh University Press, 2011.

La Monte, John L. *Feudal Monarchy in the Latin Kingdom of Jerusalem, 1100–1191.* Cambridge: Medieval Academy of America, 1932.

———. "The Viscounts of Naplouse in the Twelfth Century." *Syria* T. 19. Fasc. 3 (1936): 272–278.

———. "The Lords of Casearea in the Period of the Crusades." *Speculum* 22, no. 2 (April 1947): 145–161.

Lewis, Bernard. "Kamal al-din's biography of Rasid al-din Sinan." *Arabica* T. 13, Fasc. 3 (October 1966): 225–267.

———. *The Assassins: A Radical Sect in Islam.* London: Weidenfield & Nicholson, 2005.

Linder, Amnon. "An Unpublished Charter of Geoffrey, Abbot of the Temple in Jerusalem." In *Outremer: Studies in the History of the Crusading Kingdom of Jerusalem, presented to Joshua Prawer.* Edited by Benjamin Z. Kedar, H. E. Mayer, and R. C. Smail, 119–129. Jerusalem: Yad Izhak Ben-Zvi Institute, 1982.

Lindner, Molly. "Topography and Iconography in Twelfth-Century Jerusalem." In *The Horns of Hattin.* Edited by Benjamin Z. Kedar, 81–98. Jerusalem: Yad Izhak Ben-Zvi, 1992.

Luttrell, Anthony. "The Earliest Hospitallers." In *Montjoie: Studies in Crusade History in Honour of Hans Eberhard Mayer.* Edited by Benjamin Z. Kedar, Jonathan Riley-Smith, and Rudolf Heistand, 37–53. Variorum Press, 1997.

MacEvitt, Christopher. "The Chronicle of Matthew of Edessa: Apocalypse, the First Crusade and the Armenian Diaspora." *Dumbarton Oaks Papers* 61 (2007): 254–96.

———. "Christian Authority in the Latin East: Edessa in Crusader History." In *The Medieval Crusade.* Edited by Susan Ridyard, 71–83. Woodbridge: Boydell, 2004.

———. *The Crusades and the Christian World of the East: Rough Tolerance.* Philadelphia: University of Pennsylvania Press, 2008.

Madden, Thomas. *The Crusades: The Essential Readings.* Blackwell: Oxford, 2002.

Madden, Thomas, James L. Naus, and Vincent Ryan. *Crusades—Medieval Worlds in Conflict.* Farham, Surrey: Ashgate, 2010.

Mahoney, Lisa. "The *Histoire Ancienne* and Dialectical Identity in the Latin Kingdom of Jerusalem." *Gesta* 49, no. 1 (2000): 31–52.

Marshall, Christopher. "The Crusading Motivation of the Italian City Republics in the Latin East, 1096–1104." *The Experience of Crusading: Western Approaches.* Edited by Marcus Bull and Norman Housley, 60–79. Cambridge: Cambridge University Press, 2003.

Mayer, Hans Eberhard. "Studies in the History of Queen Melisende of Jerusalem." *Dumbarton Oaks Papers* 26 (1972): 93, 95–182.

———. "Carving up Crusaders: The Early Ibelins and Ramla." *Outremer: Studies in the History of the Crusading Kingdom of Jerusalem, presented to Joshua Prawer.* Edited by Benjamin Z. Kedar, H. E. Mayer, and R. C. Smail, 103–118. Jerusalem: Yad Izhak Ben-Zvi Institute, 1982.

———. "The Succession to Baldwin II of Jerusalem: English Impact on the East." *Dumbarton Oaks Papers* 39 (1985) 139–147.

———. "The Double County of Jaffa and Ascalon: One Fief of Two?" In *Crusade and Settlement.* Edited by Peter W. Edbury, 181–190. Wales: University College Cardiff Press, 1985.

———. "Angevins versus Normans: The New Men of King Fulk of Jerusalem." *Proceedings of the American Philosophical Society* 133, no. 1 (March 1989): 1–25.

———. "King Fulk of Jerusalem as City Lord." In *The Experience of Crusading.* Vol. 2. Edited by Peter Edbury and Jonathan Phillips, 179–188. Cambridge: Cambridge University Press, 2003.

Metcalf, D. M. "Describe the currency of the Latin Kingdom of Jerusalem." In *Montjoie: Studies in Crusade History in Honour of Hans Eberhard Mayer.* Edited by Benjamin Z. Kedar, Jonathan Riley-Smith, and Rudolf Heistand, 189–198. Variorum Press, 1997.

Murry, Alan V. "Dynastic Continuity or Dynastic Change? The Succession of Baldwin II and the Nobility of the Kingdom of Jerusalem." *Medieval Prosopography* 13, no. 1 (spring 1992): 1–35.

Nader, Marwan. *Burgesses and Burgess Law in the Latin Kingdoms of Jerusalem and Cyprus.* Aldershot: Ashgate, 2006.

Nicholson, Helen, ed. *The Crusades.* New York: Palgrave Macmillan, 2005.

Nicholson, Robert Lawrence. *Jocelyn I, Prince of Edessa.* Urbana: University of Illinois Press, 1954.

Ouerfelli, Mohamed. *Le sucre: production, commercialisation et usages dans la Méditerranée mediévale.* Leiden: Brill, 2008.

Painter, Sidney. "The Houses of Lusignan and Chatellerault 1150–1250." *Speculum* 30, no. 3 (July 1955): 374–384.

Parnell, David. "John II Comnenus and Crusader Antioch." In *Crusades—Medieval Worlds in Conflict.* Edited by James L. Naus and Vincent Ryan, 149–160. Farham, Surrey: Ashgate, 2010.

Phillips, Jonathan. *Defenders of the Holy Land: Relations Between the Latin East and the West 1119–1187.* Oxford: Clarendon Press, 1996.

———. "A Note on the Origins of Raymond of Poitiers" *English Historical Review* Vol. 106, No. 418 (Jan. 1991) 66–67

Phillips, Jonathan and Martin Hoch, eds. *The Second Crusade: Scope and Consequences.* Manchester: Manchester University Press, 2001.

Pringle, Denys. "Magna Mahumeria al-Bira: The Archaeology of a Frankish New Town in Palestine." In *Crusade and Settlement.* Edited by Peter W. Edbury, 147–168. Wales: University College Cardiff Press, 1985.

———. "Aqua Bella: The Interpretation of a Crusader Courtyard Building." In *The Horns of Hattin.* Edited by Benjamin Z. Kedar, 147–167. Jerusalem: Yad Izhak Ben-Zvi, 1992.

———. "The Castle and Lordship of Mirabel." In *Montjoie: Studies in Crusade History in Honour of Hans Eberhard Mayer.* Edited by Benjamin Z. Kedar, Jonathan Riley-Smith, and Rudolf Heistand, 91–109. Variorum Press 1997.

Porée, Brigitte. "Études des installations techniques artisanales et industrielles dans le Royaume de Jérusalem: note sur les site d'extraction saline d'Athlit Château-Pèlerin et de l'Île de Mèlah." In *Dei Gesta per Francos: Etudes sur les croisades dédiées à Jean Richard/ Crusade Studies in Honour of Jean Richard.* Edited by Michel Balard, Benjamin Z. Kedar, and Jonathan Riley-Smith, 269–276. Burlington, VT: Ashgate, 2001.

Redford, Scott. "Excavations at Gritille 1982–1984 The Medieval Period, a Preliminary Report." *Anatolian Studies* 36 (1986): 103–106.

Richard, Jean. *Le Comté de Tripoli sous la Dynastie Toulousaine 1102–1187.* 1945. Reprint, Paris: Geuthner, 1999.

———. "Note sur l'archidiocése d'Apamée et les conquêtes de Raymond de Saint-Giles en Syrie du nord." *Syria* T. 25, Fasc. 1/2 (1946–1948): 103–108.

———. *The Latin Kingdom of Jerusalem.* Translated by Janet Shirley. Amsterdam: North-Holland, 1979.

———. "Hospitals and Hospital Congregations in the Latin Kingdom during the First Period of the Frankish Conquest." In *Outremer: Studies in the History of the Crusading Kingdom of Jerusalem, presented to Joshua Prawer.* Edited by Benjamin Z. Kedar, H. E. Mayer, and R. C. Smail, 90–102. Jerusalem: Yad Izhak Ben-Zvi Institute, 1982.

———. *Croisés, missionaires et voyageurs.* London: Varioum Reprints, 1983.

———. *Francs et Orientaux dans le monde des croisades.* Aldershot: Ashgate, 2003.

Rice, D. S. "Medieval Harran." *Anatolian Studies* 2 (1952): 36–84.

Riley-Smith, J. S. C. "Peace Never Established: The Case of the Kingdom of Jerusalem." *Royal Historical Society,* 5th ser., 20 (1978): 87–102.

———. "Some Lesser Officials of Latin Syria." *The English Historical Review* 87, no. 342 (January 1972): 1–26.

———. "The Venetian Crusade of 1122–1124," *I Communi Italiani nel regno crociato di Gerusalemme,* ed. G. Airaldi and B. Z. Kedar, Genoa (University of Genoa), 1986.

———. *The First Crusaders, 1095–1131.* Cambridge: Cambridge University Press, 1997.

———. "Early Crusaders to the East and the Costs of Crusading 1095–1130." In *Cross Cultural Convergences in the Crusader Period: Essays Presented to Aryeh Grabois on his Sixty-fifth Birthday.* Edited by Michael Goodrich, Sophia Menache, and Sylvia Schein, 237–257. New York: Peter Lang, 1995.

———. "King Fulk of Jerusalem and 'the Sultan of Babylon.'" In *Montjoie: Studies in Crusade History in Honour of Hans Eberhard Mayer.* Edited by Benjamin Z. Kedar, Jonathan Riley-Smith, and Rudolf Heistand, 55–66. Variorum Press, 1997.

Rogers, R. *Latin Siege Warfare in the Twelfth Century.* Oxford: Clarendon Press, 1992.

Runciman, Steven. "Some Remarks of the Image of Edessa." *Cambridge Historical Journal* 3, no. 3 (1931): 238–252.

——. *A History of the Crusades. Vol. II: The Kingdom of Jerusalem and the Frankish East 1100–1187.* Cambridge: Cambridge University Press, 1968.

Salibi, Kamal S. "The Maronites of Lebanon under Frankish and Mamluk Rule 1009–1516." *Arabica* T. 4, Fasc. 3 (September 1957): 288–303.

Sargent-Baer, Barbara N., ed. *Journeys Toward God: Pilgrimage and Crusade.* Kalamazoo, MI: Medieval Institute Publications, 1992.

Sassier, Yves, *Louis VII,* Fayard, Paris, 1991.

Schein, Sylvia. "Women in Medieval Colonial Society: The Latin Kingdom of Jerusalem in the Twelfth Century." In *Gendering the Crusades.* Edited by Susan B. Edington and Sarah Lambert, 140–153. Cardiff: University of Wales, 2001.

Seton, Lloyd and William Brice. "Harran." *Anatolian Studies* 1 (1951): 77–111.

Smail, R. C. "Crusader's Castles of the Twelfth Century." *Cambridge Historical Journal* 10, no. 2 (1951): 133–149.

——. *Crusading Warfare 1097–1193.* Cambridge: Cambridge University Press, 1956.

——. "Latin Syria and the West, 1149–1187." *Transactions of the Royal Historical Society,* 5th Ser., 19 (1969): 1–20.

Spinka, Matthew. "Latin Church of the Early Crusades." *Church History* 8, no. 2 (June 1939): 113–131.

Sumption, Jonathan. *Pilgrimage: An Image of Medieval Religion.* Totowa, NJ: Rowman and Littlefield, 1975.

Tabba, Yasser. *Constructions of Power and Piety in Medieval Aleppo.* University Park, PA: Pennsylvania State University Press, 1997.

Throop, Palmer A. "Criticism of Papal Crusade Policy in Old French and Provençal." *Speculum* 13, no. 4 (October 1938): 379–412.

Tibble, Steven. *Monarchy and Lordships in the Latin Kingdom of Jerusalem 1099–1291.* Oxford: Clarendon Press, 1989.

Tyerman, Christopher. *God's War: A New History of the Crusades.* Cambridge, MA: Belknap Press, 2006.

Whalen, Robert E. "The Discovery of the Holy Patriarchs: Relics, Ecclesiastical Politics, and Sacred History in Twelfth-Century Crusader Palestine." *Historical Reflections/ Réflexions Historiques* 27, no. 1 (spring 2001): 139–176.

——. "God's Will or Not? Bohemond's Campaign against the Byzantine Empire." In *Crusades—Medieval Worlds in Conflict.* Edited by James L. Naus and Vincent Ryan, 111–126. Farham, Surrey: Ashgate, 2010.

Wolff, R. L. "The Kingdom of Cilician Armenia." *The Later Crusades, 1189–1311.* Edited by H. W. Hazard. Madison, WI: University of Wisconsin Press, 1969.

Yewdale, Ralph Bailey. *Bohemond I, Prince of Antioch.* Amsterdam: Adolf M. Hakkert, 1970.

Ziadeh, Nicola. *Damascus Under the Mamluks.* Norman, OK: University of Oklahoma Press, 1964.

Zouche, Abbès. " Zangi, Stratège averti 522/1128 à 541/1146? Réexamen des Sources Latines et Arabes." *Bulletin d'études orientale* T. 56 (2004–2005): 63–93.

INDEX

ACKNOWLEDGMENTS

FIRST OF ALL, THANKS TO MY AGENT, CRISTINA CON-cepcion, who has had to deal with my neuroses most of her adult life.

Thanks to my editor, Elisabeth Dyssegaard, who adopted the book when it was orphaned and spoon fed it until it could survive on its own.

Historians Penny Adair, Malcolm Barber, Andrew Buck, Karen Nichols, Helen Nicholson, Denys Pringle, and Dorothea Weltecke were all of great help in pointing out sources and sending copies of their articles. It's wonderful to be part of such a generous community of scholars.

Marilyn Smith and Elizabeth Chadwick sent information on William Marshal and were kind enough to let me know that the event I remembered came from medieval fiction, not fact.

And, for moral support, laughter, and occasionally giving me a swift kick when I whined (in random order): Kathleen, Laurie, Marcia, Cora, Sue B., Sue S., Audrey, Kathy, Helga, Kaye, Linda, Ann, Rosa Lee, Dee, Michelle, Judy B., Judy P., Judith, Suzanne, Joan, Shirley, Chris, and the free radical, Surya. If I've forgotten anyone, it's because you don't come to the deep end of the pool where I can see you.